Parliaments and Legislatures Series

Samuel C. Patterson, General Advisory Editor

Parliaments and Legislatures Series

General Advisory Editor
Samuel C. Patterson, The Ohio State University, USA

The aims of this series are to enhance knowledge about the well-established legislative assemblies of North America and Western Europe and to publish studies of parliamentary assemblies worldwide—from Russia and the former Soviet bloc nations to Asia, Africa, and Latin America. The series is open to a wide variety of theoretical applications, historical dimensions, data collections, and methodologies.

Committees in Post-Communist Democratic Parliaments: Comparative Institutionalization

EDITED BY
DAVID M. OLSON AND
WILLIAM E. CROWTHER

The Ohio State University Press
Columbus

Library of Congress Cataloging-in-Publication Data

Committees in post-Communist democratic parliaments : comparative
institutionalization / David M. Olson and William E. Crowther, eds. p. cm.
— (Parliaments and legislatures series)
Includes bibliographical references and index.
ISBN 0-8142-0912-2 (hardcover : alk. paper)
    1. Legislative bodies—Europe, Central—Committees. 2. Legislative
bodies—Europe, Eastern—Committees. I. Olson, David M. II. Crowther,
William E. III. Series.
JN96.A71 C66 2002
328.3'65'0947—dc21
2002007840

Paper (ISBN: 978-0-8142-5743-2)

Jacket design by Sans Serif, Inc.
Type set in Sabon by Sans Serif, Inc.

CONTENTS

LIST OF TABLES

FOREWORD

THE AUTHORS OF THIS BOOK DISSECT PARLIAMENTARY COMMIT-
tees in seven new democracies in Central Europe—in Hungary, Poland,
the Czech Republic, Bulgaria, Estonia, Lithuania, and Moldova. Although
these countries have endured varied governmental experience, including differential authoritarianism and external control in the four decades or so of
post–World War II Soviet hegemony, more-or-less European-style parliamentary institutions emerged and coagulated in the wake of the collapse of
the Soviet system in the 1990s. Some of these parliaments—the Polish Sejm,
the Hungarian National Assembly (*Országgyülés*), and the Czech Republic's Chamber of Deputies (*Poslanecka Snemovna*)—carry a modicum of fa-
miliarity to Western scholars and other observers of Central European
politics. Although these authors devote their major attention to parliamentary life after the "democratic transitions" of the 1990s, in these three
countries (particularly in the Polish case) a national parliament existed
beforehand.

In the remaining cases, it would be fair to say that the nations' parliamentary institutions are virtually invisible outside their countries. A few
may be vaguely aware of the existence of a parliament in Bulgaria, the National Assembly (*Narodno Sobranie*). But in the smaller Central European
countries, virtually absorbed by the Soviet Union, parliaments are unfamil-
iar bodies. This certainly is true for the small-country parliaments analyzed
in this book—the Estonian Riigikogu, the Lithuanian Parliament (*Seimas*),
and the Moldovan Parliament. Accordingly, the studies in this book serve
to expand our knowledge about the political, parliamentary world.

Apart from their visibility in the outside world, these seven parliaments
exhibit various familiar organizational features. Of course, these political
systems differ in their political histories and cultural environments. Their
parliaments vary in size, membership, legislative powers and activity, and
political party representation. Poland and the Czech Republic are homes
for bicameral parliaments, although the analyses here concentrate on committee life in the lower houses. The other five parliaments are unicameral.
Finally, as the authors of this book so fully demonstrate, the committee systems in these parliaments display considerable diversity.

Committees are ubiquitous for parliamentary institutions. It is difficult to find a national parliament with no committees. In principle, one can imagine a committee-free parliament, where all decisions were made by the plenary, a committee of the whole. Nascent parliaments, those in their infancy, may operate for a time without committees, as did the U.S. Senate in the late eighteenth century. But as parliaments mature, become consolidated, establish roots in the constitutional regime, and wield influence over public policies, the urgency of a division of labor and distribution of power becomes irresistible. In the case of the U.S. Congress, a committee system in each house evolved over the years, beginning in earnest in the early nineteenth century. The British House of Commons is an interesting case study because for many decades its committees were largely procedural and temporary, but ultimately the House established a substantive committee system. Readers of this book may marvel at how quickly and effectively, though to different degrees, parliaments in the new democracies of Central Europe acquired nearly full-blown committee systems.

The authors of this comparative study are concerned primarily with investigating the process by which seven parliamentary bodies in a region of the world characterized by rapidly emergent parliaments, namely Central Europe, came to acquire organizational complexity, stability, rootedness in the national political culture, and played important roles in national development and public policy making. In a word, they ask, how do parliaments become *institutionalized*, and to what extent? Here, the raw materials for inquiry are rich. While the developmental sequences for these seven countries were not identical, all faced similar political problems of postcommunist adaptation. These chapters provide a pioneering baseline for the Central European parliaments. The authors carefully describe the structures and processes of these parliaments, making comparisons across the seven parliaments and their committee and party components.

Capitalizing upon a major opportunity for comparative political analysis, the authors delve into each parliament's committees, examining subcommittees and other organizational features operating within the larger committee systems. There is a natural nesting: committees are nested within parliaments and, in turn, subcommittees are nested within committees. The comparative analyst can, accordingly, compare across parliaments, across committees within and across parliaments, and across subcommittees within committees, across committees, and across parliaments. These authors open up fertile avenues for acquiring new knowledge about parliamentary institutions through the kaleidoscopic perspective of committee-centered analysis and cross-committee comparison.

U.S. scholars have long considered that an understanding of legislative committees was fundamental to explaining how legislative or parliamentary institutions work. From Woodrow Wilson to Richard F. Fenno Jr. and beyond, we have sought to account for committees of the legislature—their proliferation, practices, and powers. We know a great deal about congressional and state legislative committees in the United States. However, today there is a much larger world of parliaments and parliamentary committees requiring careful nurture and study. The authors of the chapters of this book have contributed mightily to that enterprise.

SAMUEL C. PATTERSON
The Ohio State University
General Advisory Editor

PREFACE

OUR COMPARATIVE STUDY OF COMMITTEE SYSTEMS IN THE PAR-liaments of new democracies of post-communism and the older parliaments of Western Europe rests upon the cooperation and participation of many persons over several years. As organizers of this cooperative international venture, the two editors have relied upon the guidance and preparatory work of the Research Committee of Legislative Specialists (RCLS) of the International Political Science Association. That group's "committee initiative" has sponsored several conferences, leading to both "The Changing Roles of Parliamentary Committees," in the RCLS Working Papers series, edited by Lawrence Longley and Attila Ágh, and to a special issue of the *Journal of Legislative Studies* (Spring 1998), which has been separately published in book form as *The New Roles of Parliamentary Committees,* edited by Lawrence D. Longley and Roger H. Davidson (London: Frank Cass, 1998).

The selection of committees as a topic for comparative research grew out of a 1994 conference near Prague. That conference prepared the first assessment of the newly democratized parliaments of post-communist countries, which was subsequently published as both a special issue of the *Journal of Legislative Studies* (Spring 1996) and as a book, *The New Parliaments of Central and Eastern Europe,* edited by David M. Olson and Philip Norton (London: Frank Cass, 1996). The conference suggested that if we were to understand parliaments as working bodies, we should examine committees as the place where the work of parliament gets done.

The research design undergirding this book was developed at ensuing conferences of the RCLS. Wlodzimierz Wesolowski of the Polish Academy of Science and Attila Ágh, Budapest University of Economics, were particularly helpful in guiding the objectives and methods of the entire project. Lawrence Longley, Lawrence University, Appleton, Wisconsin, and Philip Norton, Hull University, United Kingdom, served as RCLS co-chairs during the inception of and work on this project.

Many organizations funded the research reported in this book. The National Council for Eurasian and East European Research has supported the research work in Central Europe. The National Science Foundation, through its support for the Parliamentary Documents Center for Central

Europe, funded transportation of our researchers and documents collectors for a conference at the University of North Carolina at Greensboro. The conference uniquely combined researchers with members of the parliamentary staff who were responsible for the preparation of documentary materials used in our research. The conference, in summer 1998, also enjoyed the financial support of UNC Greensboro, the Tannenbaum-Sternberger Foundation of Greensboro, and the Volvo Truck Corporation of North America. In addition, each author has relied upon the support of personnel and equipment, as well as funds, available in their parliaments and research institutions.

Each chapter is a team project. Our authors have extensive experience in their respective parliaments; we have urged them to use their best judgments when, as was often the case, hard data were either unreliable or nonexistent. The whole team greatly benefitted from the perspectives of Hilmar Rommetvedt for Norway, Magnus Hagevi for Sweden, and Reuven Hazan for Israel, to provide perspective from more established parliaments to understand the new parliaments. They have participated with us from beginning to end of our data collection and analysis.

During 1999, Olson was privileged to work in Berlin through Hans-Dieter Klingeman, at the Abteilung institutionen und sozialer Wandel, Wissenschaftszentrum Berlin für Sozialforschung, and in Prague, through Michal Illner and Lubomir Brokl of the Sociologicky Ustav, Akademie ved Ceske Republiky. In Prague, Zdenka Mansfeldová of the Institute of Sociology, and Jindriška Syllová at the Parliamentary Institute, together with their associates and staff, were helpful in every way in the preparation of the materials in this book.

As organizers and editors, we have relied upon the active support of our university, instrumented through the Parliamentary Documents Center for Central Europe. The Center has provided space and computer equipment, as well as the skills and energy of many students. Our student assistants, both graduate and undergraduate, included Jacquelyn Crace-Murray and Kristin Effle. We particularly benefitted from the university's exchange program with Wroclaw University, through which we have had the benefit of a Polish student with us for several years: Piotr Chruszczewski, Adam Gorski, Marcin Starnawski, Artur Sikora, and Mariusz Ziemecki. The manager of the Documents Center, Christopher Leslie, a graduate student in economics and participant in the Wroclaw exchange, made the conference a workable and enjoyable experience. He coauthored with Olson the first paper to explore our findings. Theodora Moleva continued his work as manager of the Parliamentary Documents Center. Jonathan Mattielo, a graduate assistant in the Master of Public Affairs program of the political science department, has had special responsibility for preparation of the tables for each chapter. We have made rigorous use of the talents of Ellen Olson as our English language editor, who has exercised her skills on computers in many countries. It has not been an easy task for any of our authors from many countries to write in a foreign language.

We express our thanks and gratitude to one and all who have contributed their time, talent, and patience to a complex task of comparative research. If our collaborative work suggests additional steps in the understanding of the democratization processes of post-communism, one of our objectives will, perhaps over another decade or more, become a reality. Our project itself has been a decade in the making.

DAVID M. OLSON
WILLIAM E. CROWTHER
October 4, 2002
Parliamentary Documents Center for Central Europe
University of North Carolina at Greensboro

PART 1

Comparative Institutionalization of Post-Communist Democratic Parliaments

ONE

Committees in New Democratic Parliaments: Indicators of Institutionalization

David M. Olson and William E. Crowther

THIS BOOK EXPLORES ATTRIBUTES OF COMMITTEES OF THE NEWLY democratized and activated parliaments of post-communist states in their first democratic decade. We examine the beginnings and subsequent development of these committee systems. To what extent have committee systems become stabilized in post-communist democratic parliaments? Do the new post-communist legislative committees as a whole reflect a pattern of committee activity that is regionally distinct, or are they characterized by substantial intragroup diversity? We examine these questions through comparative cross-national analysis of the first decade of legislative activity in seven post-communist legislatures.

The rapidly changing parliaments of Central Europe provide both a challenge and an opportunity to examine how democratic institutions begin and develop during and after an authoritarian system transformation. Legislatures are central institutions in developed democracies, performing, at least potentially, complex and interactive functions in policy formation, interest representation, and administrative review. Their committees are the prime organizational means by which parliaments act independently of the executive in all of these functions. We therefore focus on the committee systems of the newly democratized parliaments of Central Europe as examples of the post-communist democratization process.

The parliaments of post-communist democracies in their initial decade provide a unique window on the processes of early institutionalization. While we cannot directly observe salient features of early legislatures in

Western Europe or North America, the contemporary efforts of new members in newly activated legislatures of post-communist democracies to build functioning and effective parliamentary bodies permit us to observe directly the beginning stages of institutional development. We concentrate on committees to provide examples of change, experimentation, and development of legislatures as whole institutions.

This chapter first considers the characteristics of the post-communist transition as the essential context for parliaments. We then present the criteria by which we seek to measure and understand legislative committee development. We conclude with a preliminary evaluation of the seven case studies of legislatures and their committees in this volume. The chapters to follow are arranged by degree of institutionalization of their country's committee systems.

Post-Communist Legislatures in the Democratic Transition

The circumstances facing the legislatures of the sudden democracies of Central Europe and the former Soviet Union are unprecedented. As noted by Linz and Stepan (1996) the transition from one party dictatorship to open competitive democracy occurred much more abruptly in Central Europe than in many of the preceding democratic transitional episodes of the twentieth century. The difficulties presented by this rapid change are evident in the efforts to reshape legislative institutions to meet the demands of the evolving political environment. Legislatures became a "central site" in the democratization process in Central Europe and the former Soviet Union (Olson and Norton 1996; Ágh 1998).

Legislatures as new instruments of democracy, however, are also transitional. The inherited structures and procedures of their half-century communist past were inadequate to cope with the new policy demands, disagreements among many parties, and uncertainty in the absence of external control by the ruling party. The post-communist parliaments were faced with the task of creating an internal structure of effective organization and regularized procedure, while simultaneously processing a wide range of policy decisions.

The new democracies, though all have experienced communism, have very different pre-communist histories, and also had different kinds of communist rule (Korbonski 1999). The most important distinction is between those countries that had been included within the Soviet Union, and the others as external "satellite" states. Only three of our Central European countries are continuous states from before World War II—Poland,

Hungary, and Bulgaria. The Czech Republic and the three post-Soviet countries of Estonia, Lithuania, and Moldova are successor states of larger but disappeared aggregates. In each, the parliament has enormous value as a patriotic and national symbol, irrespective of its present or even past condition.

Research on the new legislatures of Central Europe is undergoing rapid change. Immediately following communist system collapse, the initial wave of research on the newly democratized legislatures of post-communism concentrated on a broad institutional description of each legislature (Ágh 1994; Olson 1997). Early comparisons within the region were based upon separately written country papers (Hibbing and Patterson 1992; Olson and Norton 1996). The second and current wave of research on the newly democratized parliaments has begun to examine more specific internal features such as parliamentary parties, interest group activity and the members (Ágh and Ilonszki 1996; Hahn 1996a; Remington and Smith 1996; Wesolowski and Pankow 1995; Ostrow 2000; Kopecky 2001).

In a review of existing parliaments, Patterson and Copeland asked both "how" and "why" institutionalization occurs in legislatures (Patterson and Copeland 1994, 2–4). There are as many examples of failed legislatures as of failed democracies and of disappeared countries. New institutions, as well as new countries, are not destined to persist much less to succeed. The new democracies of post-communism provide the opportunity to see how new democratic institutions begin and take shape. Their varied experiences of independence and communism provide a unique opportunity to chronicle the beginning stages of institutional development. Their current efforts permit us to turn the analytic developmental clock back to the beginnings.

Legislatures and Committees

The central place of parliaments in the democratization process as transitional institutions provides the essential context within which their committees exist and function. Committees are at the heart of the internal attempt by legislatures to cope with external tasks. They have been identified by as "focal points" of legislative activity (Mattson and Stroem 1995, 149), at least in established democratic parliaments of Western Europe. But in a much larger set of struggling parliaments, it was also observed that committees were the location of expertise (Mezey 1979, 64). In semi-authoritarian regimes, in which parliaments are permitted to exist and to attempt to become more active, it is through committees that they can gain sufficient knowledge to attempt to exercise power against their executive (Blondel 1973). The slow growth of committees within two communist-era parliaments has been noted in both Poland and Hungary (Olson and Simon 1982; Zakrzewski 1982; Mason 1991; Racz 1989). Most research on committees, however, is on the U.S. Congress (Eulau and McCluggage 1985). Only recently have the committees of post-communist legislatures begun to receive scholarly attention (Longley and Ágh 1997; Longley and Davidson 1998).

Committees, like all other components of the system of governance, are not unidimensional. For each of its potentially constructive contributions to the work of parliament, there is a corresponding potential liability; or, at least, legislators will argue over whether a given committee characteristic is more an asset or a liability within any one parliament and set of circumstances.

If committees are relatively autonomous from sources of external control, are they also capricious? If they hold jurisdiction over a sector of public policy, do they pursue their own self-interest? If they are a means to protect minority rights within parliament, do they thwart majority will? If they avoid partisanship in their internal deliberations, are they "islands" of interest group politics (Mueller-Rommel 1990, 326; Rommetvedt 1998)? Committees, by their very existence, raise all of the questions within parliament that are commonly expressed about parliament itself, of representation, accountability, accessibility, and of rights and obligations. The more powerful the committees, the more important these questions become.

Committees are found in most of the world's legislatures, however inactive or marginal they may be (Shaw 1998), as well as in the U.S. state legislatures (Francis 1985). Committees exist in a wide variety of institutional settings, and function through detailed rules and procedures, all of which vary from one parliament to another, but many of which are not considered in the analytic literature (Mattson and Stroem 1995, 303).

A recent analysis of the procedural and structural features of eighteen Western European parliaments identified characteristics of the committee system to be among the attributes of parliaments most closely related to the ability of parliaments to function independently in the policy process (Döring 1995b; Mattson and Stroem 1995). Autonomy of committees from the government was found to be a critical component of the policy-making capability of the larger institution. These findings confirmed the observation in an earlier worldwide examination of committees in eight legislatures that committee autonomy from government and party control is the key element in an active and influential legislative committee system

(Shaw 1979). The characteristics of a particular parliament's committees thus may serve as a useful indicator of the status of parliament as a whole.

Institutionalization

Our main concept, institutionalization, expresses the extent to which the organization and activity of committees becomes established and regularized in new legislatures. The many definitions of institutionalization all revolve around the idea of stability, continuity, and predictability (Huntington 1968; Polsby 1968; Sisson 1973; Hahn 1996b, 8–11; Copeland and Patterson 1994, 151; Patterson 1995, 15; Stroem 1997). Broadly stated criteria for institutionalization in established legislatures typically include: 1) organizational differentiation from the environment; 2) organization complexity and functional differentiation; and 3) use of universalistic rather than particularistic or discretionary standards.

Though these criteria may be limited in their applicability to new institutions because of their inherent volatility, examining the early developments in Central European parliaments is important because institutionalization processes are likely to be rapid at first and less noticeable later (Hibbing and Patterson 1994). Early decisions can, at least in retrospect, be seen as crucial in the subsequent pattern of institutional development (North 1990; Kitschelt et al. 1991).

Studies of legislative institutionalization often use the entire legislature as the unit of analysis, for which committee system attributes are indicators (Hahn 1996b, 250; Wilson 1999, 548; Carey et al. 1999). By contrast, committees themselves are the object of our analysis. Clearly, a close symbiotic relationship exists between the legislature as an entire body and its component parts (Loewenberg and Patterson 1979, 204–5; Olson 1994, 56–73). Multicountry surveys have shown that committees closely reflect attributes of the entire legislature (Lees and Shaw 1979; Döring 1995a). Parliamentary committees are a prime example of organizational complexity, one of the broad criteria of institutionalization (Hahn 1996b; Patterson and Copeland 1994, 5–6; Stroem 1997).

We focus on the institutionalization of committees because of their potential centrality to the activities of the legislature as a whole. Committees provide an essential division of labor among members that can and often does, over time, become a specialization of function. The extent to which committees are defined by their specialized functions, and the extent to which they are active in those functions, constitute evidence for the degree of institutionalization of parliamentary committee systems.

Our data will also provide evidence about the possible functional role of committees as providers of information (Shepsle and Weingast 1994), as instruments of party influence (Cox and McCubbins 1993), and as claimants to special rights within the rules and procedures of the parliament (Krehbiel 1991).

Comparison of Committee Systems in Post-Communist Parliaments

We directly measure committee phenomena at the initial stage of legislative development by comparing the newly democratized post-communist parliaments. While the Central European legislatures are not fated to evolve inevitably in the direction of their Western European counterparts, we derive our initial indicators from the established parliaments of the West. The Western European cases provide us with clear expectations regarding committees that currently function within the context of well-established legislative institutions. In addition to seeking temporal trends, even within the short period of one decade, we also search for emerging cross-national patterns among legislatures, seeking to understand those factors that shape variation in institutional outcomes.

Following Döring (1995a) we suggest seven sets of indicators of differential degrees of committee system institutionalization. These indicators, abstracted from a region-wide survey of Western parliaments, include: structural attributes, membership characteristics, the party system, committee relationships with parliamentary parties, committee autonomy, floor control, and relations with the government.

As measures of differential degrees of institutionalization, we express in hypothesis form what we anticipate finding on the seven sets of indicators (see Appendix 1.1):

1. Committees in institutionalized parliaments would be permanent in existence and jurisdiction, and would parallel the structure of ministries. Such committees would be moderate in both number and in size. Though Western European parliaments vary greatly, we take as an empirical guide the median measures from the eighteen Western European parliament studies (Mattson and Stroem 1995). In them, both the number of committees and their size were related to broader measures of committee power (Mattson and Stroem 1995, 301). Numbers have implications for both specialization and efficiency in the committee system.

2. As committees become increasingly institutionalized, committee membership should have greater significance for the entire legislative body and for individual members. As indicators of institution-wide significance, incumbency would be higher, and mid-session changes lower on committees in more developed parliaments. As indicators of personal significance for individual members, committee assignments would more clearly be relevant to member constituency and skills. Increased incumbency rates in turn increase specialization, and have clear informational and distributional implications for committees (Mattson and Stroem 1995, 254, 276).

3. Party ratios in membership and officer positions on committees would be proportional and consistent across committees in institutionalized parliaments. Proportionality in committee membership and officers is a consensus-building practice, protecting both minority and opposition parties from majority and/or government domination of the policy process (Kraatz and von Steindorf 2001). Consistency of proportionality across all policy committees and over a series of electoral terms with different majorities would be a measure of institutionalization. This practice has been related to broader measures of committee procedural autonomy in Western European parliaments (Mattson and Stroem 1995, 301).

4. The relationship between committees and parties should be clearer and more predictable in more established parliaments. Committee members should have more accurate knowledge of the policy views of their own parties and would more consistently participate in the development of party views on topics within their committee jurisdiction. Though parliamentary parties and committees are inversely related in their importance and strength in some parliaments (Shaw 1979), they can also evolve in mutually supportive and "interlocking" structures and functions (Longley and Davidson 1998). Based especially upon German and Swedish examples, we estimate that institutionalized committees and institutionalized parties would develop stable and active interactions (Patzelt 1997).

5. Committees in established legislatures should have greater autonomy than those in less institutionalized ones. They should have more control of their schedules, have greater latitude in the initiation and amendment of legislation, and make more use of minority reports. There should be more consistent intercommittee coordination, and in bicameral systems, committees would more directly mediate relations between the chambers. This diverse set of measures indicates committee autonomy from both majority party (or coalition) and government control (Mattson and Stroem 1995, 285, 301).

6. Committees in more highly institutionalized parliaments should have more control over floor proceedings on legislation within their jurisdiction than their counterparts in less institutionalized parliaments. Committees would consider legislation prior to significant floor decisions, and more proposed legislation would be examined in committee rather than on the floor. Since not all bills are referred to committees in either the British parliament or in some of the new parliaments, the sheer frequency of committee referral is itself a variable. A more complex question is whether committees or party leaders are in control of floor proceedings on bills that have been referred to committee. This practice in turn is related to the source of the floor text—whether the committee or the government (Mattson and Stroem 1995, 286). A party majority or government would usually have either the formal power of written rules or the political power of the vote to both bypass committees and to manage floor proceedings. But the exercise of that power can vary.

7. Our final set of indicators of committee institutionalization examines potential interactions between committees and government ministers, ranging from informal discussions to more formal review and documents access (Mattson and Stroem 1995, 293–95; Andeweg and Nijzink 1995, 172–73). Committee relationships with ministries would, in institutionalized parliaments, be more varied and regularized, including personal meetings with ministers, discussions prior to formal legislative introduction, and a variety of reporting and monitoring procedures.

Sources of Institutionalization

The intraregional analysis of post-communist legislatures also allows us to undertake an examination of factors that shape the early development of new legislatures. What variables explain emerging differences among the committee systems of post-communist parliaments? We propose that six broad groups of factors underlie different institutionalization forms and processes across the region (see Appendix 1.2). These include the institutional legacy from the communist regime, the policy environment of the transition, the party system, the institutional environment of other governmental actors with which the legislature interacts, the legislature as a critical environment for the committees, and, finally, the resources available to committee.

1. We would anticipate that both the pre-communist and the communist experience of a half-century defined the inheritance of newly democratized parliaments. While we consider the divide between former Soviet republics and the Central European countries to be particularly salient, this factor has varied in intensity among Central Europeans as well.

2. The policy environment differs significantly across the former Soviet Union and Central Europe. Across the region, particular issues have differing levels of intensity and salience. Ethnic conflict, lustration debates, privatization, and constitutional reform each produced deep division in some cases while they are of little importance in others. We suggest that the more complex transition policy environments, characterized by multiple highly salient issues, would hinder the consolidation of legislatures.

3. The party system, often fluid in new democracies, has a direct impact on parliamentary organization and activity. We expect that in either one party dominant, or in highly fragmented parliaments, that committee institutionalization would be lower than in conditions of both stable and moderate party competition. In single party dominant systems there is a clear tendency for policymaking authority to pass to extra-parliamentary forces, and for the parliament and its internal structures to languish (Crowther and Roper 1998). This tendency is reinforced in the post-communist context, in which the tradition of external party control remains strong. Intense fragmentation, on the other hand, threatens to produce such a high level of partisanship and volatility that no regularization of procedure can occur.

4. Since committees interact with the government and ministries, how this relationship is organized and functions will define a critical environment for both the legislature and its committees. Executive dominant systems would present obstacles to legislative institutionalization. While of less concern in established democratic systems, this issue is of central importance in the post-communist transitions, in which the pre-transition political systems are characterized by weak legislatures and strong executive bodies. As in the case of extra-parliamentary party control, it is difficult to imagine that executive domination of the policy process would be conducive to efforts by actors within the legislative branch to develop the institutional capacity to assert countervailing influence.

5. Differential degrees of institutionalization of the committee system will reflect different degrees of institutionalization of the entire

parliament. As subsets of parliament, committees will both reflect and contribute to institution-wide attributes.

6. Committees in more institutionalized parliaments will have more resources than in parliaments that are less developed. They will have access to more resources and skilled personnel. While this factor is related to the resources provided by the parliament for itself and thus reflects the prior hypothesis, we list it separately as a critical and specific component for our understanding of committees and their ability to play a significant role in the legislative process.

Post-Communist Legislatures: An Initial Assessment

The parliaments discussed in this book illustrate both our broad themes and many variations of detail. The parliaments of Poland, the Czech Republic, and Hungary are currently the most institutionalized of our cases, while Estonia, Lithuania, and Moldova are the least. The Bulgarian parliament occupies an intermediate category. The following chapters are grouped by these categories of analysis.

The least stable parliaments illustrate two formative influences upon institutional development. All three were part of the Soviet Union and bear the imprint of that political system in which parliaments were stable but inactive. Their legacies of long-term communism within the political and economic structures of the former Soviet Union are distinct from the experiences of Central European "satellite" states. The two Baltic States, however, did have a prior period of independence. This suggests a further distinction between them and Moldova, which is our "bracketing" case. All three of our chapters in this set of post-Soviet states emphasize the first legislative terms of post-communist democratization. They illustrate the vulnerabilities and tenuousness of the beginning years.

The examples of clear institutionalization of parliamentary committee systems in Central Europe are post-communist, not post-Soviet. The parliaments of Poland, Hungary, and the Czech Republic are more stable than the others. Their committees are more continuous, party ratios more constant, and levels of activity higher in these three parliaments than in the other post-communist parliaments examined here.

These "high institutionalization" cases are differentiated from the others by two background factors: in Poland and Hungary, as Wesolowski and Karpowicz, and Ilonszki, respectively, point out, flexible communist systems permitted their parliaments to develop an active internal structure that became the basis for their current committee structure and practice. In

the Czech Republic, by contrast, as the direct successor to the Czechoslo-
vakian Federation, the interwar experience of a continuously elected democratic parliamentary government was quickly revived and copied in the
post-communist period.

All three relatively institutionalized parliaments exhibited in their
early years the frenetic and experimental behavior also seen in the less institutionalized parliaments of the post-Soviet Republics. But the three stable parliaments have reorganized their committee systems to thereby
regularize both their structure and their behavior. Over a series of electoral-parliamentary cycles, they have gained an increasing proportion of
incumbent members, permitting the development of experience with and
learning of institutional behavior. Incumbency at the committee level,
however, is not identical with reelection to parliament. These cases illustrate the importance of dual incumbency: within a chamber-wide incumbency rate, committees vary greatly in the extent to which their members
had served previously on the same committee.

Finally, the Parliament of Bulgaria occupies an intermediate category
of institutionalization among post-communist countries. Karasimeonov
shows that it has developed a committee system that, in broad outline, resembles the structure of the other post-communist parliaments. Each new
government majority, however, has altered the number of committees for
its own purposes, and committees seem to be more amenable to external
party and government preferences than in the more institutionalized parliaments. The evidence on this last-mentioned criterion is the most difficult
to establish unambiguously of all our criteria.

Taken together, this diverse set of countries illustrates the growth, development, and continual change of the transition parliaments. The variation in our measures of institutionalization suggest that broad themes of
legislative analysis require detailed examination, both intensive and comparative, to better understand the dynamics of institutional growth and
development.

Individual chapters reflect the unique attributes of each parliament
and of the varying sources and types of data for each. Throughout,
however, we seek to understand the organization and practices of each
parliament and its committees from the broader perspective of institutionalization that informs this book. Together, the following chapters illustrate
the rich variety of detail and the complex interaction of context and people who try their best to make democracy work. We shall return to these
themes in our final assessment chapter.

Appendix 1.1
Committee Institutionalization Indicators

Indicator	Low	High
1. Structure		
a. Permanence	temporary	permanent
b. Principle organization	other	agency parallel
c. Number	few or many	10–20
d. Size	40+ members	under 40 members
2. Membership		
a. Number/member	none or many	1–3 committees/member
b. Incumbency	low	high
c. Mid-session changes	high	low
d. Constituency links	weak	strong
e. Member skills	not relevant	relevant
f. Member attendance	sporadic	constant
3. Party Composition	majoritarian	proportional
4. Party Relationships	unstructured	structured
5. Committee Autonomy		
a. Schedule control	no	yes
b. Initiate legislation	no	yes
c. Amend bills	no	yes
d. Minority reports	no	yes
e. Prior to floor	no	yes
f. Bicameral participation	no	yes
g. Intercommitee coordination	low	high
6. Floor Control		
a. % bills referred to committees	low	high
b. Floor debate management	party	committee
7. Government Relations		
a. Meetings with ministers	seldom	frequent
b. Agency reviews	few	more
c. Require information	no	yes
d. Public hearings	no	yes

Appendix 1.2

Institutionalization Source Indicators

1. Institutional Legacy	Communist experience	Democratic experience
2. Policy Tasks	complex, interconnected	functionally specific
3. Party System	fluid, unstable	stable
4. Government	centralized or factionalized	flexible coordination
5. Parliament		
Institutionalization	low	high
a. Party membership	fluid	stable
b. Party internal structure	undefined	differentiated
c. Leadership	unspecified	stable
6. Resources		
a. Rooms, space	small, shared	more, separate
b. Staff	few, shared	more, separate
c. Budget	low	high
d. Documentation	few	many, varied

References

Ágh, Attila, ed. 1994. *The Emergence of East Central European Parliaments: The First Steps.* Budapest: Hungarian Centre of Democracy Studies Foundation.

———. 1998. "Changing Parliamentary Committees in Changing East-Central Europe: Parliamentary Committees as Central Sites of Policy-making." *Journal of Legislative Studies* 4, no. 1 (Spring): 85–100.

Ágh, Attila, and Gabriella Ilonszki, eds. 1996. *Parliaments and Organized Interests: The Second Steps.* Budapest: Hungarian Centre of Democracy Studies Foundation.

Andeweg, Rudy B., and Lia Nijzink. 1995. "Beyond the Two-Body Image: Relations Between Ministers and MPs." In *Parliaments and Majority Rule in Western Europe,* edited by Herbert Döring. New York: St. Martins Press.

Blondel, Jean. 1973. *Comparative Legislatures.* Englewood Cliffs, N.J.: Prentice-Hall.

Carey, John M., Frantisek Formanek, and Ewa Karpowicz. 1999. "Legislative Autonomy in New Regimes: The Czech and Polish Cases." *Legislative Studies Quarterly* 24, no. 4 (November): 569–604.

Copeland, Gary W., and Samuel C. Patterson. 1994. "Changing an Institutionalized System." In *Parliaments in the Modern World,* edited by Gary W. Copeland and Samuel C. Patterson. Ann Arbor: University of Michigan Press.

Cox, Gary, and Matthew McCubbins. 1993. *Legislative Leviathan: Party Government in the House.* Berkeley: University of California Press.

Crowther, William, and Steven Roper. 1998. "The Institutionalization of the Romanian Parliament." *Southeastern Political Review* 26, no. 2 (June): 401–26.

Döring, Herbert, ed. 1995a. *Parliaments and Majority Rule in Western Europe.* New York: St. Martins Press.

Döring, Herbert. 1995b. "Time as a Scarce Resource: Government Control of the Agenda." In *Parliaments and Majority Rule in Western Europe,* edited by Herbert Döring. New York: St. Martins Press.

Eulau, Heinz, and Vera McCluggage. 1985. "Standing Committees in Legislatures." In *Handbook of Legislative Research,* edited by Gerhard Loewenberg, S. C. Patterson, and M. E. Jewell. Cambridge, Mass.: Harvard University Press. 395–470.

Francis, Wayne. 1985. *The Legislative Committee Game: A Comparative Analysis of Fifty States.* Columbus: Ohio State University Press.

Hahn, Jeffrey W., ed. 1996a. *Democratization in Russia: The Development of Legislative Institutions.* Armonk, N.Y.: M. E. Sharpe.

Hahn, Jeffrey W. 1996b. "Introduction: Analyzing Parliamentary Development in Russia." In *Democratization in Russia,* edited by Jeffrey W. Hahn. Armonk, N.Y.: M. E. Sharpe. 3–25.

Hibbing, John, and Samuel Patterson. 1992. "A Democratic Legislature in the Making: The Historic Hungarian Elections of 1990." *Comparative Political Studies* 20: 430–54.

———. 1994. "The Emergence of Democratic Parliaments in Central and Eastern Europe." In *Parliaments in the Modern World,* edited by Gary W. Copeland and Samuel C. Patterson. Ann Arbor: University of Michigan Press.

Huntington, Samuel. 1968. *Political Order in Changing Societies.* New Haven, Conn.: Yale University Press.

Kitschelt, Herbert, Zdenka Mansfeldová, Radoslaw Markowski, and Gabor Toka. 1991. *Post-Communist Party Systems.* Cambridge: Cambridge University Press.

Kopecky, Petr. 2001. *Parliaments in the Czech and Slovak Republics: Party Competition and Parliamentary Institutionalization.* Aldershot, UK: Ashgate.

Korbonski, Andrzej. 1999. "The New Democracies in East Central Europe and the Legacies of Communism." In *Power and Social Structure,* edited by Aleksandra Jasinska-Kania, Aleksandra, M. Slomczynski and M. Kohn. Warsaw: Wydawnictwa Uniwersytetu Warszawskiego. 199–211.

Kraatz, Susanne, and Sylvia von Steindorf. 2001. "Government Majority and Opposition in Post-Communist Parliaments." Paper presented to European Consortium for Political Research Congress, University of Kent, Canterbury UK, September 6–10, 2001.

Krehbiel, Keith. 1991. *Information and Legislative Organization.* Ann Arbor: University of Michigan Press.

Lees, John D., and Malcolm Shaw, eds., 1979. *Committees in Legislatures: A Comparative Analysis.* Durham, N.C.: Duke University Press.

Linz, Juan, and Alfred Stepan. 1996. *Problems of Democratic Transition and Consolidation.* Baltimore, Md.: Johns Hopkins University Press.

Loewenberg, Gerhard, and Samuel C. Patterson. 1979. *Comparing Legislatures.* Boston: Little, Brown.

Longley, Lawrence, and Attila Ágh, eds. 1997. *Working Papers on Comparative*

Legislative Studies II: The Changing Roles of Parliamentary Committees. Appleton, Wis.: Research Committee of Legislative Specialists, IPSA.

Longley, Lawrence, and Roger Davidson, eds. 1998. "The New Roles of Parliamentary Committees." *Journal of Legislative Studies* Special Issue 4, no. 1 (Spring).

Mair, Peter. 1997. *Party System Change: Approaches and Interpretations.* Oxford: Clarendon Press.

Maltzman, Forrest, and Steven S. Smith. 1994. "Principals, Goals, Dimensionality, and Congressional Committees." *Legislative Studies Quarterly* 19, no. 4 (November): 457–76.

Mason, David S. 1991. "The Polish Parliament and Labor Legislation during Solidarity." In *Legislatures in the Policy Process,* edited by David M. Olson and Michael L. Mezey. Cambridge: Cambridge University Press. 179–200.

Mattson, Ingvar, and Kaare Stroem. 1995. "Parliamentary Committees." In *Parliaments and Majority Rule in Western Europe,* edited by Herbert Döring. New York: St. Martins Press.

Mezey, Michael L. 1979. *Comparative Legislatures.* Durham, N.C.: Duke University Press.

Mueller-Rommel, Ferdinand. 1990. "Interest Group Representation in the German Bundestag." In *The U.S. Congress and the German Budestag: Comparisons of Democratic Processes,* edited by Uwe Thaysen, R. Davidson, and R. Livingston. Boulder, Colo.: Westview Press.

North, Douglas C. 1990. *Institutions, Institutional Change and Economic Performance.* New York: Cambridge University Press.

Norton, Philip, and David M. Olson. 1996. "Parliaments in Adolescence." In *The New Parliaments of Central and Eastern Europe,* edited by David M. Olson and Philip Norton. London: Cass.

Olson, David M. 1994. *Democratic Legislative Institutions.* Armonk, N.Y.: M. E. Sharpe.

———. 1997. "Paradoxes of Institutional Development: The New Democratic Parliaments of Central Europe." *International Political Science Review* 18, no. 4: 401–16.

Olson, David M., and Philip Norton, eds. 1996. *The New Legislatures of Central and East Europe.* London: Cass.

Olson, David M., and Maurice D. Simon. 1982. "The Institutional Development of a Minimal Parliament: The Case of the Polish Sejm." In *Communist Legislatures in Comparative Perspective,* edited by Daniel Nelson and Stephen White. London: Macmillan.

Ostrow, Joel M. 2000. *Comparing Post-Soviet Legislatures: A Theory of Institutional Design and Political Conflict.* Columbus: Ohio State University Press, 2000.

Patterson, Samuel C. 1995. "Legislative Institutions and Institutionalism in the United States." *Journal of Legislative Studies* 1, no. 4 (Winter): 10–29.

Patterson, Samuel C., and Gary W. Copeland. 1994. "Parliaments in the Twenty-First Century." In *Parliaments in the Modern World,* edited by Gary W. Copeland and Samuel C. Patterson. Ann Arbor: University of Michigan Press.

Patzelt, Werner. 1997. "German Mps and Their Roles." *Journal of Legislative Studies* 3, no. 1 (Spring): 79–90.

Polsby, Nelson W. 1968. "The Institutionalization of the U.S. House of Representatives." *American Political Science Review* 62 (September): 144–68.

Racz, Barnabas. 1989. "The Parliamentary Infrastructure and Political Reforms in Hungary." *Soviet Studies* 41, no. 1 (January): 39–66.

Remington, Thomas. 1994. "Partisan Competition and Democratic Stability." In *Parliaments in Transition,* edited by Thomas Remington. Boulder, Colo.: Westview Press.

Remington, Thomas, and Stephen Smith. 1996. "The Early Legislative Process in the Russian Federal Assembly." In *The New Legislatures of Central and Eastern Europe,* edited by David M. Olson and Philip Norton. London: Cass.

Rommetvedt, Hilmar. 1998. "Norwegian Parliamentary Committees: Performance, Structural Change, and External Relations." *Journal of Legislative Studies* 4, no. 1 (Spring): 60–84.

Shabad, Goldie, and Kazimierz M. Slomczymski. 1999. "The Formation and Institutionalization of a New Political Class in East-Central Europe: Continuities and Discontinuities." Paper presented at 1999 Annual Meeting of American Political Science Association, Atlanta, Georgia.

Shaw, Malcolm. 1979. "Conclusion." In *Committees in Legislatures: A Comparative Analysis,* edited by John D. Lees and Malcolm Shaw. Durham, N.C.: Duke University Press.

———. 1998. "Parliamentary Committees: A Global Perspective." *Journal of Legislative Studies* 4, no. 1 (Spring): 225–51.

Shepsle, Kenneth A., and Barry R. Weingast. 1994. "Positive Theories of Congressional Institutions." *Legislative Studies Quarterly* 19, no. 2 (May): 149–79.

Sisson, Richard. 1973. "Comparative Legislative Institutionalization: A Theoretical Exploration." In *Legislatures in Comparative Perspective,* edited by Allan Kornberg. New York: McKay.

Stroem, Kaare. 1997. "Rules, Reasons and Routines: Legislative Roles in Parliamentary Democracies." *Journal of Legislative Studies* 3, no. 1 (Spring): 155–74.

Wesolowski, Wlodzimierz, and Jacek Wasilewski, eds. 1992. *Poczatki Parlamentarnej Elity.* Warsaw: Institute of Philosophy and Sociology, PAN.

Wesolowski, Wlodzimierz, and Irena Pankow, eds. 1995. *Swiat elity politycznej.* Warsaw: Wydawnictwo IFiS PAN.

Wilson, Rick K. 1999. "Transitional Governance in the United States: Lessons from the First Federal Congress." *Legislative Studies Quarterly* 24, no. 4 (November): 549–68.

Wilson, Woodrow. 1956 [1885]. *Congressional Government.* New York: Meridian Books.

Zakrzewski, Witold. 1982. "Die gesetzgeberische Tätigkeit des Parlaments (Sejm) der Volkerepublik Polen in der VIII Legislaturperiode bis 13, Dezember 1981." *Ost-Europa Recht* 3, no. 4: 210–14.

PART 2

Institutionalized Parliaments of Central Europe

TWO

A Functional Clarification of Parliamentary Committees in Hungary, 1990–98

Gabriella Ilonszki

THIS CHAPTER WILL SHOW HOW THE COMMITTEE SYSTEM WAS established and consolidated in the Hungarian parliament. After two legislative terms and three democratic elections, the direction of the transformation and the trend toward stabilization of parliamentary institutions can be evaluated. In Hungary there have been two full parliamentary terms, the first from May 1990 to April 1994, and the second from June 1994 to April 1998. The parliamentary party framework remained relatively straightforward during these eight years. The same six parties were elected to parliament in the first and second elections. There have, however, been some changes to the parties and to the coalitions formed by these parties. In 1998 one party disintegrated and was replaced by a new one. The coalition in power changed in each of the three sessions. In the first term a center-right coalition was in power, in the second term a center-left coalition took over, and in the third term a conservative coalition was in power.

This chapter will demonstrate that legislative committees consolidate their memberships, organizations, and activities. These developments can be understood under the broader term of functional clarification, a process through which the legislative, oversight, and stabilization functions of committees become settled and clear after initial uncertainty. This chapter seeks to show that committees bring stability to the parliament, and that they contribute to the prominence and complexity of the Hungarian legislature. Thus, they are forerunners and agents of parliamentary institutionalization. This chapter will examine first, how committees were

21

established, second, their consolidation in terms of membership, and then, their activity in the context of internal organization, differentiation, and external connections. Finally, their functional transformation in terms of constraints and freedoms will be presented.

The Formation of the Committee System

During the democratic transition, both the elite and the public had concrete assumptions about how parliament should work in a democracy that affected the formation of parliamentary committees. These assumptions were based on two different premises. One assumed a talking parliament with independent members of parliament with more emphasis on discussion and debate, and the other, a working parliament with effective legislative capacity. Committees were assumed to fulfill several functions regarding legislation and oversight. The process of committee formation and transformation will show how committee developments contributed to the clarification of these initial assumptions and debates.

Since parties were the main actors in the transition, the parliamentary party groups became the major actors in parliament. As a result, the party groups, and not the committees, obtained the available financial resources. Party and political "talk" was emphasized in the first legislative term, but it was criticized on the grounds that it inhibited the "professional" work of the parliament. Despite this criticism, the reality of the evolving parliamentary system of government with its focus on elite and parliamentary-centered parties made parliamentary party groups the engines of parliamentary politics.

During an extended debate following the 1990 elections, the extremes of large French-type committees and a more structured and specialized committee system were discussed. Eventually a "continental type" committee system was established. The parliamentary parties worked out a political agreement (parliamentary resolution no. 1990/41) to establish a relatively modest number of committees. A general agreement prevailed that the evolving standing committee system should follow the logic of governmental functions, and committees should follow the distribution of ministries. Of course, there are committees, such as the Budget Committee, that could receive bills affecting many ministries.

The most unusual case is that of the House Committee consisting of the Speaker, Vice Speakers, and leaders of the parliamentary party groups. Although it was established as a type of standing committee, its functions are more political and managerial. For example, it was given the responsi-

bility to set the agenda for the parliament. As an institutional development, from November 1990 on, the agenda for next week's plenary session was set and the draft agenda for the next two weeks was discussed at
a meeting of the committee chairs with participation from the speaker or
vice speaker. The committee chairs justified this action on the grounds that
the agenda depended on how committees proceeded with the bills referred
to them. Also, a Committee Office was formed to manage the committees.

Ten standing committees and five special committees were formed. In
many respects, the regulations concerning their functions reflected the different assumptions about parliament. On the one hand, committees were
given special powers to initiate legislation, to discuss and report on legislative initiatives, to hold hearings and issue written reports, and to receive
information from outside experts to achieve these aims. On the other
hand, it was not the committees but the parliamentary party groups that
received financial resources needed to hire experts. The parliamentary parties became the locus of policy formation, because the external parties remained weak and did not have time to work out their programs during the
period of fast systemic change.

The 1990 agreement included the distribution of committee membership and leadership by proportional representation of the parliamentary
parties. Thus, the opposition parties got committee chair positions in an
attempt to ensure that one party could not dominate. It is no wonder that
the place of committees was initially controversial. The chair positions
were actually determined by a bargaining process among parliamentary
party groups. Changes in the parliamentary party distribution of the
House were reflected in the committees' memberships during the first two
terms.

The committee system was modified in the autumn of 1992. The number of committees increased to twelve with the addition of the committees
on education and agriculture, and the number of special committees increased to six. After the 1994 elections, the new majority in the House
soon accepted new Standing Orders, which changed the number of standing committees to seventeen by abolishing the special committees as a category and converting the existing special committees into standing
committees. At the same time, a temporary committee category was created, and was in fact vested with substantial prestige.

Temporary committees included both investigative committees, which
examined controversial political and economic affairs, and case committees, which looked into concrete but wide-ranging and important social
topics. This development also signaled a change in political orientation.
Although it was possible to establish investigative committees in the first
legislative term, only one such committee was set up during the entire

four-year period. Under the new Standing Orders, it became possible to create investigative committees at the written request of one-fifth of the MPs. The opposition groups used these new committees to scrutinize the government more extensively. As a result, a larger number of case and investigative temporary committees were set up, and a clear distinction was made between the standing and temporary committees.

In the summer of 1995, two new standing committees were added to the list. The Committee on Social Organizations followed the regular pattern of standing committees. The Committee on Constitutional Preparation was composed of an equal number of MPs from each parliamentary party with the task preparing a new constitution. With this development, the committee system was completed (see Table 2.1).

Table 2.1 also shows the membership figures. The size of a committee may indicate its relative importance. The membership of Social and Health Affairs, Environmental Affairs, and Cultural Affairs Committees decreased in the second term. Except for those three committees, the stability is striking. The logic used to form the committee system did not change substantially. The only exception is the Committee on European Integration, the membership of which increased considerably.

Table 2.1 also indicates whether the chair positions of a given committee was in government or in opposition hands. Some committees are led by the opposition irrespective of the distribution of parties in the House. For example, interior affairs and budgeting were in opposition hands in both legislative terms. In contrast, after the change of government in 1994, the new government kept the Foreign Affairs and the Human Rights Committee chair positions that it had held while in opposition. While committee leadership functions are often considered technical rather than political, the importance of committee chairs cannot be ignored. Seniority does not prevail; instead, parties tend to nominate well-known experts in the given field as committee chair and vice chair(s).

The importance and influence of the committee leadership became obvious in the second legislative term when the government—despite its large majority of 72 percent—made gestures towards the minority opposition by introducing more consensual elements into parliamentary procedures. For example, as already mentioned, an initiative by one-fifth of the MPs can establish an investigative committee. As another consensual gesture, the new 1994 Standing Orders gave the minority parties more rights than in the previous term. The minority opinion of the committee could be presented to the plenary session, and the committee minority could initiate a ministerial or other committee hearing.

Consensual methods made committee chair positions more important. In those committees with a government chair, the chair regularly worked

Table 2.1

Standing Committees in the Hungarian Parliament with Membership Size, and Government or Opposition Chairmanship, 1990–1997

| | 1990 May | | | 1992 Oct | | | 1994 Nov | | | 1995 Dec | | | 1997 Dec.* | | |
| | | Chm | | | Chm | | | Chm | | | Chm | | | Chm | |
Committee	N	G	O	N	G	O	N	G	O	N	G	O	N	G	O
Constitutional Affairs	26	x		25	x		27	x		27	x		27	x	
Interior Affairs	25		x	26		x	27		x	27		x	26		x
Foreign Affairs	23		x	23		x	27	x		27	x		26	x	
Defense	24	x		22	x		19	x		19	x		19	x	
Budgeting	26		x	26		x	27		x	27		x	26		x
Economic Affairs	26	x		26	x		27	x		27	x		27	x	
Social and Health Affairs	26	x		28	x		19	x		19	x		19	x	
Environmental Affairs	23	x		23	x		19	x		19	x		19	x	
Cultural Affairs	25	x		25	x		19	x		19	x		19	x	
Human Rights	25		x	25		x	19	x		19	x		20	x	
Educational Affairs	-	-	-	19	x		19	x		19	x		19	x	
Agricultural Affairs	-	-	-	19	x		27	x		27	x		27	x	
Immunity and Credentials	-	-	-	-	-	-	8	x		8	x		10	x	
National Security	-	-	-	-	-	-	9		x	9		x	11		x
European Integration	-	-	-	-	-	-	15		x	15		x	23		x
Auditing	-	-	-	-	-	-	13	x		13	x		14	x	
Employment	-	-	-	-	-	-	13		x	13		x	14		x
Social Organizations	-	-		-	-		-	-	-	16	x		16	x	
Constitutional Preparation	-	-		-	-		-	-	-	25	x		25	x	
Total	223	6	4	287	8	4	334	12	5	375	14	5	387	14	5

Note: *At the end of 1997 actual membership figures were occasionally lower because one of the parliamentary party groups disintegrated in 1997.
G = Government Parties; O = Opposition Parties; Chm = Chairmanship

with two vice chairs (one from the government, one from the opposition). In the committees with an opposition chair, the two vice chairs were always from the government. In key committees, three government vice chairs counterbalanced the opposition chair. This party pattern demonstrates that chairs were regarded not only as keepers of timetables and agendas, but also as managers of committee work.

These developments can be placed in a logical sequence. First, despite the several changes that have occurred, the original structure was basically maintained. This continuity agrees with the findings of the "institutionalization" literature that the initial steps may remain decisive in later periods. Second, in many cases, functional needs explained the transformation of the committee system. For example, as European integration approached, the Committee on European Integration became a standing committee, and its membership increased dramatically. The Committee for Constitutional Preparation was formed in response to a concrete demand.[1] The separation of educational affairs from cultural affairs on the ministerial level followed by the establishment of a new committee on education also served functional needs. In other cases, the committee itself initiated the change. For example, the Agricultural Committee was first established as a subcommittee of the Economic Committee. Third, the general demand to have a clearer committee system can force transformation. The extinction of the special committee category is a case in point.

The consolidation process went beyond an enlargement of the committee system. Due to the experiences of the first term, the new Standing Orders in 1994 introduced measures to increase the role of committees in some areas. The effect of these changes will also be examined in the section concerning the functional clarification of committees.

Membership and Professionalization

Continuity ensures that members become more skilled and can use the potential, or develop the potential, of a given institution fully. In return, membership continuity fosters stable structures. Continuity is a delicate issue in democratizing countries because turnover rates are regularly high in the first terms. In 1990, the Hungarian legislature had a mere 7 percent incumbency rate. Even in 1994, it had only a 36 percent and in 1998, 47 percent. My hypotheses are that: a) membership continuity and consequently professionalization patterns will be more pronounced in committees than in the entire parliament; b) parties will show different professionalization patterns; and c) the comparative importance of committees can be detected by membership continuity figures. Thus, in the following I shall examine committee membership with respect to: a) the entire parliament; b) the parties; and c) the differences between committees.

Parliament

Large turnover rates in new democracies are a feature of the party-political scene and do not come from the performance of parliament. Thus it is important to test how the efforts to establish stability, and to professionalize parliamentary work, can be detected in parliament and in committees.

The number of committee seats has constantly increased. At the beginning of May 1990, the number of seats in the standing and special committees together was 300. At the end of 1997, it was 415. Even if we exclude the seats in temporary committees, seats in standing committees at the end of the second legislative term outnumber by one the number of seats in the entire House (387 versus 386). As we noted in the previous section, expansion was often due to functional needs, functional clarification, and committee initiatives. We must add that committee seats are financially rewarding for the members.[2] Also, important committee positions can bring visibility to individual members.

The demand to ensure proportional representation for the parties also increased membership. Not only functional needs, but also personal and political interests affected the increase in committee positions. Nevertheless, many MPs do not have a committee seat while others occupy more than one. Although the number of MPs without a committee seat has decreased almost continuously, the number was still relatively high near the end of the second term (sixty-three MPs, or approximately 16 percent).[3] In contrast, as of July 1997, sixty-six MPs had two or more standing committee seats. The number of MPs without a committee position and those having more than one position was almost identical.

There is a group of MPs that is more embedded, and another that is less embedded in parliamentary work than the average member. The first group is made up of a more professional segment of the parliamentarians as shown by the background of those who have multiple committee positions. According to the first hypothesis, incumbency would be more pronounced among committee members than in the House as a whole.[4] Indeed, while the incumbency rate was 36 percent in the entire parliament in 1994 (137 MPs from a total of 386), it is close to 60 percent among those with several committee seats (sixty MPs of the 101 that have two or more committee positions). The rate is more than 90 percent if we exclude the less important investigation committee positions (sixty MPs are incumbents of the sixty-six who have two or more standing committee positions). Experienced MPs acquire more committee positions than newcomers.

Parties

Professionalization patterns will be different in different parties. The number of MPs with multiple committee positions was the highest among the two governing parliamentary parties between 1994 and 1998. The MSZP (Socialists) and SZDSZ (Free Democrats) held twenty-two and twenty-three positions respectively. Since these parliamentary party groups are larger than the opposition parliamentary groups, larger numbers do not mean higher proportions. In fact, members in smaller parliamentary party groups more often serve on two committees, otherwise their party could not fill in the committee seats available to them.

Incumbency rates in the individual parties were diverse, ranging from the lowest, 15 percent of the MSZP, to the highest, 75 percent of the SZDSZ. The Fidesz-MPP (Young Democrats) and the MDF (Forum) also belong to the highest level incumbency group of parties (70 percent and 68 percent respectively). In the two most stable parliamentary party groups, the Free Democrats and the Young Democrats, incumbents have multiple committee positions in a larger proportion than their highest incumbency rate (82 percent versus 75 percent, and 78 percent versus 70 percent). Thus, while incumbents generally tend to have more committee positions than nonincumbents, this trend is even more explicit in parties that show high stability. We can conclude that the performance of the entire party helps professionalization trends. Even in the FGKP (Smallholders) and the KDNP (Christian Democrats), the rate of multiple positions is higher among the incumbents than the party's general incumbency pattern (54 percent versus 27 percent, and 40 percent versus 36 percent respectively).

The large governing Socialist parliamentary party group seems to be the exception to the rule for several reasons. First, the general incumbency rate of the party was very low because many new members were elected in their landslide victory of 1994, and second, the party does not provide the incumbents with multiple committee seats, but has them serve in the government.

Thus, it seems that there are at least two ways to reward incumbents: government positions and committee positions. The Socialist incumbents are a good example of the former. In all the other parties a high proportion of the parliamentary incumbents serve on committees. Virtually all the 137 parliamentary incumbents have a committee seat or a government post.

Committee

The third hypothesis is that in more important committees personal continuity will be even higher than average. To test this hypothesis, personal continuity within the same committee will be examined. This comparison will be made between the first and the second legislative terms (interterm comparison) and then within the second legislative term (intraterm comparison). The MDF (Forum) and the MSZP (Socialists), the leading forces of the first and second democratic elections respectively, are omitted from the analysis of the interterm personal continuity, because of a large variation in their size in the two terms.

In the second term, among the remaining four parliamentary parties, eighty committee members were incumbents, and among them, thirty-four served in the same committee both in the first and the second terms. This group almost exclusively consisted of Free Democrats and Young Democrats, the two parties that demonstrated professionalization trends in other respects as well. Although these figures may be lower than in established legislatures with long democratic traditions, they are signs of continuity in Hungary, considering its low level of parliamentary incumbency.

The table on intraterm continuity (see Table 2.2) provides a general view of the stability of committee members and demonstrates committee differences as well. The second column indicates the total number of MPs serving in a committee during the second legislative term (1994–98). In the third column, the percentage figures represent the proportion of these members to the number of committee seats, while the last column indicates the consistency of committee members as a proportion of seats.

The number and share of committee members compared to the size of committee ranges from 110 percent (twenty-one served in the Education Committee while the committee size was nineteen) to 165 percent (thirty-three served on the Human Rights Committee while the committee size was twenty). These figures do not necessarily indicate consistency, because a few seats could have changed hands several times while the majority of the seats were stable. Thus the last column in the table shows the actual membership consistency, that is, the number and share of MPs who served in the same committee without interruption throughout the period, ranging from 30 percent (Immunity Committee) to 81 percent (Foreign Affairs). Some important committees perform relatively badly, for example, the interior committee with 50 percent consistency. At the other extreme, Foreign Affairs, Education, Agriculture, Cultural Affairs, Defense, Economic and Cultural Affairs are above the two-thirds consistency level. It can be assumed that parties tend to select the members of these committees more carefully.

Table 2.2

Stability in Committees in the Hungarian Parliament Second Term, 1995–1997

Committee	Committee Size End of 1997	Anytime During the Period N	% of Committee Size	N	% of Committee Size
		Persons Serving in Committee		*Members with Continuous Committee Service*	
Constitutional	27	35	130%	18	67%
Interior	26	37	142%	13	50%
Foreign Aff.	26	31	119%	21	81%
Defense	19	25	131%	13	68%
Budgeting	26	40	153%	16	62%
Economic	27	35	129%	18	67%
Social	19	24	126%	16	84%
Environmental	19	29	152%	11	58%
Cultural	19	26	136%	13	68%
Human Rights	20	33	165%	10	50%
Education	19	21	110%	15	79%
Agricultural	27	34	125%	20	74%
Immunity	10	16	160%	3	30%
Nat. Security	11	18	163%	4	36%
European Int.	23	32	139%	9	39%
Auditing	14	21	150%	9	64%
Employment	14	17	121%	9	64%
Social Org.	16	22	137%	11	69%
Const. Prep.	25	31	124%	12	48%
Total	387	527	—	241	—

Professionalization of the parliament becomes manifest if we examine the professional background of committee members. The democratic parliaments were highly educated with 88 percent of MPs having a university degree in the first parliament and 91 percent in the second. In the first parliament the three dominant degrees were humanities (30 percent), law (20 percent) and engineering (14 percent), while in the second parliament humanities (24 percent) economics (20 percent), and law (18 percent) ranked the highest.

Different committees show different professional degree patterns. For example, in the Constitutional Committee (63 percent), Constitutional Preparation Committee (77 percent), and Immunity Committee (46 percent), the number of law degrees is much higher than the parliamentary average; while economics degrees dominate in the Budget (47 percent),

Economy (44 percent) and European Integration Committees (71 percent), and humanities degrees in the Education Committee (62 percent).

We conclude that the three hypotheses about membership patterns were supported by the evidence. Committee positions could be associated with a well-defined membership group, the incumbents. There were significant differences between the parties in this respect. In some parties professional politicians are more numerous than in others. Both the interterm and intraterm committee continuity tends to indicate that committees began to work as agents of parliamentary institutionalization. We also found that the consolidation of membership went further, and that specific professional background patterns began to appear in certain committees.

Committees at Work

The work of committees is mainly determined by the Standing Orders, but in practice, committee activity can be analyzed from two perspectives: 1) how committees actually work internally; and 2) how they relate to other parliamentary actors. These activities reveal the consolidation process of the committees.

Internal Activities

Each committee prepares an agenda for itself. As they set the agenda, they consider the government's legislative agenda that the prime minister publishes at the beginning of each year. Then they consult the agenda of the ministry or ministries to which they are related. Committees will consider certain proposals of their members and even the suggestions of other actors or organizations. This sequence shows the hierarchy of importance. The third and fourth sources are often neglected in the process of forming the internal agenda. Members of committees often complain that they are under the pressure of the government's agenda. If the committee has a preference in setting its agenda, it has only limited means to push its case. To increase the potential of committees to set agendas would require a joint action of different committees at the Meeting of the Committee Chairs.

Committee meetings are weekly, and their working period is clearly specified. While plenary sessions take place on Mondays and Tuesdays, committees regularly meet on Wednesdays. Committee meetings are public except when the committee decides to meet in closed session. The media are hardly ever interested in committee meetings to the dismay of committee members and leaders. The public gets information only on "scandalous" committee cases and plenary sessions.

The number of committee meetings did not increase steadily. In some cases the number remained constant; in other cases it even decreased. The committee itself determines the schedule of committee meetings, with the committee chair presenting a proposal. While committee chairs are not senior figures with authority, their proposals are not challenged but accepted quickly because the proposals are embedded in the legislative agenda already decided elsewhere and in the discipline of the parliamentary majority. The committee gets professional and secretarial help from the small committee office of three staff members for each committee in the first cycle and four staff members in the second.

External Activities

An important external activity of the committees is connecting with experts. There are virtually no permanent experts connected to committees, but they are invited to give their expertise in specific cases. The resources available to prepare background materials are very limited, although there has been some increase since a democratic parliamentary government was established. The committee chair frequently invites the experts, but members can propose them as well. A majority of the committee must agree on the suggested person. Despite limited opportunities, there are big differences in whether committees use experts and how often they use them. There is also a difference in whether the experts are more closely tied to the chair or to the committee as such. A chair with a strong position in the party hierarchy and/or one who is closely tied to the professional field of the committee will play a more activist role. This is also true of external connections. Whether or not to invite the press, and how often, if at all, to hold a public meeting will largely depend on how the chair perceives the function of the committee.

Other important external connections are to organizations and interest groups. Committees seek to involve them, and thus they invite groups that they think would be interested in a given bill. In the first parliamentary term this tendency was still relatively vague, but in the second term, committees frequently informed and invited interested groups to their meetings. This practice became more common after a register of interest groups, or a lobby list, was put together by the Chief Clerk of the House. The lobby list is a public document, published in an official format.

Committee Activity and Functional Clarification: Realities and Perceptions

In addition to the above consideration of the internal and external environment, committee activity can be approached from a functional perspective. Legal regulations and the Standing Orders provide broad functions to committees in both legislation and oversight. In the first part of this section I will argue that in both major areas committee activity became more complex and developed as functional clarification took place. In the second part of the section, the perceptions and views of MPs themselves will add a different perspective to this argument.

Institutional Functions

With respect to legislation, committees have the right to initiate and amend bills, but their right to reject bills is limited to private members' bills. In concrete terms, the overall legislative performance of the Hungarian parliament is impressive in the number and range of laws. In the first term 432 and in the second term 498 new or amended laws were passed. Committees had a substantial but changing role in this process. In the beginning, committees participated actively in initiating legislation, presumably because the first new government was not well prepared to fulfill this function. In the first full year (1991) they proposed close to two dozen laws, while in the second parliamentary term the entire number of laws initiated by the committees was not much higher. The government had an increasing role in the initiation of bills, while the role of committee diminished, and the role of individual MPs somewhat decreased.[5] The share of committee-initiated legislation was 7 percent in the first term and a mere 2 percent in the second term. Their success rates improved: twenty-six were accepted in the first term (50 percent) and eleven (68 percent) in the second term. The success rate of government bills was 94 percent in the 1994–98 period, while the success rate of individual members' bills was a mere 18 percent.

The role of committees was meant to increase as compared to the role of individual members, according to the new Standing Orders of 1994. The committees were given the right to accept or reject the motions and amendments of individual MPs. Previously, all the motions of the individual MPs reached the plenary session, causing an enormous workload. Now, the committees act like a filter, because they do not have to forward an individual MP's motion to the plenary if it does not get at least one-third support in committee. This saves a lot of work at the plenary level and has an impact on the activities of parliamentary party groups and individual MPs. It is the Speaker of the House with the House Committee and the less powerful but important Meeting of Committee Chairs that decide to send the bill to committee(s) for the first proper review.

There were some changes between the two legislative terms in this complex process. Bills were forwarded to more committees in the first cycle than in the second one. The majority of bills were sent to both the Constitutional and Legal Committee to help with codification, and also to the committee(s) functionally related to the bill. Occasionally a committee might ask for a bill even when it is not originally referred to it. Table 2.3 shows the number of bills referred to individual committees as well as the number of bills discussed but not referred to committees. The workloads of the committees are very different.

There are two further stages in the legislative process in which the committees have a role. After both the first and second reading in the plenary when amendments to bills appear in large numbers, the committee discusses the amendments and takes an active part in legislation. The committee itself is entitled to propose amendments. The amending procedure in the committee is finalized with a vote. If there is a minority opinion in committee, it will be sent forward to the plenary also.

The obvious area for committee activity lies not with the actual bill preparation but in other parts of the legislative process. For example, in the first term, committees proposed 760 amendments to bills. In the second term, in addition to amending bills, they successfully filtered motions. The committees now are entitled to prepare and present broad discussion materials to the plenary session for general debate to clarify the implications of a particular piece of legislation. These measures point towards a working parliament in which the role of committees is expanding. The internal complexity of committees grew, particularly in the second term. Initially subcommittees were less well organized. Although thirty-seven subcommittees had been formed in the first term, their position was unclear, and many had been formed but rarely or never worked. They were established on two grounds. The subcommittees either dealt continuously with a field or area within the committee framework, or for a limited time on a concrete case. Initially the subcommittees working on a case were more numerous, and then this trend changed. These subcommittees were the test tubes for more professional committee activity from the start, because non-party considerations were less important to them. Subcommittees mushroomed in committees where it was easy to divide the committee's policy field.

In the second term the number of subcommittees was seventy-one, and, with a few exceptions, they were all working bodies. Moreover, membership continuity and professional orientation were more explicit

Table 2.3
Number of Bills Referred to Committee and Number of Other Bills Discussed in Committee, Hungarian Parliament, 1995–1997

Committee	Bills Referred to Committee			Other Bills Discussed in Committee		
	1995	*1996*	*1997*	*1995*	*1996*	*1997*
Constitutional	56	46	86	5	20	14
Foreign Affairs	30	34	28	0	0	0
Interior Affairs	49	45	47	0	0	0
Budgeting	51	50	70	3	8	2
Economic Affairs	54	43	40	0	0	0
Defense	13	9	13	0	0	0
Social Affairs	21	31	29	1	1	3
Environmental	16	16	20	3	2	0
Cultural	16	15	21	0	0	0
Human Rights	17	25	35	7	1	2
Agricultural	41	27	7	0	0	0
Education	13	15	22	4	0	0
European integration	9	4	5	0	0	0
Auditing	11	8	9	2	1	0
Employment	17	25	24	0	4	0
National Security	3	3	3	1	2	0
Immunity	0	1	1	0	1	0
Social Organizations	0	0	0	0	0	0
Constitution Prep.	0	0	0	0	0	0
Total	417	397	460	26	40	21

than in the committees themselves. The functional diversity of the subcommittees contributed to the institutionalization of the parliament.

Oversight took several forms. All citizens must appear before committees when requested. In addition, committees have formal and informal hearings. Formal hearings are related to the nomination of new officials to certain posts. Informal hearings are regularly held when the committees seek information and hear opinions on certain issues from outside actors who are invited to present their viewpoints. Subcommittees are often organized with the aim of overseeing the implementation of a law. Special committees of investigation are formed occasionally to examine a certain problem area that is not properly handled in the opinion of the members of parliament.

Oversight is the function not only of committees but of the entire parliament. In several cases, however, parliamentary oversight is transferred to committees. The compulsory reports provided by members of the government and other national organizations are placed before a committee. The committee's evaluation is placed in turn before the plenary which then decides to accept or reject the report. There are many formal elements in this process, because the party division both in the committee and in the plenary would ensure the acceptance of these reports. Nevertheless, quite often the government and the national bodies do not fulfill their constitutional duties and do not present their reports. Thus, the oversight function of parliament is injured.

Committees held more hearings on average in the second legislative term than in the first one. Some committees proved to be pioneers in establishing new forms in several areas. Committees developed public relations by organizing open days. Some utilized expertise more effectively than others. The amount the committees could spend for hiring experts was raised under committee pressure, although party groups still have much wider resources. Committee connections to external interest groups, civic organizations, etc., became more transparent because committees officially invite, and, if possible, seek to involve the groups affected by the legislative bill under discussion.

Member Perceptions

In addition to these concrete changes and developments, MPs became more interested in and more conscious of the committees, demonstrated both by a questionnaire survey and by interviews about committee work.[6]

In the questionnaire, the MPs were asked to evaluate three fields of committee activity: legislation, government oversight, and public relations. Legislation was regarded the most successful area, although it only received a middle grade (2.4 on a 5 point scale; 1 = excellent), while government oversight was graded lower, and public relations the lowest. Government and Opposition MPs' answers did not differ significantly. The lack of a significant difference agrees with the findings of the interviews, namely, that a common committee position sometimes diminishes the importance of party-political loyalty, and helps a common committee rationale to develop.

Another question asked what the MPs thought about the government's attitudes towards committee work. Their opinions are diverse. An insignificant number of MPs from the government and the opposition (8 percent) think that the government is not receptive to the committees' work. In contrast, the differences are high between government (32 percent) and opposition (5 percent) respondents who believe that the government cares about the committees' activities. This difference can be explained by the fact that the government majority in committees is better connected to governmental groups than the opposition. A large majority believes, however, that government is not very receptive.

The interviews confirmed what our earlier data also show: that parties tend to nominate an MP to a committee position if he/she had some experience and/or a genuine interest in the given field. On the other hand, the interviews revealed what is difficult to prove by other measures: namely, that the parliamentary party groups to a large degree determine the committee environment. This finding is not surprising, considering the reality of party government and the importance that parties acquired in the new Hungarian democracy.

The MPs' double position in the parliamentary party group and in the committee helped to develop a clear-cut internal organization within the parliamentary party groups, the working group system. The members of a parliamentary party on the same committee constitute a working group. In this way, working group members connect the parliamentary party to the committee. In relatively large parliamentary party groups, the working groups overlap the committee structure, and the leader of the working group is the highest-ranking MP in the committee. Smaller parties cannot establish such a functionally refined working group system. Consequently, in large parties, members have the luxury of specialization, while in small parties, they have to struggle with a variety of issues at the same time.

Committee members in the working group will be responsible for a certain legislative motion in their party. The responsibility is shared if there are several members in the committee from the same party group. Working group members acquire information, meet lobbyists, inform the parliamentary party, discuss the case with experts, and make decisions. The parliamentary party regards the working groups as the competent authority in their own fields. This institutional development partially results from the party leaderships seeking efficiency and from their understanding of the importance of connections with committees. Since all parliamentarians are knowledgeable in only a handful of policy fields, the parties must rely on the judgment of the working groups, or the representative of the working group. For example, the working group might suggest how to vote on a bill to the parliamentary party in the plenary.

Constraints and Freedoms

The above analysis suggests that committees exist under particular constraints while they also have broad freedoms. Their controversial position will be elaborated upon from the perspective of the chapter: the consolidation of the committee system and consequently of the entire parliament.

The committees can initiate institutional changes within parliament, particularly those concerning the committees themselves. For example, as a functional differentiation, subcommittees might develop into proper standing committees. This is what happened to the Agricultural Committee. Initially it existed as a subcommittee within the Economic Committee, but it developed into a standing committee in the face of functional demands. Subcommittees are worth considering from other respects as well. Different committees can form a joint subcommittee. This provides an opportunity for introducing new forms of cooperation and diversification, while the activities of the MPs are removed from party restraints. For example, the subcommittee that considered the law on ethnic minorities within the Human Rights Committee developed into an all-party forum of cooperation in its field while remaining connected to the committee.

Subcommittees embody the tendencies that many parliamentarians report missing and would like to envisage as dominant future trends. That is, professional viewpoints are more pronounced in subcommittees with regard to both membership and policymaking behavior. At the same time subcommittees are less strictly formalized. For example, there is no quorum for decision making. Anybody can participate with the right of discussion, and invited experts can join in the discussion without the formal vote and special permission that prevails in standing committees. Advisers, who really can contribute information and expertise, can substitute for members of the subcommittee although they are not entitled to vote.

While subcommittees might acquire an increasing role in the legislative function of committees, committees have potential in oversight. The oversight function of committees is much wider than that of the plenary session. Due to their external connections and rights, the committees can control public officials and make them report to the committee. They can also examine the implementation of laws and the general consequences of a piece of legislation. Each committee is involved in budget issues, which are a special field, related to both legislation and oversight. Analysts generally agree that committees still do not utilize their oversight opportunities to the extent that is possible under the laws and Standing Orders.

It would be possible to widen the committees' potential by establishing circles of experts around each committee. Despite financial constraints, it will be in the interest of each party to ensure an intellectual resource for committees irrespective of party membership. This will happen when it is understood and accepted that each party can be in the opposition, and thus would need expertise independent of the parliamentary party group and government resources. In fact, all MPs, when asked about their needs, admit that this development is essential.

It is possible and desirable, MPs say, to involve interest groups more fully in the work of committees. Of course, these changes would reinforce each other. A larger policymaking or oversight role will attract more external input from experts or interest groups, and external inputs will increase the influence of the committees.

The above potentials embedded in committees are important to note for three reasons related to the theme of functional clarification. First, the committees exceed the opportunities of the plenary sessions because party restraints are less obvious within committees. Second, due to their size, inclination, functional position, etc., committees might be the forerunners of some tendencies that can develop in the wider parliamentary framework. And third, an increase in the functional importance of committees is very much in harmony with the members, who, according to interviews, seek the ways and means to turn from party-centered to more policy-centered parliamentary institutions.

With respect to limitations, differences between committees become obvious. The subject area of a committee will determine how seriously governmental or external experts consider the committee. This is reflected in the number of bills referred to a committee, in the number of reports it receives, and so forth. On the other hand, relatively weak committees might compensate for their limited strength in some areas by increased activity in other areas, for example, by attracting more external attention.

Another difference results from special constitutional regulations regarding certain subjects of legislation. That is, several policy areas require a two-thirds majority vote. Although this was not a problem in the second legislative term when the government had a safe majority both in the House and in committees, important decisions that would otherwise take place in the committee are transferred to all-party bodies with respect to these bills requiring a two-thirds vote. Although these committees are important due to their subject areas, they lose their importance in the concrete processes.

A growing limitation on committees is that they are often forced to sit during plenary sessions because they have so many duties and obligations. This draws the attention to the dilemma between the reality of a working parliament and a talking parliament. Still to come are the conceptual decisions together with the provision of different resources that will determine future tendencies in this respect.

Very often, of course, the weaknesses or shortcomings of committee work are not rooted in the committees themselves. Committees cannot be well prepared if the government's programs are not precise. Although the government puts forward its prospective legislative plan, some of it is never or belatedly placed in front of parliament. Others appear unexpectedly, which does not provide the committees with the opportunity to prepare their positions. In addition, the ministries have diverse attitudes towards committees. While the ministries' working programs could be a major source of assistance with committee work, committee members report that cooperation with the ministries largely depends on personal and party sympathies and the professional connections between the ministerial staff and committee members.

The life of opposition committee members is made difficult due to several other reasons. For example, minority experts only rarely are invited to committees. Most often it is the expert of a majority parliamentary party group who helps the committee. This means that minority opinion cannot be supported by the opinion of a minority expert.

In addition to these mainly party-related problems, a major complaint of committee members is that their role in deciding the agenda is secondary. That is, they cannot report in advance on issues that they find important. They cannot draw the attention of government to certain subject areas where action would be necessary. Of course they can put pressure on their parliamentary party, but this is only useful if the party is in government. In opposition, they can try to pursue a case with a private member's bill, the success rate of which is low.

Conclusion

The development of parliamentary committees in Hungary proceeded through several stages. Initial agreements evolved into institutional solutions. Then, stabilization occurred in working practices and personnel. Finally, adaptation to new challenges took place with the clarification of external and internal functions and with the establishment of new organizations such as subcommittees or the working groups.

In this process, the place of parliamentary committees has changed in comparison to other intraparliamentary actors such as the individual members, the parliamentary party groups, and the plenary sessions. In the first term, the individual MP seemed to be a major actor partially due to weak party discipline and partially due to the assumptions prevalent in the transition when both the liberals and the left demanded power for the parliamentarian. This view was also strengthened by the communist legacy. In this period the parliamentary party groups were the engines of parliamentary activities because they established standards of professional party politics, helped clarified party policies in parliament, and trained new party politicians who had not learned political skills before. The committees, however, had an impact on how the Hungarian parliament was institutionalized. If parliamentary party groups have been the engines in establishing a working notion of parliament, committees have been the oil in this process.

New dimensions of parliamentary work began to appear mainly through committees. Committees were more stable than the entire House. Their members were more professional in terms both of continuity and skills. Their orientation could challenge the party and individualistic approach. Interparty cooperation was easier in committees. They were able to establish new methods in performing their activity and could contribute to the development of a more work-oriented attitude through the working group system. All in all, committees proved to be agents of parliamentary institutionalization.

What are the basic dimensions of change? First, a functional clarification is taking place between parliamentary institutions. This means the decreasing activism of parliamentarians and a more balanced connection between committees and parliamentary party groups. Second, there are obvious signs that the position of committees in the Hungarian parliament is being rethought. Both the members' attitudes and the institutional changes in Standing Orders point in this direction. This implies a turn towards a more active, working parliament. We can assume that the development of a German-type system in which the position and connections between parliamentary party groups and committees are more balanced is on its way. Third, it is manifest that functional clarification is taking place in parallel with the institutionalization and professionalization processes of committees.

Functional clarification partially resulted from the 1994 Standing Orders and partially evolved spontaneously. Occasionally it was due to political changes. In this process one cannot neglect the pressures of committee members to establish efficient and stable parliamentary institutions. The intention of committee members on both sides of the political spectrum to extend committee powers runs in contrast to party logic that still tends to dominate committee work and parliamentary decision making. The executive is also reluctant to draw committees into the legislative and policy-making process more substantially. It does so only when it needs support due to the sensitivity of the given issue.

Notes

1. Hungary is the only country in East-Central Europe where a new constitution has not yet been accepted.
2. Each MP is entitled to a monthly honorarium, which is about four times the average Hungarian salary. In addition, committee members will receive another

identical sum as their honorarium; if someone serves in two committees, the sum of course is doubled; committee chairs receive an extra honorarium, double the amount of simple membership. As a result, some MPs have higher salaries than government ministers do.

3. One must take into account that members of government cannot occupy a committee position in Hungary.

4. Professional literature is similarly diverse on the concept of professionalization as it is on the concept of institutionalization. Here, professionalization is used in the sense put forward by Sartori (1971) that he largely focused on personnel stability (or fluctuation, rotation) as a means of acquisition skills.

5. With regard to individual members' bills we must add however that they are often due to unsatisfactory government work. That is, individual MPs on the government side enter the legislative procedure at the request of the government: they propose amendments to correct the government initiative.

6. The questionnaire survey was conducted in autumn 1995, when a mail questionnaire was sent to all the 386 MPs. One hundred thirty-two filled in and returned the survey, 113 committee members among them. The interviews were based on the combination and reframing of two research approaches by Eulau and McCluggage (1985) and Fenno (1973). Although the former represents a more outward-looking approach (in addition to members and the committee itself it emphasized the committee's connections in the larger legislative system) and the latter a more inward-looking approach (with intracommittee features and policy making in the focus), they both sought to find the committee's place in the legislative system. Thus both proved to be very useful for marking the place of committees and their potential directions of changes in the Hungarian case. The interviews covered a sample of thirty-nine committee members, roughly representing the prevalent divisions of a) party; b) type of mandate (whether list or direct mandate); c) the position in the committee, regarding whether a new or old member; d) gender; e) leadership position in committee; and of course, f) the committee itself. For a fuller analysis see (Ilonszki 1997).

References and Bibliography

Eulau, Heinz, and Vera McCluggage. 1985. "Standing Committees in Legislatures." In *Handbook of Legislative Research,* edited by Gerhard Loewenberg, S. C. Patterson, and M. E. Jewell. Cambridge, Mass.: Harvard University Press. 395–470.

Fenno, Richard F. 1973. *Congressmen in Committees.* Boston: Little, Brown.

Ilonszki, G. 1996. "From Marginal to Rational Parliaments." In *Parliaments and Organized Interests: The Second Steps,* edited by A. Ágh and G. Ilonszki. Budapest: Hungarian Center for Democracy Studies Foundation. 451–65.

———. 1997. "Some External and Internal Dimensions of Parliamentary Committees in Hungary: Western Research Frameworks and Central European Experiences." In *Working Papers on Comparative Legislative Studies II: The Changing Role of Parliamentary Committees,* edited by L. D. Longley and A.

Ágh. Lawrence, Wis.: Research Committee of Legislative Specialists, International Political Science Association. 471–88.

Sartori, Giovanni. 1971. "The Professionalization of Italian MPs." In *European Politics,* edited by Mattei Dogan and Richard Rose. Boston: Little, Brown and Co. 408–15.

Schüttemeyer, Suzanne S. 1994. "Hierarchy and Efficiency in the Bundestag: The German Answer for Institutionalizing Parliament." In *Parliaments in the Modern World: Changing Institutions,* edited by Gary Copeland and Samuel Patterson. Ann Arbor: University of Michigan Press. 29–59.

Soltész, István. 1995. "The Committee System of the First Hungarian Parliament." In *The First Parliament 1990–1994,* edited by A. Ágh and S. Kurtán. Budapest: Hungarian Center for Democracy Studies.

THREE

Committees of the Polish Sejm in Two Political Systems

Ewa Karpowicz and Wlodzimierz Wesolowski

A N UNQUESTIONABLE DESIRE OF THE PEOPLE LIVING IN COUN-
tries freed from communism is to establish a democratic political system in which representative bodies are paramount. The transformation of
the Sejm (the parliament) and its functions were of prime importance in
the peaceful Polish revolution of 1989, initiated by the nationwide social
movement, Solidarity.

The Sejm as a representation of "the nation" has always played a
major role whenever the Polish people's democratic aspirations were at
stake. As one of Europe's oldest parliaments, it was a symbol of national
independence and individual freedom both when Poland was partitioned
and in the decades following World War II when the country's sovereignty
was limited.

In the Polish People's Republic (under communist rule), the formal
prerogatives of the Polish parliament were great, equal to parliaments in
Western democracies. Communist ideology, however, included the concept
of the "leading role" of the community party, which limited the function
of the parliament. In the formation of governments, parliament was
merely a rubber stamp.

In this chapter we will review the real role of the Sejm before the political breakthrough in 1989. Then we will discuss the shaping of the new,
democratic parliament after 1989, and the critical role of the parliament's
extraordinary constitution-drafting committee. We next consider the role
and activity of the Sejm's standing committees in a new democratic period,
and examine the activities of four specific committees in their administrative review function.

Historical Antecedents and the
"Contract Parliament," 1989–1991

In the Communist Constitution of 1952, "the principle of unity of authority and the state supremacy of the Sejm" was declared. The Sejm was "the representative organ of the State's uniform authority," "its highest organ," "the highest body expressing the will of the Nation, appointed to realise its sovereign rights." Its political rank was higher than any other institution of authority. At the same time, however, the elimination of free and competitive elections, the political domination of the Communist Party, and other features of the communist political system made these declarations spurious. In this respect, the situation was uniform throughout the Soviet block.

The two non-Communist parties, the United Peasant Party and the Democratic Party, normally had their representatives in parliament, and a few ministerial offices were allocated to their leaders such as the ministry for agriculture, the ministry for trade, or the agency for small industry and craft. There was no conflict, however, over policy issues. The Communist Party consulted its "satellite parties" at closed meetings and minor differences of opinions were resolved at such meetings. The practice of one common list of parliamentary candidates and the way in which the names on the list were ordered gave the Communist Party complete control of the electoral results.

Some attempts at modifying the internal structure of real power within the communist state occurred in 1956, in the period of political debate within the Communist Party that followed the death of Stalin.

The new period in the political history of People's Poland was started by the workers' mass protests in August 1980 and the formation of the "Solidarity" trade union movement. The August events paved the way for decisive political changes. As in former periods of political crises, the public's demands centered around political freedoms and the role of the parliament. The public wanted the legislative body to have greater power in relationship to the government and to be free from Communist one-party control. These events ended with the imposition of martial law by General Wojciech Jaruzelski in December 1981.

The following eight years convinced the party leadership that there was no way out of the crisis except to negotiate with the political opposition. The Round Table talks of February–April 1989 opened the door for adjustments and compromises. The gradual transformation to democracy was negotiated during the Round Table Talks.

The two sides agreed to hold parliamentary elections. The agreement stated that the elections to the Sejm, the Lower Chamber, and to the newly created Senate, the Upper Chamber, would be partly "free" and partly pre-arranged. The communist party and its allies were to have two-thirds seats in the future Sejm while one-third of the seats were open to other parties. The Senate seats were open to all the parties. Solidarity won all of the open seats in the Lower Chamber and 99 percent of the seats in the newly created Upper Chamber (Senate).

The half-democratic elections of 1989 brought unexpected political results. When the "Contract Parliament" convened, the communist party was not able to form a government because of the radical, democratic climate among all strata of the population. Under mounting pressure, the former satellite parties refused to cooperate with the Communist Party (PZPR). They allied with the Solidarity representatives and the "new majority" was formed to select the first non-Communist prime minister of the Soviet bloc, Tadeusz Mazowiecki. These circumstances opened the chances for a "peaceful revolution."

The Contract Parliament started the reconstruction of the legal system of the state. It was a tremendous task for the people who were new to the job. Solidarity deputies never considered themselves legislators. Deputies of the former ruling party, now transformed into the Social Democratic Party, were mostly young activists, who had no prior experience in parliamentary work, either. Only a limited number of deputies, who were members of parties in the "former regime," had the knowledge and experience needed for legislative work. Some of the leaders of the democratic opposition were lawyers, economists, and academics with only theoretical knowledge about political and legislative processes.

The new bills concerned the highest organs of authority, the administration and the judiciary. They also addressed the parliamentary process. Within the Sejm a new statute of legislative procedures and structure was confirmed, which stressed the reconstituted committees' crucial prerogatives in discussing and preparing the final versions of bills. This newly introduced practice gave committees the power to investigate some issues independently from the government. The new politically pluralistic structure of the committees forced them to function democratically. On the whole, the contract Sejm was empowered with real prerogatives and burdened with new real duties.

Both the achievements and the emerging political difficulties of this period quickly made new elections necessary. All the new political groups that evolved out of the Solidarity movement wanted to test their real strength. President Lech Walesa aimed at creating a party of his own that could form a permanent basis for his political leadership. The former Communist Party, now the Social Democracy of the Republic (SdRP), and its former allies, the Polish Peasant Party (PSL) and the Democratic Party (DP) sought democratic legitimation through popular election. Consultations between the parties and groups led to a common decision that ended this parliament, formally designated as the Tenth Term, continuing the numbered series of communist-era parliaments.

The Democratic Terms

The New Democratic Sejm, the First Term, 1991–93

The First Term of the fully democratic Sejm also lasted two years (October 1991–May 1993). It held forty-five sessions in 136 days and its committees met 2,237 times. One hundred and nine bills were passed, and 135 resolutions were adopted.

There was no single vision of the functions of the parliament and the executive branch. Within the common "democratic" option several detailed ideas were formulated. On the most general level one can distinguish between proposals aimed at constructing a strong parliamentary-cabinet system that retained the "highest" power of the parliament and proposals aimed at a presidential system, which included the strong policy and nominating powers of the president. There were numerous minor divergent points of view on other issues, such as how much power should be given to local government. The most important of these was a proposal to change the old constitution by amending it via the bill called "The Small Constitution."

The aim of that bill was to rearrange the prerogatives of the president, prime minister and his cabinet, and the parliament, primarily the Lower Chamber. The predominant thought was that a period of systemic transition needed a stable executive branch of the government. Many right-wing politicians wanted to strengthen the power of the president. Some leftist politicians also hinted at the need for an "authoritative" power. The new president, Lech Walesa, openly declared that he needed more power for himself as the leader of the transformation. The composition of the Sejm elected in 1991 indicated that in principle these demands could be satisfied. In the Sejm, the great majority of the new political parties had grown out of the Solidarity political movement. The Solidarity Trade Union also had a separate group in parliament. Problems arose, however, due to the great fragmentation of opinions and concrete proposals.

The final text of the "Small Constitution" was a result of many compromises, and not a single party fully supported the bill. The parties gave their deputies the freedom to vote according to their individual opinions, and positive votes were dispersed across the whole spectrum of political groupings.

One thing was clear: the president, elected by the whole nation, had a special role. He controlled the nomination of the minister of the interior, minister of defense, and minister of foreign affairs. He also had a great influence on the selection of the prime minister. The practical need to change the prime minister and the composition of the whole cabinet quickly revealed that the division of prerogatives between the parliament and the president was not clear at all. These practical difficulties, and the broader need to completely rewrite the constitution, led to the formation of a special constitution-drafting committee.

The first fully democratic Sejm ended its term "incidentally" on the vote of no confidence against its own government, proposed by the Solidarity Trade Union. The vote was not intentionally aimed at abolishing the government, but it did. It caused the dissolution of parliament and new elections.

The Democratic Sejm, the Second Term, 1993–97: The New Constitution

The second term of the Sejm lasted four years. It held 115 plenary sessions with a total of 297 days of discussions. Eight hundred and twenty-six draft laws were submitted in parliament, and 473 laws were passed. Sejm committees held 6,522 meetings, including 6,070 meetings of permanent committees. Two hundred and eighty desiderata were adopted.

The 1993 parliamentary election was won by the left-wing parties. The Social Democracy of the Republic in alliance with OPZZ Trade Unions, both successors of former communist organizations, and PSL, the transformed peasant party that existed in the former regime, together held a safe majority. Another important feature of that parliament was its political fragmentation on the right. "The right" was the self-characterization of many small post-Solidarity parties. Towards the end of this parliament's term there were five party caucuses and six smaller parliamentary groups. During the term, there were many changes in party affiliation on the right. The mobility of deputies who moved from one caucus (in Polish: "parliamentary club") to another was greater than ever before in the history of parliament.

The second parliament was the first to serve its full term after the 1989 change of Poland's system of government. The greatest achievement of this Sejm was the adoption of a new constitution, which replaced the Constitution of 1952 and the Small Constitution of 1992. We examine the "battle for the constitution" to show the role of the parliamentary committees and the search for political compromises. The intense search for compromise was a new feature of Polish democratic politics.

Over two years, 1995–97, through a tough bargaining process, the completely new democratic constitution was forged and adopted. The work was done in the forty-five member Constitution Committee of the National Assembly. The National Assembly consists of the members of both legislative chambers meeting as a single body. It is not so much bicameral as supracameral.

The Constitution Committee, likewise, was not a joint committee of Sejm and Senat but a single committee of the National Assembly. The committee members were chosen by the Sejm and the Senat, at informal and formal meetings of political leaders of several political groupings inside and outside National Assembly, and at the plenary sessions of the Sejm and the Senat. Its membership consisted of constitutional experts and leaders of the parliamentary parties.

The parliamentary majority had the majority in the Constitution Committee. This majority was opposed from the beginning by the committee members who were preparing a "social" draft under the auspices of Solidarity Trade Union and by some political leaders affiliated to the union. They were supported by the formal Solidarity caucus in the Senat of ten senators, three of whom were members of the official parliamentary committee drafting the constitution.

When the "social" draft was in its final form, Solidarity activists collected two million signatures of citizens in support. This draft was sent to the parliament to be considered on equal terms with the one prepared by parliament. The proponents of the "social" draft pushed the symbolic issues of the role of religion in public life, and the "threatened" national identity of Poles, to the forefront. In short, the "Citizen's Proposal" of the constitution opened one political front by expressing the views of one set of political forces.

A second political front formed within parliament, first of all in the Sejm and the Committee on the Constitution, composed of deputies coming mostly from the ruling coalition within the Sejm, the social democratic, post-communist SdRP and the transformed peasant party, PSL. The aim of the ruling coalition was to win the support of the liberal party (Freedom Union), which had a relatively large share of the deputies within the Sejm. Collectively these two groups had two-thirds of the votes needed to pass the constitution.

We have described the political "landscape" of the battle to illustrate the complexity of the situation within which a compromise was reached. Those who forged the compromise earned credit for being responsible politicians, who had learned the art of negotiation and mutual accommodation. For the Polish parliamentarians it was a new and important experience.

First, within the parliamentary committee, representatives of SdRP and the Labour Union (the post-Solidarity party that was strongly anti-confessional) opted for declaring "the neutrality of the state" in religion. They strongly opposed two suggestions: the first was to mention any role for the Catholic Church in public life and, the second was to mention God in the constitution. Liberal Catholics could not share this position. The deadlock ended when Tadeusz Mazowiecki, a liberal Catholic (and the first post-communist prime minister), proposed to put in the Preamble a sentence saying that the constitution is established both by "people believing in God as the source of truth, good and beauty and those who get their inspiration from another source." Including such a statement eliminated the reference to God's will as the inspiration of the constitution and made the constitution the product of citizens' will. The acceptance of this formulation by the majority of the committee, against strong opposition from the Solidarity senators, paved the way for reaching agreement within the committee on that and related issues. State-church relations were declared to rest on the principle of cooperation and non-interference in their respective spheres of activity.

A second compromise solution was found for the controversy over the people to whom the constitution refers and gets inspiration from: the Polish nation or the citizens. Liberals argued that Ukrainians, Belorussians, Germans, Jews, and other minority groups that inhabit Poland cannot be called members of the Polish nation. Deputies in parliament and politicians outside of parliament of the many groups of nationalist or "patriotic" persuasion argued for the need to give expression to the "Polish identity" and the Polish cultural uniqueness that guides patriotic, positive emotions. The solution found by the conciliatory-minded politicians for the dilemma of "Nation" or "Citizens" was neither conceptually satisfying nor stylistic, but it allowed parliament to move ahead and pass the constitution. The phrase adopted reads "We the Polish Nation, members of the society . . ." (or "citizens" in some parts of the text).

The third compromise solution was found for the differences of opinion on how to characterize important and general features of the economic order and the key social functions of the State. The Peasant Party (PSL) demanded that a declaration that the "family farm is a model for Polish agriculture" be put into the constitution. Because of the numerical strength of Peasant Party representatives in the Sejm, this demand was accepted, although liberals felt uneasy.

On April 2, 1997, in the concluding vote in the National Assembly,

451 out of the 560 members of both chambers supported the text of the constitution, forty opposed and six abstained. All the deputies of SLD, Freedom Union, and Labour Union voted "yes." One hundred and thirty-one representatives of the PSL said "yes," six said "no," and five abstained. Members of smaller centrist groups supported the constitution, whereas smaller rightist groups rejected it.

Open opposition to the parliamentary constitution was declared by the Solidarity Trade Union leadership. It called for its rejection in the ensuing referendum. The Catholic Church hierarchy voiced its dissatisfaction with the parliamentary proposal, which meant its rejection. Liberal Catholics within the Freedom Union and within society at large had to take individual responsibility for their support of the parliamentary proposal that they helped to design.

Despite this opposition, the proposed constitution was approved by voters in the referendum. It was not an overwhelming victory, only a modest one. With only 42.9 percent of eligible voters taking part in the referendum, 52.7 percent supported the proposed constitution, and 45.7 percent opposed it.

On the whole, it was a liberal-democratic constitution. It eliminated the domination of the president over the cabinet and removed elements of president's direct influence on the selection of prime minister. Return to the parliamentary-cabinet system was the general idea behind this constitution and was also the wish of President Kwasniewski.

Standing Committees

In this and succeeding sections, we turn to an examination of the standing legislative committees, beginning with the Sejm of the communist period.

Under the Communist Regime

In the People's Republic of Poland, parliamentary committees were called "auxiliary bodies of the supreme representative body." Nonetheless, doctrinal disputes arose over what the "auxiliary role" actually was, and what were the resulting limitations to the committees' activities. Committees made "their own" decisions, but they were acting on behalf of the Sejm. Controversies especially concerned whether or not committees were able to act outside the organizational framework of the parliament when they tried to enforce an order, or "desideratum," to a state administrative body.[1] The opinion prevailed that the auxiliary functions of a committee could and should include extraparliamentary activity. The authorization to control and pass desiderata and interpretations, or "opinions,"[2] meant that committees were able to influence the activity of administrative bodies. In reality, committees as a matter of course acted on their own initiative. The committees' autonomy was not a direct result of legal regulations,[3] but was rather a practice that later became the rule. Desiderata and opinions are the Parliament's instruments of administrative control.

Based on the Sejm's regulations and the People's Republic practice, committee activities were the following: preparing bills initiated by the Sejm or the committees; analyzing and evaluating proposed legislation submitted by an extraparliamentary body such as the government or the Council of the State; examining concrete cases, and suggesting decisions, such as an appointment to a governmental post; examining controversial issues to inform the Sejm, specifically, the Committee of Petitions and Motions; conducting first reading of bills replacing the Sejm in plenary session; analyzing and evaluating some activities of certain extraparliamentary bodies; performing administrative review or oversight on behalf of the Sejm; and suggesting decisions to extraparliamentary bodies through desiderata and opinions.

The postwar Sejm had standing and also special or temporary committees. Most of the committees dealt with a sphere of economic, social, or political life. Their division closely resembled that of the administrative branches of the state economy. Some of the committees had specific but broad roles, such as the Constitutional Committee and the Legislative Committee. Others coordinated the work of specific committees, for instance the Budget Committee and the Committee for the Economic Plan. This classification is sometimes called a division into branch, problem, and functional committees.

Committees were empowered to create standing or temporary subcommittees to pursue specific aims. Committees gradually grew in both numbers and importance during the communist period. During the first session (1952–56) committees met 247 times, for an average of 61.7 times a year. During the sixth session (1972–76) they met 1,057 times, for an average of 264.3 times a year. In general, the meetings of the committees and subcommittees were closed, except for the nonmember MPs, who could attend at any time. Committees issued a report, as well as routine information for the press, after each meeting.

Changes in rules in the 1970s and 1980s reflected a general trend toward broadening the powers of committees. The most important changes in 1972 and 1980 were the following: The presidium of the Sejm could ask the appropriate committee for its opinion on the nomination of a new member to the Council of Ministers; committees gained the right to require explanations from any state officer, as well as from any economic or social institution; the Committee of Petitions and Motions was created, which gave the committees additional oversight powers; and the Committee on Constitutional Responsibility was appointed.

Though it is not easy to evaluate the activity of the parliamentary committees under the communist system, their weak points can be listed as follows:

1) There were too many committees, and they paralleled the structure of economic branch ministries. This feature was partially the expression of the Sejm's inertia. For instance, a government reorganization in 1981 did not automatically start changes in the parliamentary committees' structure;

2) The lack of certain committees may demonstrate the Sejm's passivity. For instance, in the 1980s, a committee for local self-government was needed but not formed;

3) The approval of committee resolutions by the Parliament during plenary sessions was automatic. On the one hand, the responsibility of the committee was less than it should have been, considering the importance of the issues. On the other hand, the MPs usually accepted the committee's opinion without properly examining it;

4) Specialized committees often tried to enforce their own solutions, which resulted in committees taking on some administrative functions. The consequence was that state administration and some of the lobbies tried to manipulate them;

5) Committee meetings were not accessible to the media and public; the consequences are characteristic traits of communist systems.

Despite these weak points, there were also some strengths of the communist period legislature that carried over and impacted positively upon the democratic Sejm. Our thesis is that in the communist system, taking part in the committees could be considered as an opportunity for people who were "appointed" to the parliament despite their formal election to show their concern for the social welfare. If they worked hard, showed their competence, and were committed to appropriate legal solutions, they had the moral right to vindicate their good name, even though they had accepted a seat in parliament from the Communist Party.

The committees also were also a venue in which some elements of a true democracy functioned. They were the places where real arguments occurred, voting was not biased toward the dominant party opinion as during plenary sessions, and different opinions were expressed. Paradoxically, a lack of political differences among the MPs enabled them to focus on the substantive arguments when discussing specific problems. Our opinion is that the committees made the image of the Sejm under the communist regime more acceptable.

Parliamentary Committees in a Democratic Sejm

Committees are autonomous bodies of the democratic Sejm. They are also working bodies for the plenary sessions. These two traits did not change after the 1989 breakthrough. The committees also function as agents of the political parties. Only this third trait changed radically because of the introduction of democratic parliamentary elections and party pluralism. The parties make sure that they are fairly represented on the committees, and monitor the committees' actions to make sure that they coincide with the parties' opinions and interests.

Legal Status. The legal status and rules of procedure of the committees did not change. The new constitution states that "[t]he Sejm appoints standing and temporary committees,"[4] and that "the Sejm can appoint investigation committees in particular cases."[5] The standing orders state that "the duties" of the parliamentary committees are the following: 1) analyzing and preparing the issues to be considered by the Sejm; 2) giving opinions in matters raised by the Sejm, the Speaker, or by the presidium; and 3) "the Sejm's committees are controlling bodies with competencies indicated in the Constitution and other bills."[6]

Functions of the Committees. The legislative and oversight functions of the committees remain in force. Legislative activity is more pronounced than in the time of the People's Republic. Now the Sejm passes more bills, which makes more committee meetings necessary. As indicated earlier, 109 bills were adopted in the first democratic term of two years and 473 in the full second term.

In the new constitution, the oversight function of the committee is very broad. In the previous "Small Constitution," it was mentioned only in the Sejm's standing orders. During discussions about the oversight function of the Sejm, the subject emerged of the suitability of traditional oversight procedures. For example, the right of the plenary sessions and committees to require government's reports, to require the presence of members of the government at plenary and committee meetings, as well as the right to express opinions and formulate desiderata were questioned.

The process of evaluating nominated state officers also went through an interesting evolution. Until this time, the committees gave their opinions about candidates for state offices to the Council of Ministers. These opinions had never been obligatory for the Sejm, but they always had some political significance. A turbulent debate at the beginning of the second session resulted in the withdrawal of this power. This decision was a victory for the governing coalition, which thereby limited opportunities of the opposition to express their opinions on this important matter.

New Types of Committees. Economic branch, as well as problem-oriented and functional committees, still exist. In recent years, temporary committees were established to consider particular issues more frequently, as the number of such issues considered by the Sejm grew.

During the third session some new committees were created, such as the Committee for Family Problems, the Parliament Representatives' Ethics Committee, the Committee for Competition, and the Consumers Protection and Small Business Committee. The first of these is a battlefield of divergent value systems; thus its meetings consist more of discussions about fundamental principles than of suggestions of concrete solutions. Similarly, the Ethics Committee has noble goals, but lacks specific powers.[7]

A new, interesting, and disturbing phenomenon is the tendency of some committees to lobby for special interests. The two other new committees listed above belong to this group. Lobbying is a growing phenomenon, and, so far, is not subject to legal regulations.

Number of Committees. Table 3.1 shows that the number of the committees is increasing gradually. During the first term, there were twenty-three standing committees, twenty-five during the second term, and twenty-eight in the third term.

Changes in the committee system have been influenced partly by the reorganization of the Polish government. The majority of parliamentary standing committees mirror the ministries, and are created as instruments for overseeing the executives in the ministries. Therefore, reorganization of the executive ministries influences the division of responsibilities in the parliamentary committee system.

A second reason for the increasing number of committees is the effort to enlarge the scope of the interest and oversight of the parliamentary bodies into new areas of social and economic activity. This tendency is reflected, for example, by the creation of the Committee for Small Business and Consumers, and also the Committee for Local Self-Government and Regional Policy, noted above.

The creation of ad hoc subcommittees to examine or settle specific issues arising in politics or social life is characteristic of a newly formed

Table 3.1

Committee Activities in the Polish Sejm by Term, 1989–1997

	X term* (04.07.89– 31.10.91)	I term (25.11.91– 31.05.93)	II term (14.10.93– 20.10.97)	III term (20.10.97–
Standing Committees	25	24	26	28
Extraordinary committees	14	12	18	12**
Committee Sittings Standing	2188	2132	6070	2230***
Extraordinary	244	151	452	
Committee Presidium Sittings	691	678	1907	770
Subcommittee Sittings	1261	860	3147	1031
Desiderata	167	82	280	154
Opinions	229	304	881	375****

Notes:
* X term is the term of Polish Sejm called "Contract Sejm" in which 35% of the membership was selected through free election. The rest were selected through communist lists of candidates.
**Ad hoc committees usually do not work for entire term.
***At the end of each term statistics are given for each type of committee separately; data for the III term not available yet.
**** Data for the III term are collected for the period 20.10.97–30.06 99

parliament. The tendency to form extraordinary bodies of this type has become stronger recently.

The increasingly large number of committees threatens to fragment the work of the Sejm. A multiplicity of committees can lead to detailed analysis at the cost of a more general or strategic perspective. Fragmentation and the economic branch character of the committees makes it impossible for the Sejm to have a broader, multidimensional view of key socioeconomic problems that goes beyond the narrow focus of the branch divisions. The coordination of so many committees is a problem also. Moreover, each committee has a small number of members, which reduces their representative character. As the shaping of opinions and decision making shifted from bigger to smaller bodies, the democratic character of the Sejm has perhaps become restricted. On the other hand, a large number of committees favor their oversight functions, while their small size increases their members' ability to work in a favorable atmosphere.

Furthermore, the most important legislative work is done in the committees. They are the battlefields where regulations and the ultimate shape of particular bills are decided. A smaller number of committees could lead to a strategy of a quicker and less careful legislative process, which could mean a diminution of the Sejm's legislative authority.

Composition of Committees. The composition of committees reflects the number of members of each party elected to the Sejm. The parliamentary party clubs have committee seats and chair positions proportional to the number of party members in the entire parliament. The parliamentary clubs also make use of an additional criterion for selecting committee members, which we label professional criteria. Some committee members are experts in the topics of interest to the committee. Most bill consideration and oversight take place in committees. When bills are discussed by MPs who are expert in the field, decisions are more likely to be soundly based.

Members of committees are often members of professional groups. The MPs are mostly members of lobbies, such as trade unions, or they represent the interests of a particular branch of the economy. The committees that we examine below are examples.

The Committee for Education has thirty members, including twenty-eight teachers; the Committee for Social Policy has thirty-six members, including two employees of the Job Centre and Social Security Office, four representatives of the women's organizations, one employee of the children's aid association, one person from the Federation of the Families with Numerous Children, one employee of a cooperative, and four representatives of an organization for disabled people; and the health committee has twenty-nine members, including thirteen physicians, one nurse, three veterinarians, and four teachers.

Taking a position in the body governing the committee (presidium) is considered to be a great honor for a deputy. The position of a chairman is especially prestigious. In practice, the chairman influences very strongly the behavior of all the participants in committee meetings and determines the committee's style of debate.

On the formal level, all of a committee's presidium members are elected by the committee members. Actually, choosing deputies for these positions is negotiated by the parliamentary parties. The list of candidates for the highest positions in the committee is always a hot issue at the beginning of each term and the final number of candidates is created after intense discussion.

At the beginning of a Sejm term, all of the parliamentary clubs create a so-called "working body" (two or three from every club) to discuss: 1) how many committees will be governed by each party, and 2) which committee will have a chair (and vice chairs) from which party. They also decide the size of each committee.

The result of these debates of the interparty "working body" is the list of candidates for the position of chair (and vice chairs) that is presented at the first committee meeting in a term to elect the presidium. If a specific candidate is not accepted, the new candidate comes usually from the same party, because all the deputies are aware of the rule of party proportionality. Generally speaking, the shape and size of every committee, the proportion of the members coming from different parties, as well as the candidates for the presidium positions, are the results of the discussions of the parliamentary clubs' leadership.

Committees vary in their attractiveness to members. Some are an honor to participate in, and many MPs would be happy to belong. Examples of popular committees include the Committee on Foreign Affairs and the European Integration Committee. The most distinguished politicians in their respective parties are willing to serve on these two committees. At the same time, there are some committees that have few, if any, prominent politicians.

How the Committees Work. The total openness of the committees' activities, guaranteed after 1989, was novel. The staff of the parliamentary party clubs, as well as the media, can attend the meetings of the committees. Representatives of trade unions, social bodies, and experts are often invited by the presidium of the committee to attend meetings. The public is not allowed, because there is not enough space in the committee rooms. The committees also publish bulletins, which provide an unofficial summary of the discussions. The dates and agendas of meetings are known in advance not only by the audit agency (the chief board of supervision) and appropriate state institutions, but also by journalists.

The principle of unlimited openness to the media has proved controversial. Opponents argue that sometimes the MPs pander to journalists. Their speeches are brilliant but scarcely concrete, which diminishes the effectiveness of work and discussion of issues. In practice, committee meetings are not generally as interesting to the media as are plenary sessions.

Joint meetings of two or more committees, which assist the MPs to see concrete problems from a broader point of view, also have became more frequent on both legislation and oversight. Below we shall present several examples of joint action in administrative review.

There has also been more frequent use of experts by committees. Under the People's Republic, experts' reports were needed only occasionally. Now, committees make frequent use of experts' reports. Parliament has funding to obtain expert's reports from outside; they are made not

Table 3.2
Incumbents in Four Committees in Polish Sejm, Terms I–III (%)

Term	Incumbents in Sejm	*Percentage of Committee Incumbents in Selected Committees*			
		Health	Education, Science and Youth	Social Policy	Culture and Media
I	23.4	8.3	25.9	14.2	16.2
II	34.5	13.7	14.2	11.9	31.0
III	48.6	28.5	38.4	27.5	20.6

Note:
"Incumbent" has served in the same committee at least twice.

only for the sake of the committees but also for the parliamentary party clubs. As a result, the quality of draft legislation and the content of the bills should be improving dramatically. Unfortunately, there is no such trend.

Committee Composition and Activities. At least two features of the way in which the committee system functions seem important for both institutionalization and professionalization processes. The aspects of institutionalization that we have in mind are the predictability of the formal procedures, the stability of attendance, and the regularity of meetings. Professionalization covers such phenomena as expert knowledge of the subject matter and knowledge about the sensitivity of various social groups to different solutions to a problem.

It seems clear that a higher rather than a lower level of incumbency in a committee is conducive to both greater institutionalization and professionalization in parliamentary committees, as expressed as an hypothesis in the opening chapter. Table 3.2 shows incumbency rates in several important committees. We define an incumbent in a committee as a deputy who was a member of the same committee in at least one of the previous democratic parliamentary terms. Incumbency in committees is lower than incumbency in the entire parliament. Deputies go from committee to committee from one term to the next.

The slow increase of incumbents from Sejm Term I to Term III reflects the fact that the increasing stability of committees parallels the overall stability of deputies in the Sejm. However, one particularity of the post-communist parliaments is a low rate of "retention" of deputies from one term to the next.

A characteristic feature of membership in parliamentary committees is the increasing number of members who are on two committees and the decreasing number of those on one committee. This tendency is rather controversial. Considering the increasing activity of the entire committee system and the greater number of issues with which each committee deals, we doubt whether involvement in the work of two committees is an efficient use of time.

There is always a group of deputies not involved in committee work. These are the members of the presidium of the Sejm and the members of the government, who, according to the rules of procedure are not supposed to participate in committees.

The figures reflecting the rate of activity of the committee members are hardly comparable among terms, for the first two terms were much shorter than the next one, Term II.

The frequency of committee meetings is increasing, which indicates the increasing activity of parliamentarians at the committee level. The increasing activity of the parliamentary committees is also shown by the greater number of desiderata and opinions (see Table 3.1), which we shall examine in greater detail below.

Desiderata of Parliamentary Committees[8]

Desiderata, or "orders," are fundamental instruments for overseeing executive bodies. The origins and the fate of several types of desiderata during the last year of the second term of the Sejm (1997) from four committees concerned with social policy issues are discussed below as examples of how committees supervise and alter the conduct of administrative agencies.

Committees differ from one another in both frequency and form in submitting desiderata to administrative bodies. Every committee develops its own customs. Some committees have never submitted a desideratum, such as the Regulations and MPs Committee, the Committee of Foreign Affairs, the Committee for the Constitutional Responsibility, and the Secret Police Committee. Other committees employ this possibility frequently. The "champion" is the Committee of Culture and Media with thirty-one desiderata within the one-year period we have examined.

Desiderata also take different shapes. For example, the health committee formulates its desiderata as general declarations, which point at problems but lack suggestions of solutions, deadlines, or descriptions of desired results. The desiderata of the Committee for Social Policy are totally different. They describe the required information and detail the changes that are necessary. The desiderata of the Committee for Education, Science, and Technical Progress, as well as those of the Committee of Culture and Media, come in the form of demands for precisely defined changes.

Contents of the Desiderata

Desiderata can be divided into two groups by the scope of their subject: 1) desiderata dealing with broad issues, which are related to the general problems of the country that influence the government's policy, and 2) desiderata consisting of interventions in the actions of individuals, as well as those aimed at specific groups or institutions.

Examples of the first type are provided by two desiderata formulated by the Health Committee. One required that a manual for sexual education not be introduced, and the other asked that the financial situation of the national health service be improved and systemic changes be made. One of the desiderata of the Committee of Culture and Media required that the property right to a location be normalized, and the other that regulations concerning the protection of historical monuments be taken under consideration in privatization procedures. As an example of the second type, the Committee for Social Policy wanted the construction of a clinic for war veterans at Dickens Street in Warsaw to be completed, and required the government to start the PHARE fund aid program.

There are two dominant modes of action, corresponding to the scope of desiderata: 1) Monitoring the government's projected legal regulations requires the government to provide information to the committee. Committees also accept the reports of ministers concerning the implementation of laws and the budget in the committee's subject areas. These methods monitor activities within the legislative jurisdiction of the committee; 2) Interventions concerning individuals, groups, or institutions to create procedures to settle problems, to correct the errors of local administration, or to find the solution to important social issues. Such measures are not directly related to specific legislative proposals.

Models of Desiderata

The analysis of specific desiderata will help us to find patterns in the procedures for their submission. Our primary questions are the following: Did the committees submit the desiderata on their own initiative? Was this activity consistent? How often did it occur? On what matters?

In the Sejm's Regulations, each desideratum is regarded as the initiative of the committee. That provision does not mean, in practice, that the only initiators are members of the committee. A whole range of interventions became the subject of the committees' interests, not on the basis of their own investigations, but from external sources. From the bulletins of the committees, and from interviews with the committee secretaries, it is clear that the MPs often learn about a problem from a nonmember or as a consequence of a public action, rather than from the committee's own work.

There are six major models of procedures for transforming problems into a committee desideratum, defined both by type of problem and by source.

Model 1: Administration in Committee Policy Sector. Most desiderata are related to acceptance of annual reports of the cabinet, or Council of Ministers, concerning the administration and implementation of the state budget. The Sejm discusses the government's annual report concerning the implementation of legislation, including the budget. Each committee evaluates that part of the report within its jurisdiction, points to irregularities or missing information, and then submits a desideratum to the government.

An example is a joint desideratum of the Committee for Social Policy and the Health Committee concerning the implementation of anti-abortion legislation, which both committees found deficient in education, contraception, and aid for the pregnant.

The sequence of events that preceded the passing of the desideratum was the following: In May and June 1994, the committees held three joint meetings to consider the government's information about the administration of the anti-abortion bill. At the first meeting, there were present, among others, the deputy minister of health, the secretary of state in the Ministry of Labour and Social Policy, and the deputy director of a department in the Ministry of Justice. The ministers' information was considered to be lacking in precision. They explained that they were unable to give details concerning the bill's implementation, since the bill had been in force for a short time. The minister also claimed that there was not enough money in the budget to implement the law. The committees declared that the officials representing the ministries had too low a rank, which showed a lack of respect toward such an important issue and the committees themselves. They decided to postpone the meeting.

The next meeting was attended by the deputy ministers and the deputy general prosecutor. This time their rank was satisfactory to the members of the committees. The committees focused on the functioning of the few shelters for single mothers and on benefits for women with small children. Another subject of discussion was a school textbook that viewed the issue of abortion from the point of view of the Christian system of values or "in the spirit of the Church's teachings." This book was strongly criticized by members who referred to the sexuality experts' published reports. The press was the initial source of the committees' information about what teaching aids were used in the schools.

During the next joint meeting, the committees critically evaluated the implementation of the abortion bill by the government. The numerous critics in the committees resulted in the submission a desideratum to the Council of Ministers.

Model 2: Budget Needs. Many desiderata accompany the process of making the new state budget; usually they concern the neglect of some issues that are important to the committee, and the lack of appropriate financing. Those portions of the government's proposals concerning the new state budget that are within a committee's jurisdiction are examined by that committee for gaps and irregularities in finances. The committee's opinions are contained in the desideratum submitted to the government.

An example of such a desideratum is from the Committee for Social Policy concerning the finances for the Polish telecommunication company, Telekomunikacja Polska S.A. The funds were intended to reduce the phone bills of war veterans.

The desideratum was formulated during discussions about the budget. In the committee's opinion, the amount allocated to cover the costs of reducing the veterans' phone bills was too low. The committee did not have the right to decide to increase this amount, as the law forbids a committee to amend the government's budget proposal. The only way to correct this miscalculation was to formulate a desideratum to the government.

Model 3: Citizen Complaints. MPs, committee members, and parliamentary party clubs receive many letters from voters either directly or indirectly through the Sejm's chancellery. Those letters can be a source of inspiration for desiderata from a committee to the government.

An example of this kind of desideratum comes from the Committee for Social Policy, which was concerned with refunding the costs of purchasing adult diapers. Diapers were not included in the category of either drugs or sanitary products. The source of this concern was the letters from the families of people with chronic diseases.

This case is a typical example of the role of the public in bringing problems to the committee's attention. Letters addressed to the Sejm, kept by the committees' staff secretaries, turned the attention of the members of the committees to a specific issue. It had been discussed at two meetings of the committee. The committee decided during the second meeting to submit a desideratum concerning this very problem.

Model 4: Administrative Agency Needs. Committees receive letters from institutions undertaking some socially important issues that they think need intervention from a parliamentary committee. The procedure is identical with Model 3, with one difference: the source of inspiration is not citizens but rather the representatives of an institution or a group of institutions.

An example is a desideratum of the Committee of Education, Science, and Technical Progress concerning the State Archives. The board of directors of the state archives informed the committee about its financial and space problems. The committee presidium, its officers, visited the archive and confirmed that the complaints were well grounded, and the decision to submit a desideratum followed.

The committee had been interested in the problems of the archives for some time. Previously, it requested an increase in funding for the archives, and that the Ministry of Finances increase the amount in the 1996 budget to enlarge the storage capacity. The committee received information about the threat to the document collections from the main board of directors of the state archives. A letter also arrived from the director of this body, with photographs showing the poor condition of the document storage facilities. The representatives of the committee paid a visit to the archives. At the committee meeting a report of the audit agency, Chief Board of Supervision (NIK), was quoted. It confirmed the bad conditions and stated that the institution in question made enormous efforts to improve working conditions by investing at the cost of current expenditures. The NIK supported the recommendation to increase the funding for the archives. The idea of submitting the desideratum received unanimous support from the committee members, and a vote was not necessary.

Model 5: Interest Groups. Among the voters, mentioned above, who inform MPs about the society from their own point of view, there are also professional groups, united by common interests, and expressing them in the form of homogenous opinions. The MPs call such pieces of information "signals from milieus." They are mostly about the material conditions of these groups. The committee analyzes letters and information from professional groups, and then submits a desideratum to the government.

The desideratum of the Health Committee concerning the deterioration in the functioning of the National Health Service is an example. The discussion consisted of exchanging opinions about the extremely difficult conditions of the health service in different towns.

An argument for a serious consideration of the problems of the health service was the report of one MP about the indebtedness of the health service to the drugstores. A deputy minister of finance was present during the committee discussion. His answers to the MPs' objections, remarks, and complaints could be boiled down to the lack of money. The MPs declared that the attitude of the government's representative was not sufficiently flexible. Since they were unable to persuade him to consider the other reasons given by the representatives of the health service, they decided to submit a desideratum, which they claimed was supported by the professional health groups.

Model 6: The Audit Agency. Another source of information for committees is the Chief Board of Supervision (NIK), the audit and investigation agency. Consideration of its reports is obligatory. Often such reports are about irregularities in the activity of the executive authorities or those of the state economy. These irregularities include infringing the law, wasteful activity, and other transgressions by the administrative institutions. Information from the NIK accompanying the government's annual report about the implementation of the bills and the budget is reviewed by the committee. A desideratum can then be submitted to the government.

An example is the desideratum of the Committee of Education, Science, and Technical Progress concerning the procedures of teacher evaluation. The desideratum states that there is a lack of objective criteria for evaluation, as well as low professional skills in the personnel performing the teacher examinations. Both statements are the result of the opinions of the NIK's inspection officers.

The NIK report cited poor supervision from the superintendents as responsible for the low teaching and administrative professional skills of the supervisors and the lack of executive regulations concerning the principles of evaluating the effectiveness of the educational process. The committee tried to find the reasons for this situation, not in the unsound system of supervision, but rather in the low pay of the superintendents.

As a result of the discussion, two versions of a committee desideratum were formulated. The shorter version demanded that the Ministry of Education prepare "the instruments of evaluating" the work of schools and directors, while the longer one included the arguments concerning the low pay of the superintendents. Ultimately, the second one was submitted to the government.

In addition to the six models, which encompass the majority of committee desiderata, there are also other cases that are difficult to include. They are, among others: First, desiderata resulting from the observation of social life not directly related to the work of parliamentary committees. An example is the desideratum of the health committee concerning the worsening of the health of the nation, and containing suggestions for fighting alcoholism and cigarette smoking, as well as a proposal to create a Fund for Health Protection. Second, desiderata following the insufficient answers of the government's bodies to MP questions. An example is the joint desideratum of the Health Committee, the Committee on Justice, and the Legislation Committee, concerning the answer of the government's representative to a question about the Polish delegates' opinion at a demographic conference in Cairo. The committee was not satisfied with the minister's answer, which asserted that the delegation would support the social teachings of the Church. The committee demanded that all the opinions found in Polish society be presented.

Committees and Desiderata

Several conclusions follow from the analysis of the desiderata of four parliamentary committees, as well as from the minutes of their meetings: First, the activity of a parliamentary committee in performing its administrative review function primarily depends on the commitment and professional skills of its members. This analysis emphasizes the enormous significance of the personal will and deeply rooted individual attitudes of individual MPs in their parliamentary work. By analyzing only one of the instruments, desiderata, used in one of the roles of the MPs, we can see that the effects of their actions are not only a consequence of the scope of the issues monitored but also of the labor and commitment of the MPs.

Examples of committee and member activity illustrate an unofficial but prevalent categorization of MPs into three types: "Motors"—well-known people, charismatic people, activists, leaders in a range of public actions, and those who put forward certain legislative projects; "Ants"—people who cooperate with more than one committee, are always present at the meetings, and almost always at plenary sessions; and "Audience members"—people who sign the attendance records, take part in "obligatory" voting, and feel free to do not much more.

An important part of parliamentary committees' activities, their oversight functions, depends almost entirely on the accuracy, scrupulousness, and competence of the MPs.

Second, no direct pressures from the parliamentary party clubs can be observed in the oversight role of the committees, including the formulating of desiderata. Each committee includes representatives of all the parties in the Sejm. The possibility of influencing decisions concerning what issue to choose and member attitudes on the issue is more or less evenly distributed among the parties. Since party interest is usually not explicit, it is difficult to document its absence.

Polish constitutional law includes a so-called free mandate, which means that the MPs have unrestricted freedom to act as they wish, as long as they have "the public good" in mind. The MP is not bound by the electorate's instructions. All of his/her decisions are taken on his/her own. Loyalty toward a parliamentary party club and party discipline play an important role in the MPs' actions. Even if formal party discipline is sometimes imposed when an important issue is voted at a plenary session, an individual MP rarely feels pressure from his/her party. In the forum of committees, the MP is the only master of his/her behavior.

Third, the activity of lobbyists, which has already begun in Poland, is reflected in their attempts to influence individual MPs, as well as parliamentary committees, by sending letters, motions, etc. The MPs call this lobbying somewhat enigmatically, "the voice of a milieu."

In summary, committees vary greatly in the frequency and type of actions that they undertake in the conduct of administrative review and supervision. Their "desiderata" activities mainly occur in six types, but each committee innovates and improvises as it encounters new problems in the administration of government policy. Up to now, it is not clear what a desideratum of a parliamentary committee should be. Is it only a signal for the government, a suggestion to undertake changes, or a document requiring changes in state policy and administration? This often-used and long-standing device is sufficiently important to generate its own controversy.

Conclusions

This chapter has examined parliamentary committees in two specific respects: First, the extraordinary constitution-drafting committee, and second, the more typical standing committees. The special constitution-drafting committee worked over two parliaments, through a complete change of party majorities and of governments. The standing committees developed procedures for review of administration. While the special committee was the prime institutionalized locale for interparty negotiations among the leaders, the standing committees permitted ordinary deputies to work without either party guidance or discipline. Both types of committees and their very different tasks illustrate the interconnections between parliamentary activity and external political forces and social organizations.

Both types of committees and their working procedures were based upon precedents developed during the communist period, illustrating both stability of form and adaptability of function to cope with the fluid circumstances of a new democratic political system. The organizational forms and procedural devices now used in the democratic Sejm are directly based upon the precedents established over a thirty-year period during the communist regime.

The development of powers and instruments in the committee, however, has not kept up with the tasks of the Sejm in post-communist Poland. Answers to the following three questions are still urgently needed:

1) Is the role of a committee only to prepare the sessions of the Sejm, or does it have other functions? A purely auxiliary role would limit both their administrative oversight and law initiation functions.

2) Should the committee enter into implementation? Though this question could be answered negatively, we observe a tendency to expand this activity. The opponents of the committees' unrestricted freedom emphasize that expanded review over executive authorities makes the government uneasy.

3) Does the increase in the committees' activities strengthen the position of the Sejm, or weaken it? Some opponents are of the opinion that the committee system's strength grows at the cost of the Sejm as a whole.

Notes

1. A desideratum is an order to undertake an action or resolve a problem.
2. An opinion is a recommended interpretation of a regulation or a rule of behavior.
3. The 1952 Constitution had not much to say about the committees, and the uncompleted Sejm's Regulations did not arrange all the possible issues in detail. More complete regulations could be found in the communist-era constitutions of Czechoslovakia, Yugoslavia, the Soviet Union, and Bulgaria.
4. Art. 110, par. 3.
5. Art. 11, par. 1.
6. Art. 18, par. 1 and 2 of the Regulations.
7. The new regulations created a Register for Material Benefits, which shows the material situation of particular MPs. The MPs were obliged to declare all material benefits (regardless of its kind) acquired during their mandate.
8. The co-author of this part is Krzysztof Przybyszewski.

FOUR

Committees of the Chamber of Deputies of the Czech Republic

Zdenka Mansfeldová, Jindřiška Syllová,
Petra Rakušanová, Petr Kolář

ON OCTOBER 28, 1918, THE CZECHOSLOVAK REPUBLIC CAME into being, as a successor state after the disintegration of the Austrian-Hungarian Empire. The Constitution of the Czechoslovak Republic was anchored by the principle of democracy through elected representatives. The parliament (called the National Assembly) consisted of two chambers—the Chamber of Deputies and the Senate. The Chamber of Deputies had 300 deputies elected for six years, and the Senate consisted of 150 senators elected for eight years. Elections to both chambers were held according to proportional representation.

The Second World War and the communist regime that followed interrupted the continuity of Czech parliamentarianism. In 1968, Czechoslovakia was proclaimed a federation of the Czech and the Slovak Republics. The parliament, which had been unicameral, was renamed the Federal Assembly and had two chambers. At the same time, parliaments were formed in both Republics, the Czech National Council and the Slovak National Council.

After the revolutionary events of 1989 ended the communist regime, further constitutional changes affected the parliament. In June 1990, the first free elections in many years to both National Councils and the Federal Assembly were held. The June 1992 elections led to the breakup of the federal state. On December 16, 1992, the Czech National Council adopted the new Constitution of the Czech Republic, which went into effect on January 1, 1993.

The former Czech National Council, elected in 1992, became the

Chamber of Deputies of the Czech Republic (CDCR) on the day that the Constitution of the Czech Republic came into effect. The period between January 1, 1993, and May 31, 1996, was designated the first term of office of the Chamber of Deputies of the Czech Republic. The first elections explicitly to that chamber were held on May 31, 1996. The Senate was not established until November 1996, when elections were held for the first time. Until then, the Chamber of Deputies carried out the functions of the Senate.

The Chamber of Deputies of the Parliament (*Poslanecká snemovna Parlamentu Ceské republiky*) has two hundred deputies elected for four-year terms according to the principles of proportional representation. The Senate has eighty-one senators elected according to the principles of majority vote. Senators are elected for six-year terms, with one-third of the senators elected every two years.

The maturing and continuing institutionalization of the activities of parliamentary committees had an impact on the Chamber of Deputies, as did the external political environment. In 1995, the rules governing the Chamber were changed, giving the work of the Chamber a firmer structure and enhancing the role of the committees. This change is documented by this chapter's comparative analysis of committee activities for the years 1995 and 1997 in the first and second terms, respectively.

Parliamentary Committees

Number and Specialization of Committees

The composition and specialization of committees in both chambers of parliament is partly determined by legal provisions. These include the constitution, which states in Article 31 that "the chamber shall establish committees and commissions to function as their organs. The activities of the committees shall be regulated by law."

The powers of committees are set out in the Act of the Rules of Procedure of the Chamber of Deputies, which was last modified in 1995. The committees are considered the main legislative working instruments of the Chamber of Deputies. The Rules of Procedure expressly define the committees' rights and duties. The committees of the Chamber of Deputies and of the Senate have been permanent. It has not been the practice to set up new ones or to abolish or divide them during a session.

In both chambers, the size of the committees varies between thirteen and twenty-three members. There are eight permanent committees in the Senate and eleven in the Chamber. Parliament did not create any joint committees because the legislative procedure in the Chamber of Deputies must be finished before the Senate can consider a bill. Joint bodies were established as delegations to parliamentary assemblies of international organizations.

In the second term (1998), there were ten permanent committees in the Chamber of Deputies with traditional committee duties, such as legislation and supervision of government activities, and an additional one dealing with internal functions. This number was the same during the CDCR's first term (1992–96).

The subject areas of the permanent legislative committees do not correspond to the division of work among the ministries. There are several reasons for this. The first is tradition. The definition of jurisdiction was taken from that of the Czech National Council and the Federal Assembly in the communist era, and changes in the orientation of committees have proceeded very slowly.

The second reason is that the ministries frequently change their jurisdictions, but the Chamber of Deputies is not willing to follow. During the first term of parliament, some ministries were abolished and others created in two waves, due to the split-up of the Czechoslovak Federal Republic. Early in 1993, the Chamber of Deputies adapted its committee system to the changed circumstances by forming a Foreign Policy Committee and a Defense and Security Committee.

In addition, the CDCR has a relatively small membership of two hundred, and would have had difficulty filling seats on sixteen committees corresponding to the government departments. After the elections in 1996, the majority of ministers were deputies. Since a member of the government may not hold a position in a chamber of parliament, including a committee membership, the number of members available to serve on committee was reduced even further.

The division of subject areas among individual ministries does not present any difficulty because of the stability and orientation of the committees. Each committee is familiar with the laws pertaining to its assigned ministries, has worked on these laws repeatedly, and has working relations not only with the respective minister but also with the civil servants, who often draft several versions of a bill. This knowledge facilitates the committees' supervision of the ministries.

The Constitution and Legal Committee followed the practice of the communist-period Constitution and Legal Committee until the new Rules of Procedure came into force in 1995. This committee, composed mostly of deputies who were lawyers, checked the constitutionality and legal admissibility of each act. Despite its work, bills frequently contained formal errors that were not discovered during the legislative procedure. The processing of all bills by the Constitution and Legal Committee took the place of multiple readings in the Chamber of Deputies, and the amended version of a bill underwent only one reading. After the new Rules were adopted, the supervisory role of the Constitution and Legal Committee was abolished, and it became a committee without any special status. Now it deals with legislation originating in the Ministry of Justice, and with all constitutional acts.

The committee structure in the smaller Senate does not differ significantly from that of the Chamber of Deputies. The Senate has eight committees. The Organizational Committee and the Mandate and Immunity Committee play the same role as the analogous committees in the Chamber of Deputies. The Senate has no Budget Committee, for only the Chamber of Deputies passes the national budget. Bills for which the Ministry of Finance is responsible are assigned to the Committee for Economy, Agriculture, and Transport. The Senate Committee for Petitions, Human Rights, Science, Education, and Culture deals with the Ministry of Education as well as the other areas in its title. Another committee deals with foreign affairs, defense and security.

Forming Committees

There are some restrictions concerning committee membership. Every deputy can be a member of two committees, but membership in the Organizational Committee and the Mandate Committee is not counted. A deputy may be chair or vice chair of only one committee. Every deputy, except for members of the government and senior officers of the CDCR, must serve on at least one committee. Committee members cannot be members of the government or chair or vice chair of a chamber. The latter, however, are always members of the Organizational Committee.

Committees meet according to their own time schedule. The chambers work in sessions that last for several weeks, while other weeks are reserved for committee work. Committees also frequently meet at other times. Their business consists primarily of items assigned to them by the chamber. In addition, they also discuss items of their own choice. They are committed to meet deadlines set by the Rules of Procedure.

Subcommittees

According to the old Rules of Procedures Act in force until 1995, committees were allowed to form commissions. These commissions were made up of deputies, who were not necessarily committee members and who specialized in some particular problem within the subject area of the committee. The chairs of the commission were always a deputy and a member of the respective committee. The commissions appointed by the committee met according to need, often at the request of the entire committee, to have a preliminary debate on some particular document or bill.

In contrast to the committees, commission members did not have to be deputies; therefore, by a commission, a committee could establish a group of experts who could assist with issues requiring specific knowledge. The experts were more interested in the work of the commission than were the deputies themselves, and the documents that the commissions drafted were often influenced by views other than purely expert opinion. Several times, experts whose opinion had not prevailed in the drafting of government documents tried to influence the committee through the backdoor. There were twenty commissions in the first term; their number varied from zero to five per committee.

Because of the attempt by experts to assert group interests in commissions set up by committees, the new Rules of Procedure denied membership in subcommittees to persons who were not deputies or senators. Subcommittees now do the job formerly done by commissions. They continue to collaborate with outside experts, who have no vote.

Any committee may establish a subcommittee to deal with a specific issue. Only deputies may be members of subcommittees. Not only members of the committee that established the subcommittee, but also other deputies may be included. This practice enables reelected MPs to continue their membership on a subcommittee even if they change committee membership in the new term. Members can use the knowledge and skills developed in the previous term and can continue to work on long-term problems. A subcommittee is always chaired by a deputy of its committee. Often the chair is one of the committee's vice chairs.

Subcommittees concentrate on exceptionally difficult issues in the subject areas of their committee. The activity of a subcommittee ensures the continuing interest of deputies, creates a better working climate with fewer participants, and raises the general efficiency of the committees.

The subcommittee work is not so frequent and comprehensive as to substitute for the committees. A draft act would never be discussed only in a subcommittee, and its conclusions would never be simply backed by the committee. The entire committee always discusses the draft and prepares its own legislative recommendation.

Structure of Specialized Commissions

In addition to committees, the CDCR can set up four types of specialized bodies: control commissions, investigative commissions, permanent commissions, and oversight commissions.

The first type of commission, composed of deputies, acts as a control mechanism over special spheres of executive activity. There are three permanent commissions: 1) Security and Information Service; 2) Operative Technology of the Police of the CR; and 3) Military Defense Intelligence.

The second type of commission, the Investigative Commission,[1] is a special agency of the Chamber of Deputies, which inquires into matters of public interest when necessary.

Third, the Chamber of Deputies and the Senate can set up other commissions at any time. The commission's members are either elected or appointed by the Chamber. Permanent commissions include: 1) for Media; 2) for the Office Work of the Chamber of Deputies; and 3) for Banking.

The fourth type of special body is the Oversight Commission for any election held by a chamber during a term (e.g., the election of the Board of the Czech Television's members). The unique role of this oversight commission is defined in the Rules of Procedure and consists of preparing, organizing, and overseeing all votes (e.g., members to committees, commissions, verifiers, etc.) in the internal bodies of the respective chamber. The Oversight Commission is the first body established by the Chamber of Deputies at the beginning of a session. All the parties delegate the members of the commission proportionally.

Membership in Committees

A deputy cannot sit on more than two committees. The Mandate and Immunity Committee, the Petition Committee, the Budget Committee, and the Organizing Committee are exceptions. This practice was applied particularly during the second session (1996–98), when the number of committee memberships exceeded the total number of deputies by almost 10 percent. In 1995, committees had from eleven to twenty-four members and averaged 18.2. By 1998 this had changed to a range of eleven to twenty-six members, with an average of 19.8. In both terms, 1992–96 and 1996–98, the size of individual committees changed slightly within a range of zero to two. The committees were of more equal size in 1997 than in 1995, but the Petitions Committee and Committee for Foreign Affairs were larger. This increase was not because those committees have special prestige, for deputies did not consider them prestigious (see Appendix 3). Typically, the special committees that are not involved in the legislative process, such as the Organizational and the Mandate Committees, had a smaller number of members.

In the course of the two years reviewed in this chapter (1995 and 1997), there were no substantial changes in the composition of the committees. With a few exceptions committee members who left were replaced by another member of the same parliamentary party. Major changes in 1997 and practically the entire second term were caused by the breakup of the government coalition and of the strongest political party, the Civic Democratic Party (ODS). The restructuring of the parties led to the party composition of the committees changing but the members were the same persons.

In the Chamber of Deputies, only deputies may be members of committees and subcommittees. According to the Rules of Procedure in force until June 1995, external members could participate in both subcommittees and commissions. Under the new Rules of Procedure, they can be members only of commissions. No data on them are available. In general, the external members of commissions are specialists on the subject area of the commission.

Experience of Committee Members

On most committees, at least half the members have had prior experience in parliament. The highest proportion of experienced members were on the Committee for Foreign Affairs. We include in this measure members who had been elected to at least one term to either the Czech National Council or the Czechoslovak Federal Assembly, in 1990 or 1992. This incumbency rate may show how political parties ranked the importance of the committees.

In 1995 in the first parliamentary term, members of the Committee for Foreign Affairs and the Committee for Public Administration had the highest incumbency rate. In the next term (1996–98), members of Committee for Foreign Affairs and Budget Committee had the highest incumbency rate (see Table 4.1). Members of the Budget Committee and the Agricultural Committee were more likely to return to their previous committee, while members of Committee for Petitions were less likely. The importance of prior experience in budgeting was especially recognized by the political parties. Generally there does not seem to be a trend for members to specialize in their committee assignments.

Connection between Districts, MPs, and Committees

A connection between the MPs' districts and committee memberships cannot be ascertained for the Czech Republic, because the electoral system of proportional representation discourages a direct relationship between a seat and a specific constituency. Generally, the leading candidates of the

Table 4.1

Parliamentary and Committee Incumbency of Members by Committee,
Czech Chamber of Deputies, Second Term

Committee Name	Number of Members	MPs in the Same Committee in Last Term		Served in Parliament the Last Term	
		N	%	N	%
Committee for Economics	20	6	30.0	9	50.0
Mandate and Immunity Committee	12	4	33.3	5	58.3
Committee for Petitions	19	1	5.3	4	36.8
Budget Committee	20	8	40.0	10	60.0
Constitutional and Legal Committee	20	6	30.0	7	50.0
Committee for Defense and Security	20	3	15.0	8	55.0
Committee for Social Policy and Health Care	19	5	26.3	7	42.1
Committee for Public Administration, Regional Develop. and Environment	26	5	19.2	8	38.4
Committee for Science, Education, Culture, Youth and Sport	26	6	23.1	8	57.7
Committee for Foreign Affairs	20	3	15.0	8	65.0
Agricultural Committee	20	7	35.0	7	45.0
Total	222	54	24.75	81	50.75

Source: Archive of the Chamber of Deputies, Parliament of the Czech Republic

political parties did not run in the district in which they lived but in the constituency that seemed to be advantageous for the party electoral campaign. In contrast, candidates in the second or third position on the party ballot frequently campaigned in their own district, because many of them were regional politicians. Members of the Chamber of Deputies who are not in positions of importance have a closer connection to their constituencies and are more likely to support their region's interests. Leaders do lobby on important economic issues, such as revitalization of the big firms in their regions. This lobbying effort is directed mostly through the party clubs.[2]

There are no indications of close connections between individual committees and specific regions. Regional lobbies attend committee meetings infrequently. With the exceptions of the Mandate Committee and the Organizational Committee, meetings are usually public.

Political Composition of Committees

Elections of 1992 and 1996 and Composition of Committees

In 1992, the second free parliamentary elections were held in the Czech and Slovak Federal Republic, to the two republic-level legislatures as well as the federal parliament. The elections and the entire post-election period after 1992 were characterized by the emergence of new political parties. Out of the Civic Forum, which represented the main reform force after November 1989, new political parties were formed. The most successful of them in the 1992 elections proved to be the Civic Democratic Party led by Václav Klaus, then minister of finance.

A right-wing government coalition was formed, which consisted of the parties ODS, ODA, and KDU-CSL, headed by Václav Klaus. On January 1, 1993, the federation ceased to exist, and an independent Czech Republic came into being. The former Czech National Council was renamed the Chamber of Deputies of the Parliament of the Czech Republic.

The elections held in 1996 seriously weakened the government coalition, whose deputies received only 99 seats of 200. Opposition deputies gained a slim majority of 101 in the Chamber of Deputies. A series of negotiations followed which were made more difficult by the fact that forty seats, i.e., one-fifth of the total, were won by the deputies of extremist parties, Communists and Republicans. Finally, a minority government was formed by the former government coalition parties (ODS, ODA, KDU-CSL), which was tolerated by the largest opposition party, CSSD. The leader of that party, Miloš Zeman, became chair of the Chamber of Deputies. In the minority cabinet, ODS obtained the post of prime minister and another seven ministerial posts.

At the first session of the Chamber of Deputies in July 1996, new parliamentary bodies were constituted, including committees. The composition of individual committees corresponded to the distribution of political forces in the Chamber of Deputies. Thus, after the 1996 elections, the coalition and opposition party members were evenly balanced on the committees.

In December 1997, a split occurred in ODS. Some parliamentary party deputies and some ministers formed a new political party called Freedom Union. This new party, together with the former coalition partners (ODA and KDU-CSL), formed a new minority government, consisting mainly of nonparty members. This government was led by the former governor of the Czech National Bank, Josef Tošovský. The rest of ODS, headed by Václav Klaus, went into opposition.

Committee Officers by Political Affiliation

There is no provision that committee chairs must be proportionally allotted according to the size of the parties in parliament. The allocation is a matter of political bargaining among the parties. This is the reason why, during the first parliamentary term, all committee chairs were held by members of the majority government coalition, which also had a majority on the committees.

A different situation arose after 1996, when the government coalition had two seats less than it needed for a majority. The representatives of political parties agreed on which chairs should be held by each party. Seven chairs of committees out of eleven belonged to government parties. The party that was originally the strongest, ODS, held five chairs, two of which were in less important committees—the Mandate and Immunity and Petition Committees. The smaller government parties provided one chairman each (see Table 4.2). The sole democratic opposition party, CSSD, held the remaining four committee chairs, all of them important ones. The slight majority of coalition parties as committee chairs was compensated for by the election of the chair of the opposition party, CSSD, to the chair of the Chamber of Deputies.

CDCR committees also have vice chairs, who frequently also head subcommittees. Another officer is the verifier of the committee, whose position is not very important. Each committee can have as many vice chairs as it wishes. Most committees have four or five. The number of vice chairs during the second parliamentary term was substantially larger than during the preceding one, because the stalemate with the minority government led to their willingness to give the democratic opposition enough posts to facilitate a vote of confidence for the government and the cooperation of the opposition to the government. In both parliamentary terms, the vice chairs were elected by their committees. The real choice of candidates for the vice chair position, however, is a result of agreement among party leaders.

Table 4.2

Number of Committee Chairmen by Party and Government Status with Change in Government, Czech Chamber of Deputies, Second Term

Government Status	Party Name	Number 2.7.1996	Number 15.3.1998
Government	ODS	5	#
Coalition	ODA	1	1
	KDU - ČSL	1	1
	US	©	2
	Coalition Total	7	4
Opposition	ČSSD	5	5
	KSČM	0	0
	SPR – RSČ	0	0
	ODS	®	2
	Opposition Total	6	7
Independent		0	1
Total		12	12

Note:

© —— did not exist at the time

® —— was part of government coalition at the time

—— was part of the opposition at the time

Source: Archive of the Chamber of Deputies, Parliament of the Czech Republic

During the first term, the distribution of committee leadership positions favored the coalition parties. During the second term, the vice chairs were mostly representatives of four democratic parties (ODS, CSSD, KDU-CSL, or ODA). Often a committee chaired by a member of CSSD had among its vice chairs two representatives of ODS as vice chair and vice versa. Some committees had a different distribution of vice chairs, but it was always the result of an agreement among political parties.

Of the two nondemocratic parties, the Communists had not been included in the bargaining concerning vice-chair posts and held none. The Republicans successfully negotiated for two vice-chair positions.

Functions of Committees

Oversight and Budget

The second most important task of the committees, after the legislative function, is to review the functioning of government. This task is the natural consequence of the system of government, in which the administration is directly and continuously responsible to the parliament. Committees are the main practical working instruments for fulfilling this responsibility.

Effectiveness of oversight depends on the ability of committees to get information from the government, ministers, and other administrative officials. MPs of the Chamber of Deputies recognized the importance of obtaining information from the administrative authorities in drafting of the new Law of Rules of Procedure. MPs have the right to compel government officials to provide information during committee meetings. Article 39. § 2 says that members of government and members of the other central administrative agencies are required to attend in person a meeting of a committee when asked and to provide the information and explanations requested.

The oversight actions of committees are initiated by the government or ministry, or by the committee. In both types of debates, committees seek to obtain detailed information. Ministers and officials who present information must answer questions in connection with their report. If the issue is initiated by the committee itself, the questions are usually more concrete and controversial and may lead to a request for further information.

Not all committees concentrate on administrative review with the same intensity. The Committee on Foreign Affairs has a high percentage of such debates. This committee asks for detailed information on most serious problems regarding the policies of the Ministry of Foreign Affairs. This information usually is presented by vice ministers or department directors. The Defense and Security Committee actively investigates various affairs dealing with security service, police, municipality, and army services.

A different type of oversight is provided during the budget process, which is complex and detailed. Individual specialized committees discuss relevant parts of the draft of the state budget. Committees may propose changes to those areas or ask another committee to make changes in another part. The budget as a whole is debated in the Budget Committee, which submits its resolution to the Chamber of Deputies. Within the budget process, individual committees have the chance to get acquainted with the financial background of ministry programs, which allows them to obtain general knowledge of the policies of the relevant ministry. The most powerful committee is the Budget Committee, which coordinates the allocation of financial resources among the individual ministries and authorities, and to which the other committees report their recommendations.

The effectiveness of administrative review is affected by the composition of the Chamber of Deputies in relationship to the composition of the government. When the government had a majority in the Chamber of Deputies, effectiveness was lower because government had a majority in each committee. In practice, the ministers and officials did not usually refuse to provide required information, but the MPs from government parties defended their ministers from excessive interference. In contrast, when there was a minority government, the effectiveness of administrative review increased, especially in committees in which the chair was an opposition MP. The program of the committee concentrated on administrative review, and the content of the debates was more substantial.

Other Functions and Committees

Three other committees have different functions: the Committee for Petitions mainly deals with petitions, but is concerned with human rights in general and ethnic rights in particular. The Mandate and Immunity Committee decides all cases concerning deputy discipline and immunity rights. The Organizational Committee is not a legislative committee, but a collective body that organizes the work of the Chamber. It is the twelfth standing committee of the CDCR.

Activities of Parliamentary Committees

With the exception of the three committees mentioned above, the standing committees are typical legislative committees with responsibilities for international treaties and the budget. We do not know the proportion of legislative and nonlegislative activities of the committees. We estimate that approximately half the decisions are the result of legislative activities, and the other half deals with other issues. Over half of the committees' time is spent on legislative activities.

We can distinguish six types of activities, with an estimated time allocation within each type of activity:

A. Legislation in the narrow sense of consideration of amendments to bills (refer to section below).

B. Executive branch
   a) Decisions on inviting officials from the executive to the committee meetings are less than 5 percent of the decisions in this category.
   b) Decisions on obtaining reports or information from ministers and other executive branch officials are about 30 percent of the decisions.
   c) Decisions on documents obtained from the government, are about 10 percent of the decisions.
   d) Decisions on institutions that are supervised by the Chamber of Deputies are about 20 percent of the decisions, but apply to some of the committees only.

C. International policy
   a) International treaties range from 50 percent of the decisions in the Committee for Foreign Affairs to 10 percent in other committees.
   b) Decisions on international organizations are about 20 percent of the decisions.
   c) Decisions in connection with bilateral relations are about 5 to 10 percent of the decisions in the Committee for Foreign Affairs.

D. Committee's internal functions
   a) Procedure on questions and elections of chair and vice chair of the subcommittees are less than 5 percent of the decisions.
   b) Proposals to the Organizational Committee concerning committee business trips are about 10 percent of the decisions.

E. Petitions sent from the Petition Committee are more than 30 percent of the decisions in the Committee for Social Policy and Health but less than 5 percent of decisions in other committees.

F. Budget. From September to November of every year budget decision making dominates in the Budget Committee. In other committees less than 5 percent of the decisions deal with the budget, but the time used is more than 5 percent.

The number of committee meetings and resolutions varied among committees. The committees in 1995 with the largest number of meetings were the Defense and Security Committee and the Constitution and Legal Committee. In the second term in 1997, the Committee for Economics and Committee for Science, Education, Culture, Youth and Sport met most frequently. In 1995, the Budget Committee adopted the largest number of resolutions, and the Committee for Foreign Affairs had the second largest number. In 1997 the Budget Committee and the Committee for Science and Education reported the most resolutions.

Legislative Activity of Committees

Submission of Draft Acts[3]

Bills, or draft acts, may be submitted by deputies, groups of deputies, the Senate, the government, or the councils[4] of higher territorial self-administered units (hereinafter "initiator" or "sponsor," after the Czech term *navrhovatel*).

Most of the bills are submitted by the government using the following

Table 4.3

Number of Bills by Committee and Source, Czech Chamber of Deputies, 1997

Committee	Total Number of Bills Discussed	Bills by Source		
		Government	Deputy	Senate
Committee for Economics	9	8	1	—
Mandate and Immunity Committee	—	—	—	—
Committee for Petitions	2	1	1	—
Budget Committee	23	16	7	—
Constitution and Legal Committee	22	8	14	—
Committee for Defense and Security	3	—	2	1
Committee for Social Policy and Health Care	11	10	1	—
Committee for Public Administration, Regional Develop and Environment	7	4	3	—
Committee for Science, Education, Culture, Youth and Sport	7	2	5	—
Committee for Foreign Affairs	—	—	—	—
Agricultural Committee	9	6	3	—
Total	93	55	37	1
Average	8.45	5	3.36	0.09

Source: Archive of the Chamber of Deputies, Parliament of the Czech Republic

process (see Table 4.3). First, the bill is prepared by a department in a ministry. Then the draft goes to the Office of the Government, which receives comments from other ministries. At the government level the bill is reviewed by the Legislative Council (an advisory body of external legal experts). The draft is then reviewed in the plenary meeting of the Cabinet. After government approval, the draft is sent to the Chamber of Deputies.

Draft acts include a justification report for the new legislation. This report evaluates the current law and explains why the new law is necessary. The justification report also includes the anticipated economic and financial impact of the proposed legislation, specifically the cost to the state budget, and the degree to which the bill is in harmony with international agreements and with the Constitution of the Czech Republic.

Draft acts are submitted in writing both on paper and in the parliament's computer system. After the committee has discussed a bill, the chairman designates a reporter from among the members. The reporter writes the committee's decision and reports the decision to the floor. Depending on the topic, committees submit their decisions to the Chamber of Deputies, to the appropriate member of the government, or to the head of an administrative agency.

The bill is submitted to the Chairman of the Chamber of Deputies, who sends it to the Organizing Committee. The chair also sends the bill to all deputies and deputies' party clubs. If the bill's originator is not the government, the chair asks for the government's written opinion on the draft within thirty days. The chair of the Chamber of Deputies takes into consideration the recommendation of the Organizing Committee, but he has the authority to decide whether or not to include bill for first reading on the agenda of the next meeting of the Chamber of Deputies.

First Reading[5]

The bill is first explained by the sponsor, followed by the committee's reporter. Following general debate, the Chamber of Deputies may return the draft to the bill initiator to be refined, or reject the draft, which happens to about half of the drafts. Otherwise, the Chamber of Deputies assigns the draft to one or more committees as proposed by the Organizing Committee or the chair of the Chamber of Deputies. To date, the first reading does not provide a barrier. Most bills, even those that have no hope of being passed, are admitted for further processing by the committees. The committee has sixty days to complete discussion of the bill, after the first reading.

Second Reading[6]

The responsible committee submits a recommendation to approve or not approve the bill to the Chamber of Deputies. If the committee recommends changes or additions to the bill, it words these precisely. A minority comprising at least one-fifth of all the members may submit an opposing report. Such a report must meet the same requirements as the committee's resolution. The committee's resolution on the draft act and the minority report are printed and delivered to all deputies at least twenty-four hours prior to the start of Second Reading of the bill.

At Second Reading, debate is opened by the bill initiator, followed by the reporter from the committee. Following general debate, the Chamber may return the bill to the committee to be discussed again, or it may decide to reject it. The Chamber of Deputies may also resolve to discuss some provisions of the bill separately. After general debate there is a detailed debate on amendments. They are printed, and the chair of the Chamber of Deputies sends them to all deputies without delay.

Third Reading[7]

A Third Reading of a bill may not be started until twenty-four hours after the delivery of proposals to correct technical mistakes in grammar and in printing. The Third Reading usually occurs only a few days after the Second Reading.

At the conclusion of the Third Reading, the Chamber of Deputies votes on amendments and other proposed changes in the bill. The bill's initiator is allowed to express his/her opinion on individual amendments. After this step, the Chamber of Deputies votes on the whole bill.

Draft acts are sometimes fundamentally changed in the Chamber of Deputies. That happened for example, in the case of the university bill. Changes are always made in cooperation with the bill initiator. If several similar legislative initiatives are proposed on the same topic, the sponsors usually cooperate.

Legislative Procedure in Committees

A committee normally has sixty days to consider a bill following its First Reading. The Chamber of Deputies may extend or shorten the deadline described above by up to twenty days. The deadline may be extended by more than twenty days only with the agreement of the sponsor.

In practice, the chair of the committee nominates a committee member as reporter of the bill and proposes the date and time for consideration of the bill in committee. After the committee approves the agenda, the secretariat of the committee invites the bill's initiator to defend the bill. Usually the appropriate minister or vice minister attends the meeting of the committee on behalf of the government. The debate is started by the representative of the bill's initiator. Then the reporter gives his report. After general debate, the bill's initiator can express his/her views and the reporter can respond. During the debate on the specific provisions of the bill, MPs may propose amendments. Those adopted are included in the committee's resolution.

Usually debate on a bill takes more than one day because of amendments. The legislative officials are often requested to draft or check the amendments, and the committee suspends consideration of the bill. In rare cases, no amendments are submitted, and the committee discussion takes only one or two days.

After completing discussion of the bill, the committee submits to the chamber chair the resolution in which they recommend whether or not the chamber should approve the bill as a whole. If there are changes or amendments to the bill, the resolution must word these precisely. A minority comprising at least one-fifth of all the members of the committee may submit an opposition report to the chair.

In 1995, the parliament debated a total of 106 bills, out of which 71.69 percent were passed. It is not possible to assess the success of individual committees in preparing the drafts of a given list of bills, due to the record keeping in that period.[8] A small majority of bills were assigned to just one committee and dealt by just one. Almost one-fifth of bills were returned to committees during first and second readings.

Among 93 bills discussed in 1997 in committees, twenty-nine bills were discussed in two committees and twelve bills in more than two committees. Some broad topics, especially social policy, were within the jurisdiction of several committees. In 1997, the parliament debated a total of ninety-three bills, out of which 79.6 percent were passed.

The Organizing Committee and Leadership of the Chamber of Deputies

The Organizing Committee has a special status in the Rules of Procedure, Chapter 6, § 46: "The Organizing Committee consists of its chair, who is the chair of the Chamber of Deputies, the vice chairs of the Chamber, and other members of the committee who are proposed by Deputies' Clubs (parties in the chamber), and it is constituted in accordance with the principle of proportional representation." The organizing committees in both chambers are de facto commissions, because their work consists in organizing the work of their chambers.

The Organizing Committee usually elects two additional vice chairs of the committee from its members. Meetings of the Organizing Committee are usually not public. The Organizing Committee organizes and coordinates the work of the bodies of the chamber, and is primarily responsible for schedules, agendas, and internal budgets and administration.

In 1995, according to the old Rules of Procedure, the Organizing Committee consisted of the Speaker of the Chamber, the vice chairs, and a number of representatives of each political party, proportionate to their representation in the Chamber of Deputies. Seats were not allotted to specific persons, but to parties as such. This practice was not changed under new Rules.

External Relations of Committees

Ministers attend committee meetings on their bills accompanied by the one or two ministerial officials who are involved their drafting. Ministers present bills and explain and justify specific provisions.

Contacts with groups representing particular interests, such as trade unions, business and employers associations, professional associations and others are not explicitly regulated, nor is their participation in the legislative process. One method that groups have for making contact with the Chamber is to send a petition to the Committee for Petitions.

Another way in which the public and interest groups may participate in the work of the Chamber of Deputies is by membership on parliamentary commissions. In contrast to subcommittees, membership in commissions is not reserved for deputies, and representatives of interest groups may be members of those bodies. However, the function of a commission is not comparable with that of a parliamentary committee, and its recommendations and reports cannot become legislation (Reschová 1995, 307).

Membership on commissions is the best way interest groups can bring their influence to bear, and trade unions, business associations, professional associations, and a number of others make use of it. There are no records of the frequency of such contacts. Representatives of the Czech-Moravian Confederation of Trade Unions, and the national federated trade union association, regularly attend meetings of a number of parliamentary committees. If they wish, they may ask for the floor. The committee members then vote on their request. So far, consent has always been given.

Committee Resources, Committee Documentary Products

Most committees have at their disposal two to three office staff and a secretary. Additional rooms for offices became available for the committees gradually as the houses of parliament were reconstructed. At present, committees have an average of three to four rooms and a staff of three. There is no separate budget for individual committees. Expenditures on committee activities are covered by the CDCR Office from the annual budget of the Chamber.

Concluding Remarks

Permanent committees do not mirror the structure of the ministries. The reasons are the instability of the division of subject areas in the Cabinet contrasted with the stability of permanent committees in the Chamber of Deputies. Individual committees have a set area of legislative activity that is not dependent on the ministry from which the bill comes. The committees may be, and usually are, in contact with the respective department even when it is moved into another ministry office.

Subcommittees (formerly commissions of the committees) were constituted by all committees in the Chamber of Deputies but not in the Senate. Their main task is to prepare reports from special materials requested by the committee, mostly in cooperation with experts. The common daily legislative work on bills was not transferred to the subcommittees.

Both chambers of the parliament are characterized by the high stability of committee membership during an electoral term, even if the MP changes party membership. In the Chamber of Deputies, there have been big changes in the membership of the whole chamber from one term to another that impact committee membership and committee chairs. Over the last two electoral terms, no committee chairman had served in both terms. Only about 30 percent of MPs continued in the same committee, with the exception of the Budget Committee.

There are no direct linkages between constituency and interest groups on the one side and committees on the other. Interest groups may have some impact through the experts working in subcommittees, but no survey affirms a more important involvement. No signs of any linkage between a committee and individual constituency were found. The interest groups' lobbying is directed more to the individual MPs and/or the party clubs.

Party composition of the committees is proportional to the parties' strength in the Chamber. In the first electoral term of the Chamber of Deputies, committee chairs were given to the majority coalition only. In the second electoral term there was no majority; therefore, the opposition parties enforced the proportional allocation of chairs and other officers of the committees by party representation.

Committees are very strong on procedural issues. The term for committee debate on a bill is usually sixty days after first reading. The chamber has the right to decide on quicker procedural rules for some bills, but that happens very rarely. The government doesn't have the right to make decisions on anything within the CDCR or to interfere in the legislative agenda of the Chamber of Deputies or its committees. On the contrary, the committees usually force the ministers to change their plans and to come to defend a bill before the committee.

In the Chamber the committees have a great deal of independence. The committee debate is usually very long, interrupted several times and many amendments are proposed, so MPs have time to learn the subject. Neither debate in first reading, nor the information obtained from the minister, discourages MPs from offering amendments in committees.

The regulation of procedures has substantially changed in the year 1995 with the passing of new rules. The most important change is the addition of more time for consideration of particular bills in committees. This change contributed to the improvement in the quality of bills considered by the committees.

Notes

1. The official name used in the Rule of Procedures in paragraph 48 is Investigative Commission.
2. Deputies may assemble in Deputies' clubs, in accordance with their membership in political parties for which they were elected. Deputies who belong to one party may form only one deputies' club.
3. More information is in the § 86–§ 89 of the Act on Rules of Procedure, 78–81.
4. The councils represent local governments that are not yet in existence.
5. More information is in Part 12, § 90 and § 91 of the Act on Rules of Procedure, 81–82.
6. More information is in Part 12, § 92 and § 93 of the Act on Rules of Procedure of the Chamber of Deputies, published by the Office of the Chamber of Deputies, May 1996, 83–84.
7. More information is in Part 12, § 95–§ 96 of the Act on Rules of Procedure of the Chamber of Deputies, published by the Office of the Chamber of Deputies, May 1996, 84–85.
8. More detailed information can be found on the Internet at http://www.psp.cz/ under the section called documents.

References

Reschová Jana. 1995. Ještě několik poznámek klegislativnímu procesu podle nového jednacího řádu. *Parlamentní zpravodaj*, roč. 1, č. 07, 306–7.

Rules of Procedure of the Chamber of Deputies, Act No. 90/1995 Coll. of April 19, 1995. Prague: Office of the Chamber of Deputies.

PART 3

*Post-Communist Parliaments:
Institutionalization in the
Middle Range*

FIVE

Bulgaria: Parliamentary Committees—Institutionalization and Effectiveness

Georgi Karasimeonov

Emergence of Post-Communist Parliamentarism

From the fall of the Jivkov regime in November 1989 until the first free elections for the Grand National Assembly in June 1990, the role of the existing parliament was limited to approving the decisions of the Bulgarian "Round Table committee." The Round Table brought together representatives of the communist regime with those of the nascent opposition to negotiate a political transition. The Round Table was de facto the real "parliament," in which the former ruling Communist Party faced the united anticommunist opposition and took major decisions leading to the dismantling of the totalitarian regime.[1]

Practically all decisions taken by the Round Table were approved by the old parliament inherited from the communist regime. Most important amongst them was the removal of the notorious Article 1, which cemented the "leading role" of the Communist Party in the country. No less important were constitutional amendments implementing political freedoms, the rule of law, and party pluralism. Among these decisions of the Round Table were the new electoral law and the law on political parties.

The birth of democratic post-communist parliamentarism followed the first free elections for the constituent assembly (the Grand National Assembly) on June 10, 1990, to adopt a constitution. Although the constituent Grand National Assembly became the arena for a confrontation

93

between the dominant Socialist (ex-Communist) Party and the anticommunist opposition, it was able to adopt a new constitution based on universal and democratic principles.

In addition to this major task, the constituent assembly had to fulfill many of the functions of regular parliaments. It adopted major changes in the legal framework inherited from the old regime. During the parliament's existence, a little more than a year, it voted into power two governments with radically different compositions and also elected a president. It adopted measures that changed the political system and brought different personnel into the administrative agencies.

The adoption of the constitution was followed by three parliamentary elections, each of which brought different political parties to governing positions. Three different legislatures with three different party compositions exemplified the dynamic, and at times turbulent political life in Bulgaria following 1991. Parliament played a major role in the process of legitimizing the new democratic order and laying the foundation for a new democratic politics.

Parliament's role in the preservation of social peace came to the fore in the dramatic events during the winter of 1997, when political instability reached dangerous proportions, leading to mass social unrest. The signing of a Declaration of National Salvation in February 1997 by the major parliamentary parties avoided civil unrest and led to the parliamentary resolution of the crisis.

The Bulgarian parliament (National Assembly) is a one-chamber legislative body. Its 240 members are elected for a four-year period. The principle of separation of powers is strictly applied. Members of parliament are not permitted to hold seats in the legislature and posts in the executive branch simultaneously.

Committee System—Structure and Composition

Structure and Organization of the Committee System

The Bulgarian Constitution provides that the National Assembly elects standing and ad hoc committees from among its members. The Rules of Organization and Procedure of the National Assembly (referred to further as Rules) is the basic legal source institutionalizing and regulating the details of the committees' structure and functions.

The current structure of the Bulgarian committee system follows the precedent laid down by the Grand National Assembly (1990–91). Two alternative committee structures were considered at that time. The first focused on a committee system corresponding to the cabinet structure. The second was to reflect the main branches of social life and the crucial aspects of the transitional process.

The second of these models was adopted initially by the Grand National Assembly and was partially followed by the next legislatures as well. After 1990 some parliamentary committees existed as counterparts of governmental departments. The number of these committees varied in all legislative periods. In the legislatures with a parliamentary majority of the left-wing Socialist Party, their number was relatively low. In both the Grand National Assembly and the 37th National Assembly, there were respectively only four and three parliamentary committees corresponding to government departments.

In contrast, the parliamentary majorities of the Union of Democratic Forces in the 36th and 38th National Assemblies preferred a larger number of parliamentary committees that mirrored governmental ministries.

There was only a slight difference in the number of parliamentary committees during the first three post-communist legislatures, which consistantly averaged about twenty. The Rules of the Grand National Assembly (Art. 22) provided for the establishment of nineteen parliamentary committees. The 36th Legislature initially established eighteen standing committees, but by the end of the term (1991–94) their number had grown to twenty-one.[2]

The 38th Parliament in 1997 substantially reduced the number of standing committees to fourteen, moving away from the pattern followed by the former legislatures. It established one new committee, the so-called "Anti-Mafia" Committee to fight corruption.

Nevertheless, the committee system of the Bulgarian parliament has a high level of continuity. Most committees have existed in all the Bulgarian post-communist parliaments. In spite of some changes of names and jurisdictions,[3] twelve parliamentary committees have functioned since 1990; two existed in three legislative periods; two in two parliaments and only five in one parliament.

The way in which the Legislative Committee, the Parliamentary Ethics Committee, and the Transport Committee have functioned has been subject to dispute during the first three legislative terms. For example, the Parliamentary Ethics Committee was established by the Grand National Assembly, closed by the 36th Parliament, and reestablished by the 37th.

The Legislative Committee also functioned in only two legislatures. Initially there was a consensus on its role in the legislative process. It was empowered to consider the legal substance of all bills, as well as to take an active part in all floor debates. The idea was to evade any legal inadequacies a result of the fast and sometimes hasty changes undertaken to adapt to the new laws with the radical political and socioeconomic changes. All draft laws needed the committee's opinion in order to be read in plenary session. This requirement substantially slowed the entire legislative process and provoked many objections to the committee's existence.

The leadership of committees has remained within defined limits, and is composed of a chairman and "no more than two deputies."

All members of the National Assembly are members of at least one committee and many of them are members of a second committee as well. At the beginning of the 37th Legislature, there were 378 seats in standing committees for distribution among members.[4] The substantial reduction of the total number of the standing committees in the present parliament reduced the number of committee seats to 312.[5]

The chair and the deputy chairs of the National Assembly cannot be elected to committees. An interesting case concerned the election of the chair of the National Assembly to head the new "Anti-Mafia" Committee. This appointment provoked many objections from the parliamentary opposition because it would give too much power to the chair.

There is a clear tendency in Bulgaria towards establishing medium to large parliamentary committees. Generally, every new National Assembly has increased the size of some parliamentary committees in comparison to the previous legislature (see Table 5.1). In every legislature since 1990, the Economic Committee, the Foreign Policy Committee, and the National Security Committee have been the largest committees.[6]

The size of parliamentary committees may affect their functioning as well as the efficiency and effectiveness of their activities. Table 5.2 shows that the largest committees in the Bulgarian National Assemblies are among the most active in the number of bills reported and the number approved for final reading on the floor.

However, size itself does not predetermine the real performance of standing committees in Bulgaria. For a country going through a process of economic transformation, it seems natural that economic committees, for instance, will be very active. In spite of their size, these committees are expected to produce many bills as quickly as possible in order to lay the legal foundation necessary for further development and implementation of economic reforms.

Although the rules of the 37th Legislature did foresee the possibility of creating subcommittees, they have never actually existed. The rules of the 38th Legislature eliminated the clause concerning subcommittees.

Composition of Parliamentary Committees

Bulgarian legislatures have, in general, applied the proportional model to choose members for standing committees. The political parties in the Grand National Assembly (1990–91) opted for a parity principle that excluded parties from having a majority in any committee. Deputies finally established a proportional rule for the election of members, as well as for chairs. To continue the cooperation between the governing and opposition parties, the latter were given the opportunity to chair some important committees such as the Economic and Legislative Committees.

The distribution of seats in the standing committees of the National Assemblies followed the procedure of the Grand National Assembly, using the same proportional rule, though there were some deviations from the general principle.

The Rules state that the leadership and the membership of the standing committees shall be elected from among the members of the National Assembly by an open vote. Usually, though, the composition of the leadership is discussed behind closed doors by the chairs of the parliamentary groups.

Party splits in all Bulgarian post-communist legislatures have impeded strict application of the proportional principle. The Rules of all post-communist parliaments in Bulgaria have not contained special provisions relating to the cases of MPs leaving their parliamentary party, establishing a new party group, joining a new one, or becoming independent.[7] These conditions were prevalent in the 36th National Assembly when both the governing and the opposition parties went through a process of party fragmentation because of internal party problems.

For the leadership of parliamentary committees, the Grand National Assembly applied the proportional rule strictly, but this pattern was not followed by the next parliaments.

In the 36th Legislature, the parliamentary majority of Union of Democratic Forces (UDF) refused to offer the opposition leadership of important committees and offered them only some chair positions of secondary significance. In protest, the opposition refused to accept any leadership positions, and consequently, members of the governing majority were appointed as chairs of all standing committees. Based on ideological concerns, the opposition (UDF) did not accept any leading positions of standing committees in the 37th Legislature, since they refused to take any responsibility for the policy of the governing Socialist Party. The 38th Parliament continued this tradition. All standing committees were chaired by the governing majority, except the Energy and Energy Resources Committee, whose chair was a member of Euroleft.

Table 5.1

Number and Incumbency of Members of Standing Committees of the 37th and 38th Bulgarian National Assemblies, 1994–2001

Committee	37th National Assembly 1994–1997					38th National Assembly 1997–2001				
	Members	MPs with Parliamentary Experience		MPs with Experience in the Same Committee		Members	MPs with Parliamentary Experience		MPs with Experience in the Same Committee	
		N	%	N	%		N	%	N	%
1. Economic Policy	31	11	35	5	16	34	5	15	6	18
2. Budget and Finance [a]	23	11	48	5	22	32	3	9	5	16
3. Government Authorities	23	11	48	8	35	—	—	—	—	—
4. Local Self-Government, Administrative Division and Regional Policy	28/29	6	21	6	21	21	2	9.5	2	9.5
5. Foreign Policy and European Integration [b]	29/31	17	55	10	32	25	11	44	5	20
6. National Security	31	16	52	5	16	21	4	19	4	19
7. Human Rights, Religious Affairs and Citizens Petitions [c]	15/17	10	59	7	41	17	1	6	1	6
8. Agriculture, Forests and Land Reform [d]	25	8	32	7	28	25	5	20	4	16
9. Education and Science	25	9	36	6	24	21	4	19	4	19
10. Culture and Media [e]	17	7	41	7	41	17	5	29	1	6
11. Radio, Television and Bulgarian Telegraph Agency	23	9	39	8	35	—	—	—	—	—
12. Environment and Waters	15	6	40	2	13	17	N/A	—	3	18
13. Labor and Social Policy	23	5	22	2	9	22	4	18	3	14

14. Health Care, Youth and Sports f	16	4	25	3	19	21	N/A	—	4	19
15. Youth, Sports and Tourism	17	2	12	1	6	—	—	—	—	—
16. Parliamentary Ethics	13	4	31	—	—	—	—	—	—	—
17. Energy and Energy Resources	15	4	27	2	13	18	4	—	—	—
18. Control of the Incomes, Expenditures and Assets of Political Parties	12	6	50	4	33	—	—	—	—	—
19. Anti-Corruption	11	3	27	—	—	—	—	—	—	—
20. Development of Mountainous, Semi-Mountainous and Border Regions	15/17	4	24	2	12	—	—	—	—	—
21. Legal Affairs and Anti-Corruption Legislation	—	—	—	—	—	21	3	14	4	19

Notes:

a—Financial Control was added in 1997, created by the Grand National Assembly (1990–91), and later re-instituted by the 37th National Assembly

b—Petitions was added in 1997, created for the first time by the 37th National Assembly

c—Integration Policy was added in 1997

d—Land Reform was added in 1997

e—Media was added in 1997

f—Youth and Sports was added in 1997

The appointment of members from the opposition as deputy chairs of committees, however, is an attempt to counterbalance their exclusion from chairmanships.

Activities of Standing Committees

Parliamentary committee have three functions: preparing legislation for the plenary; providing expertise; and overseeing the executive.

According to the Bulgarian Constitution, only the individual members of parliament and the cabinet may initiate legislation. Parliamentary committees do not have that right. However, the legislative process in Bulgaria provides committees with special significance because their deliberation on bills is compulsory.

The number of meetings of parliamentary committees, and the number of bills reported, amended, and read in plenary (see Table 5.2), give an indication of parliamentary committees' activity. The number of committee sittings is usually ten times greater than the number of plenary sessions in the same period. In the short period of May through November 1997, Bulgarian legislators in the 38th Legislature participated in 270 committee meetings. In a period of nearly the same duration (January–May 1996), the members of the 37th National Assembly attended 271 meetings while having six more committees than the present legislature.

The Economic Committee, the Budget and Finance Committee, the Legal Affairs and Anti-Corruption Legislation Committee, National Security Committee, Agriculture and Agrarian Reform Committee, and Labor and Social Policy Committee were among the most active at the beginning of the 38th Legislature.

Parliamentary committees usually meet once a week, preceding the plenary sessions which start on Wednesday. Their meetings are open, though in some cases committees may opt for closed meetings. They meet for three to four hours. There are special regulations permitting the National Security Committee and the Foreign Policy and European Integration Committee to have closed meetings, except when they decide otherwise. In the 37th Parliament, the Parliamentary Ethics Committee held its meetings behind closed doors. Matters of the economy took proportionally more time to discuss because of the urgency to establish a market economy and to overcome the legacy of the old socialist regime.

In the 37th National Assembly, the parliamentary majority of Bulgarian Socialist Party (BSP) introduced a new quorum regulation that allowed sessions to be held and decisions to be made by one-third of committee members, if an absolute majority was not available within thirty minutes.

The Socialists explained this change as a further step toward improving the effectiveness of the legislative process, though it provoked strong objections from the opposition (UDF, Patriotic Union [PU], Movement for Rights and Freedom [MRF]). They claimed that these procedural changes were "anti-democratic" in character and favored the establishment of institutional barriers to "legitimate counter-balancing parliamentary devices." In the 38th Parliament, the former opposition is the governing majority (UDF and PU). Not only did it preserve this institutional amendment but it also further reduced the time necessary for reaching an absolute majority to fifteen minutes.

Stages of Legislative Process

The legislative process in the Bulgarian parliament includes four stages. First, preliminary deliberation on a bill occurs within the standing committee assigned by the chair of the National Assembly. After that, the National Assembly deliberates a bill in a plenary session ("first reading"). The bill is returned to the respective committee for an additional deliberation before its final consideration by the National Assembly ("second reading").

All bills enter a specialized parliamentary register and are initially addressed to the chair of the National Assembly, who is the only person empowered to assign bills, within three days, to standing committees. The Rules of both the 37th and the 38th National Assemblies required that the National Assembly's chairperson designate a standing committee to be the main reporting committee on a bill at his/her own discretion. Some topics, especially when money is concerned, also need the opinion of the Committee on Finances and Budget, which often seconds the main committee.

To facilitate a rapid consideration of the government program, standing committees must report and give opinions on bills initiated by the Council of Ministers no later than one month after their introduction. In contrast, the period of consideration of a bill proposed by a private MP is three months (Art. 64). The chair of the main committee may also ask for the opinion of the Council of Ministers or a certain minister about bills introduced by individual MPs.

The bills, together with the report of the main committee, must be presented in printed form to the MPs no later than twenty-four hours before the start of a sitting. In general, the first reading of a bill includes a debate on its principal provisions. Prior to the assembly's consideration, the main

Table 5.2

Committee Activity in the 37th and 38th Bulgarian National Assemblies, 1994–2001

Committee	37th National Assembly 1994–1997				38th National Assembly 1997–2001			
	Meetings	Bills Reported	Bills Amended	Bills with Final Reading on Floor	Meetings	Bills Reported	Bills Amended	Bills with Final Reading On Floor
1. Economic Policy	73	146	13	63	24	27	17	17
2. Budget and Finance [a]	N/A	110	44	81	31	39	29	29
3. Government Authorities	112	137	24	39	—	—	—	—
4. Local Self-Government, Administrative Division and Regional Policy	60	30	11	12	12	16	1	1
5. Foreign Policy and European Integration [b]	N/A	133	0	17	15	22	2	2
6. National Security	N/A	12	4	6	23	11	6	0
7. Human Rights, Religious Affairs and Citizens Petitions [c]	37	37	5	6	8	18	1	1
8. Agriculture, Forests and Land Reform [d]	92	24	6	6	22	10	5	5
9. Education and Science	69	21	3	4	17	12	3	3
10. Culture and Media [e]	60	15	2	5	20	19	6	6
11. Radio, Television and Bulgarian Telegraph Agency	64	7	1	1	—	—	—	—
12. Environment and Waters	42	26	4	12	12	10	4	4
13. Labor and Social Policy	27	29	7	8	22	18	5	5

14. Health Care, Youth and Sports [f]	87	15	3	5	17	15	4	4
15. Youth, Sports and Tourism	53	5	1	2	—	—	—	—
16. Parliamentary Ethics	N/A	3	0	0	—	—	—	—
17. Energy and Energy Resources	42	11	1	5	16	4	3	3
18. Control of the Incomes, Expenditures and Assets of Political Parties	20	7	0	0	—	—	—	—
19. Anti-Corruption	36	3	0	0	—	—	—	—
20. Development of Mountainous, Semi-Mountainous and Border Regions	40	10	1	1	—	—	—	—
21. Legal Affairs and Anti-Corruption Legislation	—	—	—	—	29	49	18	18
Total	914	781	130	273	268	270	104	98

Notes:

a—Financial Control was added in 1997

b—Petitions was added in 1997

c— Integration Policy was added in 1997

d—Land Reform was added in 1997

e—Media was added in 1997

f—Youth and Sports was added in 1997

reporting committee and the other committees concerned make their reports, and the bill's author gives an opinion.

To speed up the legislative process, all bills dealing with the same matter are required to be considered simultaneously. Afterward, the bills are voted upon separately. Those approved in the first vote are consolidated into a single bill by the reporting committee and then introduced for further written proposals.

The committee's suggestions on which bills are to be consolidated play a major role in debate on the floor. The Rules require the main reporting committee to be ready with a revised bill after taking all proposals made by MPs into account within fourteen days after the period for receiving them has ended (one week to three weeks). These time limits are usually not kept. Many bills may stay in committee for months. The reason is the need for substantial revisions and amendments, especially on complicated matters. A typical example is the pension law to which the first draft needed serious additions and revisions.

The second reading of a bill proceeds in a more detailed manner than the first, since the legislative body debates and votes on bills chapter by chapter, title by title, or paragraph by paragraph (Art. 69). At that stage the main reporting committee presents a report on the written proposals made by the committee, MPs and other committees, together with the committee's own opinion.

As many political observers argue, parliamentary committees often rework a bill's original text because of the great variety of opinions, which are hard to reconcile. Though drafting amendments to bills is permitted, committees seem to be constrained from making substantial changes because they must be consistent with the general principles of a bill already approved by the National Assembly in its first reading.

Conditions that emerged during the 38th session were such that single party majorities dominated the assembly, and most opinions presented by the committee dominated by the same majority are adopted by the assembly.

Oversight Functions of Parliamentary Committees

Bulgarian parliamentary committees are vested with the power to exercise some oversight functions, including the right to conduct investigations, inquiries, and hearings on issues of state or public interest. Most experts on Bulgaria share the view that parliamentary committees have extensive formal powers in this area, but that committee oversight activity is not efficient in practice.

Parliamentary control exerted by standing committees is usually performed at meetings in which representatives of the executive branch are asked to answer questions related to a draft bill.[8] This type of control is informative in character and has not proved to be an effective mechanism for parliamentary oversight.

The activity of ad hoc committees is intended to be more significant and influential than that of standing committees. The Constitution includes a provision for creating select committees to conduct inquiries and investigations (Art. 79 [3]). Parliamentary Rules further stipulate that their election and appointment shall result from a motion of the National Assembly chair or at least one tenth of its members (Art 30 [2]). All structural, organizational, and operational issues concerning standing committees relate to ad hoc committees as well (Art. 30 [4]).

For the entire 36th Legislature, twenty-three ad hoc committees were created. Only ten of them produced reports with a subsequent decision of the parliament; three committees produced reports without any parliamentary decision on the issue, and seven committees did not actually produce a report at all because of internal committee disagreements. Three other ad hoc committees were authorized by parliament but were never created.

The experience of the 37th and the 38th National Assemblies supports the view that legislatures with stable parliamentary majorities are not prone to create a great number of select committees. On the other hand, those few created have been able to produce reports for the National Assembly. For instance, the 37th Parliament only authorized five ad hoc committees. They all produced reports on the results of their activity. The 38th Legislature formed only three select committees, each of which reached a decision.[9]

Problems of Institutionalization and Effectiveness of Parliamentary Committees

In the following analysis I will attempt to answer three sets of questions pertaining to the development of Bulgaria's parliament: a) What are the sources of the institutionalization of parliamentary committees; b) what is their level of institutionalization; and c) what is the relationship between institutionalization and the effectiveness of parliamentary committees and their role in the consolidation of democratic regimes?

Sources of Institutionalization

The institutionalization of parliamentary committees depends on the stability of the democratic system itself and on the affirmation of the principles of liberal democracy. The slowdown in the process of democratic consolidation, together with frequent changes of the governments in power, including the deep political crisis of 1997, acted to undermine legislative institutions.

Legacies

Both direct and indirect dominance by the former Communist Party and its allies in the first legislature were evident. First, they were not interested in forging the reform process. Second, many of their MPs brought the legacy of the authoritarian culture of the past to the activity of the committees. Both of these factors, especially the second, limited the development of parliamentary committees as an independent factor in the legislature by preserving them as one of the instruments of party decisions and party discipline.

A counter-tendency did become noticeable, particularly in the first democratically elected parliament in 1990. Parliamentary committees became an arena of intense political activity and confrontations, as the parliament itself became the major focus of political change. Parliament was the institution that had to create a new constitution and adopt major new laws adapted to the new political reality. Consequently, conformity as the legacy of the past and radical new political behavior resulting from the newly born pluralism confronted each other in the early stage of parliamentary development. Parliamentary committees became more an arena of political strife than a laboratory of expert work. This conflict limited the effectiveness of committees in the legislative process and led to the low level of institutionalization.

At the same time, committees became one of the institutions in which the foundation of professional legislative behavior was laid. Parliamentary committees were a reflection of political realities, but at the same time they were molding a new pluralistic political system.

Two Post-Communist Periods

The first two legislatures (1990–94) were a product of fluid, unstable majorities, interparty strife, and changes of allegiances within parliamentary groups, leading also to weak and unstable governments. These conditions had a negative impact on the legislative process and on the activity of parliamentary committees. Governmental disabilities led to delays in adopting necessary legislation, and to the low quality of the laws enacted.

This period (1990–94) was also marked by the activity of a very powerful Legislative Committee. The committee's activity was controversial and contested because the power concentrated in its hands was detrimental to all other committees. Its existence was partially a legacy of the communist parliament. In the early stages of the transition to democracy, the Legislative Committee was needed to concentrate know-how and expertise in legal matters. It played a positive role as an intermediate institution between the parliamentary committees and the plenum. That is why it was labeled by some as "mini-parliament."[10]

The second period in the development of the post-communist legislature was marked by a significantly different political and party configuration. The elections of 1994 and 1997 brought single-party majorities.

The effect on the parliamentary committees was twofold. First, committees were more closely tied to party discipline and less flexible in their activity. Committees were less independent even though they were "liberated" from the shadow of the Legislative Committee. Secondly, committees became more focused on policy and processed bills faster as a result of the expansion of the role of the government in drafting bills.

The negative aspect of this development was that committees lost part of their role as institutions of pluralistic politics and became more focused on fulfillment of party policies and government proposals. Their role as an independent source of legislation diminished as a result also of rule changes that limited time for discussion and deliberations. The nongovernment parties accused their respective counterparts in the 37th and 38th Parliaments of being authoritarian and not receptive to proposals.

Party System

Two different processes in party development have affected the institutionalization of parliamentary committees. The first process, immediately after regime change, was characterized by fluidity and fragmentation of the party landscape, with many new emergent parties. This fluidity led to a lesser degree of party control over MPs' activities in the committees. In this period, committees' activities were more unpredictable and less effective. The legislative process was to some extent chaotic and more an expression of personal and group interests than of party influence.

The party system stabilized after the transformation of the UDF coalition into a party and the major opposing force into the Socialist Party.

The lessening of the fragmentation process has stabilized the committees themselves.

The role of incumbents has increased as the number of political parties and party families stabilized at four to five in the 1997 elections.

The importance of incumbency is especially true of committee leadership. In the 38th Legislature, about 40 to 50 percent of the committee chairs and vice chairs were one- or two-term incumbents in the same committees. We may be seeing the formation of a parliamentary elite.

Parliamentary groups dominate parliamentary committees on the one hand by determining the legislative agenda, and on the other by using the tool of party loyalty and discipline for MPs in the committees. Parliamentary groups, especially those of the UDF and BSP, apply the rule that decisions taken by the group guide MPs' activities and voting in committees. MPs cannot be forced to abide by this rule, but if MPs do not follow the leadership this might have political consequences for their future career.

Generally the parliamentary group of the majority follows the government's stand on bills and very rarely is there any other proposal. For the opposition, when a bill is initiated by the majority, the group takes a position on the bill as soon as it is placed for discussion in the committees, but not later than the first reading.

Government Stability

After 1989, Bulgaria witnessed frequent government changes. Governments had different party compositions and different types of internal relationships. In particular, the role of the prime ministers changed depending on the composition of the cabinet and parliamentary groups that supported or opposed them. All of these factors had a direct influence on the role that parliamentary committees played in the legislative and overall political process.

When cabinets were formed on a coalition basis, committees were more active as partners of government and were one of the venues in which compromises were achieved on the legislative agenda (1990–91). Committees played a different role during the period of the weakest cabinet, which was based on the lukewarm and fragile support of three parliamentary groups (1992–94). Then the prime minister was a more of a balancing figure, without a firm party base or support. Therefore, in his relations with parliament, his position was weak. Committees had a more active and independent relationship with the government and greater influence on the content of bills. Government agencies were more apt to consider both the MPs' and committees' views on legislation.

The parliamentary committees were most dependent on government proposals and decisions during the period of one-party governments supported by stable parliamentary majorities (1994–96 and 1997–2001). Committees played a subordinate role and found their activity limited by party discipline and government dominance in initiating bills. In both governments (composed by different parties), the prime minister was the government and party leader, which gave him and the cabinet an advantage vis-à-vis parliamentary committees.

Democratic Political Culture

The attributes of Bulgarian political culture (as dominant political values and attitudes) have also had a negative impact on the process of institutionalizing parliamentary committees. Political conflicts among the parties are often transferred to the parliamentary committees, impeding their effectiveness. The transition to democracy has witnessed the predominance of confrontational over consensual politics.

It has become evident that the work of parliamentary committees is more effective if dialogue and tolerance dominates rather than one of strife and rivalry. A rare example of such productive activity is the work of the Foreign Policy Committee. This committee has generated several consensual decisions, such as the declaration on Bulgaria's relations with Russia, a document that received the approval of almost all parliamentarians in the autumn of 1997. A similar example was the signing of a memorandum with NATO on the use of Bulgarian territory for the transfer of troops in 2000.

The signing of the Declaration of National Salvation in May 1997, which brought an end to the deep political crisis in the country after the fall of the socialist government in January 1997, led to greater tolerance within parliamentary committees. Moreover, the transformation of the bipolar party system to a more pluralized one, has had a positive impact on the work of parliamentary committees. We are witnessing the formation of different majorities on some specific issues that are reflected in the committees.

Internal Resources

The lack of adequate expertise and assistance is a serious problem. The National Assembly had a special "Parliamentary Research Department" within its administrative structure to assist parliamentary committees in their work. Though only two years old, the department was disbanded in

October 1997 when a new majority won the parliamentary elections. The Legal Department consists of only about ten people and does not have adequate resources to help all committees.

In principle, each MP receives a special allowance for expertise and other technical assistance. This allowance represents two-thirds of one MP's salary. These allowances are redistributed among parliamentary parties for expenses. Parliamentary committees themselves do not have the financial resources to maintain sufficient experts and staff. They have usually one or two paid experts.

The Level of Institutionalization

Structure

The number of parliamentary committees has been fluid. Committees do not follow the ministerial structure. Each legislature has changed the number of committees and their area of activity, creating and removing committees or changing their names in the same term. Committee size has also fluctuated.

Membership

Not all MPs are able to occupy committee posts, especially in the 38th Legislature, due to the lower number of committees in comparison with past legislatures. Some MPs are assigned to two committees, which leaves some newcomers without a committee seat.

Frequent elections have brought four democratic legislatures into being. This situation has led to a relatively high incumbency rate of three to four terms for a minority of MPs, particularly those occupying leadership posts in the committees. At the same time, the majority of MPs in recent legislatures are newcomers to parliament and most will experience committee assignments for the first time.

Changes occur mid-session due to parliamentary group fragmentation, which is typical for the first transitional years. With the stabilization of parliamentary groups, mid-session changes have diminished.

Constituency links are weak. One reason is the weak linkages between civil society interest groups and MPs. There is in general a lack of public interest in MPs' activities in parliament. The media, for example, rarely focus on parliament.

Another reason is the hidden links with economic lobbies that influence the MPs' behavior and often lead to corruption. Many MPs are engaged in activities that might represent a conflict of interest (as members of various boards in state companies, or keeping their law practice). The present National Assembly is trying to set up a clearer legal base on this topic.

Since post-communist parliaments are young institutions, professional skills are only a partial requirement for committee assignments. Some experts discern a deprofessionalization of parliamentary committees compared to earlier years. That is why some MPs have launched an initiative for the reestablishment of the Legislative Committee, which existed during the first three years after the start of the transition.

Member attendance at committee meetings is higher than their attendance at plenary sessions. There are a few cases when a committee has failed to start its meeting due to the lack of a quorum. Rules allow committees to work with relatively few MPs present.

Party Composition

The composition of the committees generally reflects the party composition of the parliament, while the composition of committee leadership clearly favors the majority and the biggest parliamentary groups. This was illustrated in the 37th and 38th Legislatures where one party had the majority. Chair positions, in principle, are allocated to the majority, while all vice chair positions are allocated to the second largest group or sometimes to a smaller group.

The allocation of chair positions to the opposition in the Grand National Assembly was an exception. In the 38th Legislature, one chair was allocated to a small minority group from the "cooperative" opposition.

Party Relationships

Usually members of committees are the party's experts on specific issues. This process is influenced by the instability of parties at the initial transitional period where the fluctuation in the composition of parliamentary groups was very high. With the advancement of the party consolidation process there is more stability and predictability in the relations of parties to committees and on the eventual committee assignments of party experts.

Committee Autonomy

Formally, committees have significant autonomy in amending bills prior to their introduction on the floor. In reality, they often amend government bills, but not in substance. Opposition opinion is often heard but rarely taken into account. Committee activity is tied on one side to the legislative initiative of the government, and on the other to the decisions taken by the party leadership and the parliamentary group. Committees are a secondary institution, which does not initiate legislation but concentrates on procedural matters.

Floor Control

Most bills are referred to committees after their first reading and floor discussion. The manager of the floor debate is the committee chair. Generally committee recommendations and amendments are supported by floor voting.

Government Relations

The relationship with the executive is marked by irregular contacts and inquiries. Parliamentary oversight is practiced mainly in the plenary, during question time, or through ad hoc inquiry committees.

Assessment of the Level of Institutionalization

The level of institutionalization of parliamentary committees in Bulgaria's National Assembly based on the above criteria is low to medium. The general tendency is toward greater institutionalization on the micro level in the parliamentary institution itself.

Parliamentary committees' legislative activity varied in the years after 1989. The first years of transition to democracy were characterized by a high degree of activity in considering and amending bills. This was especially true during the period when the former Communist Party was in a parliamentary defensive position, despite its domination within the executive.

In the earlier stages of democratization, the parliamentary institution was in the center of public life and more adequately reflected public interests. Moreover, the composition of the Grand National Assembly (1990–91) was characterized by the presence of some distinguished professionals and intellectuals. This is not the case in the National Assemblies that followed.

At present, standing committees are constrained to wait for bills introduced by the government. Bills introduced by the opposition and other parliamentary factions are not considered unless the Cabinet's proposal is also introduced. The domination of single-party majorities, the BSP majority from 1994 to 1996, and the UDF majority in 1997 and after, has resulted in less legislative activity in parliamentary committees than previously. Usually opposition groups complain that the majority does not consider their bills.

The dependence of MPs on centralized party leaderships, which overlap with major positions in the executive, hinders MPs' independent actions. Some change results from the higher incumbency rate and the increasing experience of MPs, chiefly committee leaders. More stable links with the electorate may in turn result.

There is clearly a need to expand the role of experts and parliamentary research to help boost committees' institutional capacities. But at present budgetary restraints hamper the appointment of more permanent experts and staff.

Institutionalization, Effectiveness, and Consolidation of Democracy

Post-communist parliaments in general and Bulgaria's Assembly in particular work under unusual circumstances. They must change an entire legal system and create a new one adapted to a democratic government and a market economy. They must fulfill this task in a relatively short historical period. This rush has led to the low quality of many bills and the necessity to amend them several times within a few years. This is reflected in the interventions of the Constitutional Court, which has declared parts of newly passed bills incompatible with constitutional provisions. In these circumstances, even a high level of committee institutionalization would not guarantee effectiveness.

The degree of parliamentary and committee institutionalization reflects the level of consolidation in the new post-communist democracies. The stability and legitimacy of the new democracies are closely linked to the expansion of the role of committees in the political process, to the greater efficacy of their legislative work, and to their ability to oversee the executive.

Notes

1. Georgi Karasimeonov, "The Legislature in Post-Communist Bulgaria." In *The New Parliaments of Central and Eastern Europe,* ed. D. Olson and P. Norton (London: Cass, 1996), 40–45.

2. Committees on Power Generation, on Transport, and on the Defense Industry were also established.

3. The Foreign Policy and European Integration Committee was slightly changed to the Foreign Policy and Integration Policy Committee in the 38th National Assembly.

4. The newly formed "Anti-Mafia" Committee is not taken into consideration.

5. Dobrin Kanev, *The Committee System of the Bulgarian Parliament,* in "Committees in Legislatures: A Division of Labour." In *Comparative Legislative Studies II—The Changing Roles of Parliamentary Committees,* ed. L. Longely and A. Ágh. Research Committee of Legislative Specialists, IPSA. June 1997, 345.

6. Ibid.

7. Ibid.

8. E. Drumeva, "Parliamentary Process in the Republic of Bulgaria: Basic Principles and Current Practices." In *The Role of Parliament,* ed. D. Kanev (Sofia: Research Department of the Parliament, 1996), 22–23.

9. Ibid., 347.

10. Karasimeonov, "The Legislature in Post-Communist Bulgaria," 47.

PART 4

*Parliaments of the
Former Soviet Republics:
Least Institutionalized*

SIX

The Estonian Riigikogu and Institutionalization of Its Committees

Jüri Ruus

ACCORDING TO ITS CONSTITUTION, ESTONIA IS A DEMOCRATIC republic in which the supreme power of the state is vested in the people. Citizens exercise this power by voting in elections to the Riigikogu, or Parliament. Estonia is a parliamentary republic which means that the government must have the confidence of the parliament to stay in power.

The first free and fair parliamentary elections took place in 1992 after Estonia regained its independence following fifty years of occupation. The second elections were held in 1995. The next regular elections occurred in 1999. The first free parliamentary elections in 1992 were for the 7th Riigikogu, numbered for continuity from the 6th Parliament, the last prior to Soviet occupation.

In this chapter I will examine the institutionalization of the committee system in the Estonian Riigikogu in the first two post-communist democratic terms. This chapter uses indicators of growing stability and consistency of committees in the post-communist transition such as party ratios in both membership and officer positions in committees, as well as changes in rates of turnover in parliamentary parties and committee membership and leadership. Further, changes should occur in the external relations of the committees, including substance and quantity of referred legislation to committees, interparty and committee coordination mechanisms, relations with parliamentary leadership, and relations with government. My assumption is that the institutionalization of parliamentary committees depends on the stablity of the democratic regime itself.

This analysis is based on published documents as well as on interviews with the members of parliamentary committees, parliamentary parties, and advisors during the 1992–98 period in the Estonian Riigikogu.

Estonian Electoral and Party System

The system of party lists is used in Estonian parliamentary elections. Candidates high on the party or electoral list are elected regardless of how many votes they themselves gained. Party lists that win at least 5 percent of the votes (electoral threshold) all over the republic enter parliament.

Nine lists were elected in 1992 to the 7th Riigikogu, making up a parliament of seven parliamentary party groups representing twenty-three electoral parties. Three parliamentary party groups, representing eight parties, formed a coalition government.

On March 5, 1995, the 8th Riigikogu was elected. Seven lists, representing fourteen parties, formed a parliament with nine parliamentary party groups. Independent candidates also took part in the elections. The new government was based on four parliamentary party groups that consisted of six electoral parties. The governing coalition numbered fifty-seven members. The Coalition Party led by Prime Minister Tiit Vähi, with forty-one legislative seats, took ten ministerial posts, while the Center Party with sixteen members took five ministries.

The winners of the 1995 elections were mainly the parties and coalitions that had been in opposition in the previous Riigikogu. The Center Party and the Coalition Party were joined by the parties forming the Rural Union. The winners stated that they would continue economic reforms but would pay more attention to social issues and agriculture.

The Reform Party that had been formed from the Liberal Democratic Party was successful, especially among urban voters. The electoral coalition "Our Home is Estonia," representing the Russian-speaking population, was also elected to the Riigikogu.

As in other post-communist states, Estonian parties at the time of independence were weak and fragmented. The largest parliamentary party, Pro Patria, won twenty-nine seats in the 1992 elections, which was well short of a majority. As the largest party group in the legislature, it took the lead in putting together the majority to form a government. The coalition numbered fifty-one members, a majority of one. Later two independent candidates joined the coalition. With such a slim majority, it is difficult to imagine a more stringent test of a political system than Estonia's first post-communist legislature.

The 1992 government consisted of nine ministers, including Prime Minister Mart Laar from Pro Patria, three from the Estonian National Independence Party (ENIP), four from moderate groups, and one independent.

Some of the main differences in the Baltic States among the Estonian, Latvian, and Lithuanian constitutional systems are the status of the president and the election systems. Both Estonia and Latvia use proportional parliamentary elections and are basically parliamentary systems. Lithuania has mixed elections and a semi-presidential system. The proportional election system in Estonia favors a fragmented distribution of seats in parliament. By contrast, half of the representatives in the Lithuanian parliament are elected from single member constituencies.

Due to the proportional system, Estonian MPs are more concerned with their inclusion and placement on the list of candidates than with their own popularity in their districts. Thus MPs tend to worry more about cultivating good relationships with their party leaders who are responsible for the candidate lists, than about developing constituent relations.

As in Sweden, government members do not retain their seats in the legislature. An alternate from their party fills the seat until the minister resigns or is removed from office, at which point the ex-minister reclaims the legislative seat.

Stability of Parliamentary Groups and Government Coalitions

Incentives for interparty collaboration in the Estonian parliament are similar to those in the West. However, Estonian parties are relatively new and unstable, and as throughout the region, legislative parties can be amorphous in the Estonian legislature.

The parliamentary parties can be divided into categories by degrees of member stability. Parties with no member defections can be characterized as stable; parties which have seen defections of single MPs, are moderately stable; and parties that have experienced splits and major defections within parliament are considered unstable.

There are clear differences among the parties. The Estonian National Independence Party (ENIP), Pro Patria, Estonian Citizens Union (ECU), and the Center Party are unstable. ECU disintegrated completely during the 7th Parliament. ENIP merged with Pro Patria in December 1995, and the Center Party survived two major splits. The Coalition Party (COP), Rural Union (RU), Independent Royalists, and People's Party of Republicans and Conservatives (PPRC) each lost one MP. The Liberal Democratic Party (LDP) and the Moderates (SPD), however, did not lose a single MP during the 7th term.

Parties are tenuous entities in Estonian society, and legislative party groups appear and disappear. Government coalitions are therefore mortal. Cabinet crises are a relatively frequent political phenomenon. The emergence of new political parties and the disintegration of others is accompanied by quantitative changes in parliamentary party groups and committee composition. Particularly as elections approach, coalitions become weaker and shift. In the last several months of the first Riigikogu before the 1995 elections, there was no governing majority. The situation was the same in 1997 and 1998 with Mart Siiman's government prior to the 1999 elections. Thus, minority governments are typical of the country's politics.

During the first parliamentary period of two and a half years, thirty-nine out of 101 MPs switched legislative group or party allegiance (Interviews). In the first two years of the 8th Parliament, 16 MPs changed party affiliation. The great instablity in the 7th Parliament, the first after independence, was reduced in the second (Interviews).

The relatively frequent shifts of party memberships have had some impact on the composition of the parliamentary committees as discussed below. Committee identities and common interests among deputies are lacking when the government does not have a stable and secure majority.

Members of the Riigikogu

The decisions of the parliament are heavily influenced by characteristics and political perspectives of its members.

One of the reasons for the shift of the 8th Riigikogu to the left-center might be explained by the composition of the parliament, in which fifty-six of the 101 MPs were former members of the Communist Party. One of them had belonged to the top Communist nomenklatura. Among the 101 members of the Estonian Riigikogu elected in 1992, by contrast only 35 percent had a Communist background (Tittma 1994, 18).

Of the 101 members in the 8th term, seven had Ph.D.s, three held master's degrees, and eighteen were candidates for advanced university degrees. The majority of the MPs (46) with higher education had studied in the University of Tartu, nineteen have studied at the Estonian Agricultural University, and seventeen at the Tallinn Technical University.

By profession, MPs in the 8th term were engineers (21), economists (13), lawyers (11), historians (10), and university graduates with a diploma in agriculture (19). Other professions include teachers, philolo-

Table 6.1

Parliament and Committee Incumbency of Members of Estonian Parliament, by Committee, VIII Term, 1992–1997

Committee name	Number of Members of Committees	Committee Incumbency N	%	Parliamentary Incumbency N	%
Finance Committee	12	3	25%	7	58%
Economic Affairs Committee	12	3	25%	5	41.66%
Constitutional Committee	12	4	33.33%	6	50%
Legal Affairs Committee	10	3	30%	7	70%
Foreign Affairs Committee	12	4	33.33%	8	66.66%
National Defense Committee	7	3	42.85%	5	71.43%
Cultural Affairs Committee	9	1	11.11%	2	22.22%
Social Affairs Committee	10	1	10%	2	20%
Rural Affairs Committee	7	1	14.28%	1	14.28%
Environment Committee	7	3	42.5%	5	71.42%
Total	98	26	—	48	—
Average	9.8	2.6	26.75%	4.8	48.55%

Notes:

Committee Incumbency: Service on same committee in previous term as in current term.

Parliamentary Incumbency: Service in previous parliament.

gists, doctors, geographers, journalists, actors and physicists ("Postimees," 21 March 1995; Riigikogu Directory 1997, 7–25).

Incumbency

Some of the MPs have had experience in a parliament. In the 1992–95 parliament, 36 percent had previous experience in communist-era legislatures. The distribution of incumbency varied among committees. The legal and cultural committees had the highest proportions of incumbents. In the 1995 parliament, the corresponding figure of parliamentary incumbency was even higher, 48.5 percent (see Table 6.1). Approximately 27 percent of the MPs had served on the same committee in the previous 7th Parliament. The tables reflect the substantial continuity of the Estonian elite during the transitional period to democracy. The continuity is greater in the key foreign affairs, finance, and national defense committees, which reveal incumbent preferences and the need for more institutional professionalism vital for state building. Obviously, in a state with a relatively small number of politicians, elite continuity tends to be somewhat inevitable.

Leadership of the Riigikogu

The Riigikogu annually elects from among its members the chair (or Speaker) of the Riigikogu and two deputy chairs, who together form the parliamentary board and direct the work of the parliament in accordance with the Standing Orders (http://www.riigikogu.ee). The Speaker comes from the same parliamentary party as the prime minister. This is the leading party in the coalition. The deputy speakers come from either the same parliamentary party or from the smaller government coalition partners.

The chair presides over the sessions of the Riigikogu, convenes meetings of the board, submits the draft agenda for meetings, and presides at board meetings and at plenary meetings. The Speaker of Estonia's legislature has mainly a formal role. He introduces speakers, states which bill is up for a vote, and announces the results. The leadership approves the meeting agenda, which is actually prepared by coalition leaders in their meetings (Interviews).

The Board of the Riigikogu divides committee seats among party groups, approves the composition of the committees, registers parliamentary parties, drafts the agenda of floor sessions, and submits it to the Riigikogu for approval. The board also refers draft bills to committees.

Parliamentary Parties

Formally, the board leadership distributes party members proportionally among the committees, ensuring that there is a coalition majority on every committee. The committees then elect chairs who are controlled by the coalition. In fact, the parliamentary party leaders present their requests about committee participation, which the parliamentary leadership confirms. The coalition majorities confirm their leaders' agreements on committee chairs (Interviews). The intended effect is to thoroughly link the parliamentary parties and the committees with a consistent majority and minority across leadership posts and committee memberships.

Parliamentary parties, which are often referred to also as "factions," can be formed by six or more members of the Riigikogu who have been elected from the list of the same party and electoral coalition. A member of the Riigikogu cannot leave one parliamentary party and join another if the new parliamentary party group was not formed from candidates who belonged to his/her former electoral list. A member of the Riigikogu can belong to only one parliamentary party.

Parliamentary parties are groups through which a large part of the work of the Estonian parliament is done. One might say that parliamentary parties are central in Estonian parliamentary work. Intercommittee coordination to a large extent is carried out in party meetings (Interviews).

In the parties, political opinions which are the basis for statements in committee, the Riigikogu or in public, are agreed upon. The party is the place for coming to political agreement. This does not mean that there can never be different opinions inside a group, since a parliamentary party group represents an electoral list which, as noted earlier, includes a number of other electoral parties.

Parties, like members of the Riigikogu and committees, have the right to initiate laws. This right guarantees that the opposition has the right to present and defend their draft laws in the Riigikogu.

Parliamentary Committees: Structure

Parliamentary committees do most of the work on bills submitted to the Riigikogu. They also have the right to initiate legislation (Estonian Constitution Art. 103). According to the Riigikogu Standing Orders, the Riigikogu forms standing and select committees and decides their personnel, authority, and duration (Art. 17).

The regulations of the Estonian Riigikogu do not fix the number of its standing committees, unlike similar provisions of many other national assemblies. However, the number of ten standing committees has been stable since 1992 elections.

Estonian committees are relatively small. Many legislative committees in western Europe are larger than the average Estonian committee. This committee size difference is explained by the fact that Estonian Riigikogu with 101 members is itself rather small compared to Western European and many other Central European parliaments as well.

The committees' jurisdiction corresponds with those of the government ministries. The structure of the Riigikogu committees corresponds roughly to the cabinet structure. Only one ministry (transport and communication) does not have a directly corresponding parliamentary committee.

The chair and deputy chairs of the Riigikogu do not belong to any standing committee. All other members of the Riigikogu belong to one standing committee and may be a replacement member on another standing committee (Art. 18).

The Estonian Riigikogu has no subcommittee system. The Standing Orders do not provide for their formation. Work that might be done through subcommittees is often carried out by parliamentary parties. Party meetings are the basic forums where parties formulate their stands on various issues for committee members.

As stated in the Standing Orders (Art. 19), the board of the Riigikogu divides the places in the committees between the parliamentary parties, keeping in mind the proportional representation of party groups and their application for committee seats. Through this procedure, the board of the Riigikogu actually decides upon the division of power among the parliamentary parties in the committees. The parliamentary parties themselves propose the committees on which they would like to serve. The party chooses the members it wishes to serve on standing committees based on the number of seats received from the board. Parties can and do, however, change the number of their seats on any given committee during a legislative term.

The internal procedure also regulates how those parliamentarians who do not belong to any parliamentary party can do their share of work in the committees. The board decides the participation of the independent parliamentarians who are not members of the parliamentary parties, based on their personal applications and the needs of the committees (Art. 20).

The basis for the selection of committee members and chairs has been debated since the country's independence. Usually the parliamentary party chooses the ordinary members of the committees according to their professional background. Given the skills and professional background of the members of the committees, the parliamentarian specialists are familiar with the committee topics. As a rule, lawyers are members of the legal committee, economists in the committee on economy, etc. (Interviews). If members were assigned to committees on which they have prior experience, the committee assignments would allow them to further specialize.

Parliamentary Committees: Activities

The main task of standing committees is to work with draft legislation. The board of the parliament sends each bill to a standing committee, which becomes the leading or main committee for that draft. Other committees may also review the bill.

Draft legislation is submitted to the leading committee before the first reading at a plenary session. The leading committee has to report back to the board of the Riigikogu within three weeks on whether to include the bill in the plenary regular schedule, or to put it aside (Art. 55). In other words, only after the submission of the leading committee's opinion is the

Table 6.2

Legislative Activity by Committee, Estonian Parliament, VIII Term, 1992–1997

Committee name	Total number of bills discussed	Floor Action	
		Bills passed	Bills not passed
Finance Committee	197	127	62
Economic Affairs Committee	223	131	71
Constitutional Committee	189	91	89
Legal Affairs Committee	193	142	42
Foreign Affairs Committee	23	22	1
National Defense Committee	18	13	5
Cultural Affairs Committee	60	40	16
Social Affairs Committee	109	52	60
Rural Affairs Committee	33	23	9
Environment Committee	37	30	4
Total	1082	671	359

Note:
Total number of bills includes all bills considered by committees, not all of which proceeded to the floor.

bill considered at a plenary session. Thus, the leading committee has the right to continue or reject draft legislation at the very beginning of the legislative process. In the 1992–97 period, the leading committee looked through proposed changes and amendments and was responsible for the bill until the Riigikogu approved it. The committee studied the draft in detail, saw if all issues had been dealt with sufficiently, and found solutions to any problems in the bills.

There has always been a problem with the workload in various standing commitees. The workload of the Committee of Legal Affairs is higher than that of most of the Riigikogu committees (see Table 6.2). The work load is not spread evenly among the committees. By far the greatest burden is carried by the finance, economic, constitutional, and legal committees. The least active committees are the Environmental Committee and the Rural Affairs Committee.

There are different reasons for the uneven workload of committees. These institutions were particularly vital for state building in the country. Estonia lacked the structure of statehood and legislation of its own, in national armed forces, governmental officials, border defense, etc.

The essence of the state is greatly determined by ownership relations and by corresponding legal regulations. Owing to the complex historical background of Estonia, any balanced regulation of ownership regulations is problematic. The key issue in the ownership reform policy is re-privatization; that is, an attempt is made to return the property nationalized by Soviet power to the legal owners of the country. Returning the property was supported by the majority of Estonian people. However, the implementation of this policy has revealed widely different positions in this matter and brought about conflicting expectations and demands.

A new legal order based on civil liberties and human rights is only in the process of taking root in peoples' practical behavior. At the same time, the historical-cultural and moral-social control and observance of the law has weakened. Because of the inadequate application of legal regulation or gaps in legislation, there are several spheres where the level of observance of the law is relatively low such as in paying taxes, service in defense forces, etc. (Estonian Human Development Report 1998, 46–47). Thus, in the transition period to democracy, there has always existed a problem of workload of various standing committees explained by the urgent tasks of state building.

Table 6.2 also shows that about one-third of bills are rejected at floor stage. Floor action largely endorses committee recommendations. This high rate of acceptance of committee recommendations is similar among the committees.

Government control is exercised in the consideration of bills in committees, since ministers have the right to participate in the committee (Art. 29). The right of other government representatives to participate is decided by the chair of the committee (Art. 29). Committees do not have the right to compel government officials to provide information during committee meetings; however, committees may send written questions to the minister. As a rule, most information gathering occurs at a plenary session.

Committees can ask for expert reports and they can also institute inquiries into the actions of administrative agencies, state-owned enterprises or other organizations. In practice these inquiries happen frequently, which demonstrates the importance of the committees functioning professionally (Interviews).

As in Austria, Iceland, Sweden, and Switzerland, Estonian committees have the right to initiate legislation (Mattson and Stroem 1995, 285). In practice this does not happen frequently since most of the bills are initiated by the government and individual MPs. In the 1996–97 period, only 10.6 percent of the bills came from committees.

Committees do, however, initiate the other types of decisions under the heading of "resolutions." They include nominations of leading state officials, confirmation of different state programs, state loans, accounts, foreign policy resolutions (for example, sending peacekeeping forces), amnesty for prisoners, etc. The large number of resolutions, and their variety, indicates the collective responsiblity of the Riigikogu, which is probably characteristic of a young democracy.

Committees pass resolutions by majority vote. Each member of the committee has the right to request a vote on his proposal (Art. 28). A committee may pass a resolution if at least one-third, but not less than three, of the members of the committee are present. The chair of the committee or the deputy chair must be one of those present (Art. 26). In extraordinary sessions, the committee may pass a resolution if at least half of the members of the committee including the chair or the deputy chair are present (Art. 27). So far there has not been a problem of meeting the quorum requirements for most of the committees.

The chair of the committee, or in his absence the deputy chair, can convene extraordinary sessions of the committee on his own initiative or on the request of at least half of the members of the committee (Art. 27). However, special sessions have not been held very frequently. In some committees such as in Defense and Foreign Affairs, committee extraordinary sessions are convened to meet foreign delegations (Interviews).

Committee Resources

A nearly complete lack of resources renders committees subordinate to party groups in the Estonian legislature. The latter shares with governmental officials space perched at the top of the old city in the palace building. In all, fifty to seventy-five rooms house the legislators, party groups, committees, and the entire technical and support staff, including library and archives. The legislature has roughly half of the building (Interviews).

Most committees have a single room for the chair that doubles as meeting room for the committee. A small adjoining room is shared by the single expert staff member and secretary. Only one or two committees, one of which is the Budget Committee, have two rooms. One is the chair's office, and the other is the committee's meeting room which is used as an office by the deputy chair when the committee is out of session.

Each committee has two or three staff persons, whose task is to register documents, prepare minutes of meetings, etc. These staff members are part of the Riigikogu Chancellery.

Outside experts are involved in committee meetings relatively frequently. Estonia has applied for membership in the European Union. Therefore, a common practice is the coordination of Estonian legislation with EU requirements, in which experts on European law participate (Interviews).

The Estonian parliament does not provide additional salary for deputies who are committee members. Only the chair of the committee gets additional income for his job. Though the chairs of the committees have different work loads, their salary is equal.

According to the Standing Orders, committee meetings occur on Mondays for three hours, on Tuesdays afternoons for an unspecified number of hours, and on Thursdays for two hours.

Committee sessions are not public. Committees could decide to invite mass media representatives to debates, but it rarely happens (Interviews).

Select Committees

In addition to permanent standing committees, the Riigikogu may form ad hoc and select committees to solve specific or temporary tasks. As of spring 1999, there were three select committees: 1) the European Affairs Committee; 2) the committee on the supervision of the lawfulness of the activities and investigations of the National Security Police Board; and 3) Committee on the Application of Anti-corruption Act (Riigikogu Kroonika 1999, 6).

The European Affairs Committee contributes at the parliamentary level to the achievement of the objectives of the association established pursuant to Art. I of the Association Agreement (Europe Agreement) between the European Union and their member states and the Republic of Estonia.

The second ad hoc committee reviews the National Security Board activities in investigations of persons who served or collaborated with the intelligence or counterintelligence services of the states that formerly occupied Estonia.

According to the anti-corruption act, the third ad hoc committee receives from members of the Riigikogu, the chief justice of the Supreme Court, the prime minister, the president of the republic, the president of the Bank of Estonia and the auditor general, declarations of their economic interests.

Ad hoc committees are established when a problem of special importance appears. These committees usually receive more external aid from outside experts than do standing committees. Ad hoc inquiry committees report their conclusions to the plenary. The final aim of the parliamentary investigations is not necessarily to draft new legislation but to analyze the essence of a problem and to make the parliament's opinion of it public.

Inquiries tend to be an instrument of parliamentary control. That explains partly why ad hoc investigatory committees were set up primarily by opposition parties. The majority of MPs agreed to their formation because of pressure from the media and public opinion.

The authority of select committees ends with the term of office of the present membership of the Riigikogu. Temporary committees must be reappointed when a new Riigikogu is elected.

Riigikogu Parliamentary Parties and Committee Composition

Every member of the Estonian parliament can be elected to no more than one standing committee and to one ad hoc committee. In addition, the Standing Orders allow parliamentary party groups to assign for every committee member two replacement members who have all the rights and duties while the member is away (Art. 9). The provision has not not been used yet; at least it has not been reflected in the official lists of committee members.

Changes in committee membership within a term can be explained by changes in the composition of the Riigikogu itself. For example, when there is a change in the cabinet and deputies became new ministers they leave the Riigikogu, and a new replacement member takes his/her committee position.

Most of the changes in committee membership come from Art. 63 of the constitution, which states that the independence of the Riigikogu must be guaranteed by the principle of exclusivity of office. According to that principle, members of the Riigikogu may not hold any other state office. If the member of the Riigikogu assumes any such office, his or her authority as a member of the Riigikogu is either suspended, as on appointment as a member of the government, or terminated. The majority of committee exits and entrances result from changes in the government coalition. As the replacement committee members come from the same election coalition list, the committee party structure has never changed much.

In the 7th Riigikogu, the most frequent changes were in the Legal Committee. Changes in the membership of this committee had some impact on implementation of the rule of law, property reform, and other highly political questions. Committee membership was more stable in the 8th (1995) Parliament. Since every MP can belong to only one standing committee, the size of committees does not change much.

Parliamentary parties, particularly those in the government, try to obtain a majority of committee seats to control both the policy products and the allocation of internal power. Chair positions are held mostly by the government coalition parties.

However, independent and opposition members have held the position of chair and deputy chair. If the seats are distributed equally between coalition and opposition, frequently independent MPs have leading positions in the committee. In both the 7th and the 8th Parliament, it was also quite common for an opposition MP to be chair of a committee.

Government coalition parties have consistently held the chairmansips of five committees, while the opposition parties only one (Legal Affairs). Government and opposition alternated chairmanships of the other committees during the first two years of the 8th term.

The governing coalition was not evenly represented in various committees. The coalition has been heavily represented in the Foreign Affairs Committee. For example, there were seven members of the coalition and one member of the opposition from 1995 to 1997. Travel and other benefits are obvious inducements to membership.

Parliamentary parties must select some committtees over others. Theoretically any party group that has at least ten members could be represented in every committeee. In the 1995 Riigikogu there were only three such party groups, the Center Party, the Coalition Group, and the Reform Party. In reality not all parliamentary parties are represented in each committee. Obviously small parties of less than ten people cannot be represented in all ten committees. Hence, some of the parliamentary party groups are not well informed about the work of the committees.

Neither are the independents. In practice there are some committees where independent MPs are completely missing, such as the Cultural Committee in the 8th term, and the Social Affairs Committee in the 7th.

Committees have an important function as the place where different political interests and opinions meet. They also are one of the main channels of communication between the government coalition and the opposition. According to the interviews, there have been hardly any committees with intense internal tensions between the coalition and the opposition. Political struggles take place more in plenary sessions than in committees. The initiatives and comments made by the opposition are usually taken into account in the committees (Interviews).

An Example of Committees at Work: The Death Penalty

The passage of a bill prohibiting the death penalty was important for Estonia to be considered for EU membership. There were three reasons why this bill is an interesting example of the work of the committees:

1. According to the polls, most people in Estonia were against the pro-hibition. Thus, this was an unpopular decision. People were op-posed to it due to the high crime rate in the country. Public opinion had an impact on the voting in the plenary session.
2. Voting in the plenary was not as strongly along party lines as it is usually (Interviews).
3. It can be considered one of the most important decisions the Ri-igikogu has made in 1998. The bill was also widely debated in the mass media.

The main institution that wanted to adopt the bill was the govern-ment. In all three readings, three different ministers were spokespersons in parliament: the minister of defense, the minister of foreign affairs, and the minister of justice.

The main proponents of the bill were the persons and groups who were responsible for Estonian foreign policies, especially in the European area. Estonia accepted the obligation of abolishing capital punishment when the country decided that it wished to enter European Union. The main proponents were the minister of foreign affairs, Toomas-Hendrik Ilves, and the member of Riigikogu, Kristiina Ojuland, who was then also the vice president of the parliamentary assembly in the European Council.

The Legal Affairs Committee became the leading committee, which was already overburdened by its extra large workload. Only one member was against the bill in the committee meeting held two days before the ple-nary session in parliament. Most of the committee members were from the government parties. Thus, the committee was under relatively strong pres-sure to adopt the bill.

This bill was not a draft law created by some government agency as legal bills usually are, but a decision embedded in the ratification of the European convention a couple of years ago. This advance preparation made the the work of the committee on the technical and juridical prob-lems much easier (Interviews). Compared to other bills, this particular bill was quite easy to handle because of the wide discussion in mass media ("Postimees," 3 March 1998). So the problems faced by the proponents of the bill were mainly political rather than legal.

The bill was passed on March 18, 1998. Thirty-nine representatives voted for the bill, thirty against, while thirteen representatives chose not to vote, and nineteen were absent ("Postimees," 19 March 1998).

As the figures indicate, it was very hard for the members of the gov-ernment and proponents at Riigikogu to persuade the majority to vote for the bill. The main opponents were the Center Party, the Rural Union, and the Pensioneers and Families Union. The latter two parties were part of the government coalition. So the actual role of the Legal Committee was much less important than on some other bills they had to adopt. Voting was not by party as usual, so deputies decided for themselves. Many MPs in the parliament considered the decision to end capital punishment premature for the country. The voting also revealed the general division on this particular issue in Estonian society.

Conclusions

This chapter examines only six years of parliamentary practice in Estonia. Therefore, we can draw only initial conclusions regarding the institutionalization of committees.

The stability of party membership within an electoral term is a basic consideration in the organization and functioning of parliaments. Political parties are the main organizers of parliament. They can support or limit executive power, and their strength and stability are crucial in the functioning of parliamentary committees. A set of stable parties can negotiate committee party ratios and develop working ties with its respective set of members on committees.

It was difficult for different committees in the first two terms to have an accurate view of their parties' policies because of the frequent splits inside the party groups. Under such conditions, when the government through its parliamentary parties failed to dominate the legislative process, there was ample opportunity for the deputies to promote their individual preferences and specialties.

Whereas the number of committees has been stable since independence, the number of different members on each committee has varied over time. Relatively high membership turnover rates affected the ability of MPs to specialize and provide policy expertise to parliament. As we have seen, the education and occupation of the MPs are clearly relevant to his/her committee assignment. Member attendance at committee sessions is high.

Some committees like foreign affairs, and also the financial committees, are clearly preferred by the government coalition parties. Some committee chairmanships, however, have been held by opposition and independent MPs.

Estonian deputies generally speak of committees as the place for specialized and intense work on legislative issues. This statement is an ideal, but the reality is far different. Neither adequate physical resources nor skilled personnel are available to committees. In fact, committees take proposals from parliamentary parties and decide what to do with them (Interviews).

Commitees consider legislation prior to significant floor decisions and more legislation is considered in committees than on the floor of parliament. The trend towards greater stability of the Riigikogu standing committees is visible in Estonian politics in the initial years of the post-Soviet transition.

References

"Estonian Human Development Report 1998." United Nations Development Programme. Tallinn, 1998.

http://www.riigikogu.ee

http://www.RK.ee/rkogu

Mattson, Ingvar, and Kaare Stroem. 1995. "Parliamentary Committees." In *Parliaments and Majority Rule in Western Europe,* edited by Herbert Döring. New York: St. Martins Press.

Postimees, 1995–98.

Riigikogu kroonika, 1993/99. Tallinn, 1993–99.

Riigikogu. The Parliament of Estonia, Directory 1997, National Library of Estonia, 1997.

SEVEN

Dynamics of Institutionalization of Standing Committees in the Lithuanian Parliament, 1990–92: The First Democratic Term

Alvidas Lukošaitis and Darius Žeruolis

A N ASSESSMENT OF THE IMPACT AND IMPORTANCE OF STANDING committees in Lithuania is not an easy task because the first parliamentary term in Lithuania (1990–92) was simultaneous with the birth of a multiparty system. First, the genesis of democratic politics was taking place in the absence of a clear and systematic expression of interest both in society and in the parliament. At the time, Lithuanian society had neither identifiably articulated interests nor competitive parties or party-like groupings attempting to exploit political conflicts (see, for example, Krupavičius 1996, 47; Žeroulis 1998). Second, the first Lithuanian parliament functioned under very unstable and temporary legal conditions. To name one example, Lithuania did not even have a permanent constitution, only *Laikinasis pagrindinis įstatymas* (Basic Provisional Law).[1] Parliament did not function within a stable and consistent framework of rules. It was inaugurated without the main guiding procedural document; hence the rules and procedures regulating parliamentary work were changed and amended often.

This chapter is the first attempt to analyze the work of parliamentary committees in Lithuania. It became evident during data collection that the archiving procedures in these turbulent times were not up to the task, and some valuable information was either missing or recorded improperly.

Institutional (Dis)Continuity and Standing Parliamentary Committees in the Context of the Institutionalization of the Lithuanian Parliament

This chapter concentrates on the first term, 1990–92, of what is now known as the Seimas. In this initial two-year period, the parliament was named Supreme Council-Constituent Seimas (AT-AS). The AT-AS laid the formal procedural and structural foundations for further parliamentary work even though it operated in a very unstable environment with no experience upon which to rely.

The Lithuanian and other Baltic revolutions are interesting because the dismantling of the Soviet system was more complex than in the countries of the external Soviet Empire. The countries of the external empire had to be watchful of Moscow's reaction to their transformation games through roundtables (Kis 1998). Their decisions were not as constrained as in the Baltic countries where the "Moscow factor" had to be considered in every decision and strategy. For example, the need to emphasize continuity of statehood to ensure the possibility of international recognition on the grounds of international law needed a fast break at the earliest opportunity. This need had to be weighed against the possibility of a *coup d'état* in Moscow, which mandated slow, gradual change. To this day, there is no scholarly agreement in Lithuania over what the systemic change meant in Lithuania—transformation of the old system or a clean break with the past. Paradoxically, it was both, because the only way the lawful revolution could succeed was through the use of existing Soviet institutions.

The 1990 elections to the last Supreme Soviet of Lithuanian Soviet Socialist Republic (LSSR) turned out to be the founding elections of the new democratic system. The sequence of the resolutions and laws passed on the first day by the newly elected parliament illuminate how the slow-track strategy was abandoned for the fast break. Based on free and fair elections, the Supreme Soviet voted to transform itself into the AT-AS, which proclaimed the Act on Restitution of Independence and then adopted a provisional constitution. The international standing of Lithuania was not jeopardized. Unlike in Latvia and Estonia, even the radical nationalists did not dispute the legitimacy of the Supreme Soviet turned into the Supreme Council of Lithuania.

The institutional legacy was palpable. The "old" Soviet Lithuanian parliament functioned according to the Regulations of the Supreme Soviet of LSSR and Rules of Standing Commissions of LSSR (*Deputatų veiklos norminiai aktai* 1985). The new parliament could not follow these outdated rules blindly; however, it could not work without some regulations.

The design of new statute proved to be a lengthy and energy-consuming process. Therefore, it had to be postponed because of other, more urgent tasks. The old Regulations were substantially amended and passed as the interim framework of the new parliament (*Lietuvos Respublikos Aukščiausiosios Tarybos ir Prezidiumo dokumentų rinkinys* 1991, 1:24, 27, 95–96, 224–25). A task-force of AT-AS was charged with preparing a new statute to govern the parliament and establish a system of standing committees (*Lietuvos Respublikos Aukščiausiosios Tarybos stenogramos* 1990, 2:228). In the meantime, committee work was regulated by the clauses on committees contained in the amended Regulations.[2] Outdated as they were, Article 27 of the old Regulations and Article 5 of the old Rules of the Standing Committees required that any set of committees must include the following standing committees: Mandates, Legislative Initiatives, Foreign Affairs, and Planning and Budget (*Deputatų veiklos norminiai aktai* 1985, 118).[3]

The challenging task of building a state from scratch quickly made even the amended Regulations an obstacle with which AT-AS could not afford to comply. Hence for more than a year, until the new Regulations were passed on April 18, 1991, adherence to the provisions of the amended Regulations was superficial. The real work on drafting of the new Regulations began on May 15, 1990, when the first serious debate was held on the floor, two months after the AT-AS first convened. On October 31, 1990, the parliament decided that the new Regulations could be passed in stages and not in any fixed order (*Lietuvos Respublikos Aukščiausiosios Tarybos stenogramos* 1990, 2:200, 7:411). The new Regulations did not ensure stability, either, because the parties realigned in AT-AS, and the *Sąjūdis* government lost its majority. From the time of adoption on April 18, 1991, to the end of the parliamentary term on November 20, 1992, AT-AS amended one-quarter of the articles of the new Regulations. The new Regulations were in place until February 17, 1994, when the current Statute of Seimas was passed.[4]

The Professional Backgrounds of AT-AS and Committee Members

The new Lithuanian parliament in 1990 was an example of sharp discontinuity with the previous Soviet parliament.[5] The voters equated the dismantling of the old Soviet system with a vote for "new faces." Thus, only a few MPs who had some parliamentary experience in the Congress of Soviet People's Deputies and in the last Supreme Soviet of Lithuanian SSR were elected. As a rule, they represented the reformist wing of the Lithuanian Communist Party (LKP). In terms of professional and educational backgrounds, the composition of the new parliament could not have been more diverse.

The vast majority of newly elected MPs did not have any experience relevant to working in parliament. Only a handful of former deputies to the all-Union Soviet People's Deputies Congress (1989–90), members of LKP apparatus and local government, had "formal" experience of "structurally constrained" politics before joining AT-AS. On the other hand, some MPs did actively participate in various political and social movements, NGOs, and newly (re)established political parties since 1988. However, experience of political activism could hardly make up for the skills required in parliament, especially in the committees.

Membership of committees became more or less stable after the 1991–92 reform, so we provide data about committee members only from the latter period onwards. The Committee on Legal System was the most homogenous in members' professional backgrounds. Seven out of ten of its members were lawyers. Similarly, five out of ten MPs in the Committee on Agricultural Affairs were agronomists and four out of ten in the Committee on Economy were economists. Other committees were very heterogeneous. The committees on Foreign Affairs, State Re-establishment, Defense and Interior were the most diverse in their members' professional background. Lack of appropriate qualifications had to be compensated by cooperation between committees. For example, if in the process of deliberation in a committee, legal and procedural issues related to proposed draft bills became too problematic, the committee would seek the opinion or recommendation of the Committee on Legal System. If the problem could not be resolved, the draft bill would be transferred to another committee.

The MPs were aware of their diverse backgrounds and on numerous occasions during the plenary sessions had to convince their opponents that the parliament was not composed of actors, singers, or music performers but of politicians representing their voters.

Procedures Establishing Standing Committees

There were no strict criteria for the assignment of MPs to standing committees when the committees were formed in March 1990. The only restricting factor was the decision of the parliament on the number and size of the committees. When this decision was made, MPs were free to choose a committee and a couple of alternatives in case all slots in their first choice had already been taken. In the absence of real parliamentary experience, the guiding factor for most MPs was their professional and educational backgrounds and experiences.[6]

The match between the committees' work and the members' background could not have been perfect, not only because of the latter's diversity compounded by the lack of political experience but also because political parties did not yet have established internal policy specialization. There was no competition or conflicts in the allocation of membership in the committees except for the Committee on Foreign Affairs, where, according to a former chairman of one of the committees, "there was a contest" for membership.[7] In the beginning MPs did not view committees as "more" or "less" prestigious. Only after some time did the MPs realize that the Committees of Budget, Economy, and Legal System were more powerful and influential than, for example, the Committee of Environmental Protection, which later had unfilled vacancies at times.

Although the composition of the committees changed frequently, the committees were reorganized only once. Standing committees were founded in March 1990 and reestablished in late 1991 to early 1992 to comply with requirements of the new Regulations (*Lietuvos Respublikos Aukščiausiosios Tarybos dokumentų rinkinys* 1990, 1:70–72; 1992, 4:160–61, 168, 177–78, 209–10, 223, 339–40). After the reform of the committees, the size as well as the structure became more or less stable.

The new Regulations of April 18, 1991, introduced proportional representation of the parliamentary parties as the most important principle in the formation of a standing committee. This procedure was implemented as follows. First, the undersecretary of the AT-AS and the chairs of the parliamentary parties had to work out the number of seats allocated to each party.[8] Then MPs applied for an assignment to a standing committee, after which each parliamentary party matched the applications with its share of seats in a committee, sorted out overlaps and mismatches, and assigned its members to committees by a letter to the secretary of AT-AS.[9] Finally this process was formally approved by a resolution of AT-AS.

The requirement of a minimal committee size of seven members was applied to all committees except for a Standing Committee on Mandates and Ethics, which could have as few as five members. This committee was formed by a special procedure whereby the ceiling on size was abolished and all parties with more than twenty members delegated two representatives each, and those under twenty delegated only one (Article 31 of the Regulations; *Lietuvos Respublikos Aukščiausiosios Tarybos dokumentų rinkinys* 1991, 3:326; 1992, 4:336).

More than half of the committee members had to be "full-time" MPs. The part-time enrollment into the legislative work of some MPs was a peculiarity of the first Lithuanian parliament. The part-timers were MPs who did not resign from their previous positions outside the parliament and chose to combine two jobs. Attendance of all plenary meetings for these MPs was not mandatory. Such practice, though not on a large scale (only about fifteen to twenty MPs out of 141), was tolerated precisely because a firm commitment to full-time professional politics by the candidates before the first elections could hardly be expected. Such practice was discontinued in subsequent parliaments.

It is striking that now, in the third Lithuanian parliament, a decade after the turn to democratic parliamentary politics, only a handful of MPs have experience dating back to the first parliament.

Standing committees had a right to establish subcommittees of at least five of its members to oversee the most important issues within the committee's jurisdiction. Only committees had the right to present an opinion or report in plenary sessions, so naturally subcommittees were neither popular nor influential (interviews with committee chairmen). Only a few subcommittees were established in AT-AS: two subcommittees of the Committee of Defense and Interior; four subcommittees of the Committee of Science, Education, Culture and Information; and two subcommittees of the Committee of Health Care and Social Protection.

According to our calculations, during 1990–92 about ten select committees were established. Characteristically, the committees' names reflected the political environment of the early days of Lithuanian independence. For three examples, AT-AS voted to establish a Select Committee on Problems of Retrieval of Lithuanian Citizens Serving in the Soviet Armed Forces; a Select Committee to Investigate KGB Operations in Lithuania; and a Select Committee on the Problems of East Lithuania.

Partisan Affiliation of Standing Committee Members

Thirteen standing committees were established in the beginning of the parliamentary term. The Standing Committee on Mandates and Ethics was the first (*Lietuvos Aukščiausiosios Tarybos dokumentų rinkinys* 1990, 1:23, 66, 70–72).[10] Committee size varied from six to twenty in the first period. Later, the distribution of membership became more even, ranging from eight to thirteen members. This standardization was carried out to accommodate the principle of proportionality in committees' formation.

To understand the party composition of the first Lithuanian parliament it is necessary to consider the context of the political situation in Lithuania in the early 1990s. Essentially, the first elections in 1990 were a contest between two political camps, namely, *Sąjūdis* and LKP.[11] The elections were contested only on one issue—the strategy for achieving independence. *Sąjūdis* favored a radical solution to the problem while LKP was gradualist in its approach. An absolute majority of seats (133 out of 141) was captured by representatives of these two political forces (see Table 7.1).

In 1990, because political forces differed so little on almost any issue save the tactics for achieving independence, for some time there was no clear distinction between the parties' positions. At the time of the establishment of standing parliamentary committees, immediately after the elections in March 1990, only the distribution of seats between *Sąjūdis* and LKP mattered. On the other hand, there was a serious attempt to accommodate all individual interests initially, so there were no big party conflicts over the assignments of MPs to standing committees.

In the beginning, *Sąjūdis* had a comfortable majority in AT-AS, so the main decisions on committee assignments were taken inside the caucus of *Sąjūdis* MPs. Other political groups, for example LKP, and especially LKP-TSKP, Polish (minority) MPs, and a couple of independent MPs, were marginal and did not have a big say in these matters. Because of insignificant political differences among parties, and *Sąjūdis*'s absolute majority, the partisan affiliation of a particular MP was not the main criterion of assignment; only competence and special skills mattered. Neither the Presidium of AT-AS nor the parliamentary parties played any role in this process. In fact, the first parliamentary party (*frakcija*) in AT-AS was officially registered only on June 21, 1990. All in all, the leaders of informal, not yet institutionalized, groups of MPs were instrumental in this process (Lukošaitis 1997, 5). By early 1992, several parliamentary parties were registered. Table 7.1 displays the party affiliation of MPs at various times during the first term.

The chairs of standing committees were elected by AT-AS before the assignment of the rest of the MPs to committees (*Lietuvos Republikos Aukščiausiosios Tarybos dokumentų rinkinys* 1990, 1:65). The only clear and predictable element in the selection of chairmen stemmed from the confrontation of *Sąjūdis* and LKP. LKP MPs did not stand a chance of being elected to a committee chair. Representatives of all the other parties (LSDP, LKDP, and LŽP) were members of a *Sąjūdis* umbrella and hence "eligible" for chair positions. Although during the elections to AT-AS, *Sąjūdis* supported candidates won 101 seats out of 141, members of the *Sąjūdis* parliamentary party (*Jungtinė Sąjūdžio frakcija*) received only five committee chair positions out of thirteen.

Chair positions were volatile and changed frequently. For example, the

Table 7.1

Changes in Parliamentary Parties in Lithuanian Parliament, 1990–1992

A. Partisan Affiliation of MPs in AT-AS in 1990 Election

Parties	MPs elected	Of Which Sąjūdis MPs
No party affiliation	73	67
LKP	41	19
LKP–TSKP	9	0
LSDP	9	9
LŽP	2	2
LKDP	2	2
LDP	3	2
Vacant	2	—
Total	141	101

B. Membership Changes in Parliamentary Parties, 1990–1992

Parliamentary parties in AT-AS, 1990–92	Registered in AT-AS Date	Membership at the end of 1990	Membership 8 May 1991	Membership October 1992
Centro frakcija (Sąjūdis Centre)	21.06.1990	20	21	20
Kairiųjų frakcija (Leftist)	25.09.1990	10	14	9
Lenkų frakcija (Polish Faction)	23.10.1990	8	8	8
Jungtinė Sąjūdžio frakcija (Joint Sąjūdis)	19.12.1990	34	34	14
Tautininkų frakcija (Nationalists)	09.01.1991	—	12	9
Septintoji frakcija (The Seventh)	23.04.1991	—	14	18
Liberalų frakcija (Liberals)	08.05.1991	—	10	9
Sąjūdžio Santaros frakcija (Sąjūdis Concord)	30.01.1992	—	—	11
Tautos Pažangos frakcija (National Progress)	14.01.1992	—	—	9
Non-aligned MPs		68	28*	31

Notes:
On 11 February 1992, Kairiųjų frakcija was renamed LDDP frakcija (Lithuanian Labour Democratic Party); Septintoji frakcija was later renamed Nuosaikiųjų frakcija (Moderates); Tautos Pažangos frakcija was established by MPs who defected from Tautininkų frakcija; Sąjūdžio Santaros frakcija consisted of defectors from Jungtinė Sąjūdžio frakcija. See Appendix II.
*Highest estimate, exact data not available.

Sources: Sources cited in Žeruolis, Darius (1998), Appendix 1, and Lukošaitis, Alvidas (1997).

Standing Committee of Defense and Interior Affairs and the Standing Committee of State and Constitution changed their heads three times during the term. The Standing Committees of Agriculture, Environmental Protection, Mandates and Ethics, Citizens Rights and Nationalities, and Foreign Affairs had two chairs. The chairs of only six committees kept their posts throughout the entire parliamentary term.

The membership of standing committees changed frequently as well. The Standing Committee on Defense and Interior Affairs holds a record of six reshuffles. The Standing Committees on Agriculture, Environment Protection, and Economy went through four reshuffles each while the rest changed their member composition two or three times. Membership stabilization was facilitated by the reorganization of the standing committees in late 1991 to early 1992, when the main principles for committee assignment became affiliation with a parliamentary party and proportional representation of all parliamentary parties. Only then did party affiliation become a matter of importance in parliamentary work (*Lietuvos Respublikos Aukščiausiosios Tarybos dokumentų rinkinys* 1991, 4:160–61, 168, 177–78, 180, 209–10, 223, 340).

The Powers, Competence, and Working Procedures of Standing Committees

Standing committees were coordinated by the Presidium of the AT-AS, the leadership body. It was composed of the chair, three deputy chairs, the secretary of AT-AS, and six other MPs. While the leadership of the parliament included the ex-officio members of the Presidium, the remaining six MPs were elected by the plenary session. The prime minister, deputy prime ministers, chair of Supreme Court, prosecutor general as well as the chairs of standing committees of AT-AS could participate in the Presidium's meetings but did not have voting rights.

It was the Presidium, not the standing committees, that held legislative leverage over the other institutions. The chairs whom we interviewed indicated that neither the plenary session nor the standing committees could equal the Presidium's influence and importance in legislative and administrative matters. The Presidium coordinated the drafting of bills and directed them through all stages of deliberation and adoption.

Article 37 of the Regulations defined the three most important functions of standing committees—initiation of legislation, review of the state budget, and parliamentary oversight. Of course, standing committees did not have the power to enforce their decisions and rulings vis-à-vis governmental agencies. However, the agencies were obliged by law to take into account the recommendations and suggestions of the committees and to report back to the committees on the agency's review of the committee's recommendations and the measures taken. Standing committees also had a right to summon any governmental official and ask for an explanation of a given issue. Standing committees could also require documents, reports on an issue, and additional data from any state institution (Articles 42–43 of the Regulations). In exercising parliamentary oversight, standing committees had a right to query the members of the government and other executive agencies (Article 45 of the Regulations).

Standing committees worked according to their own agenda, which was produced in advance of the parliamentary sessions in the spring and autumn and coordinated with the session's agenda. During the session, meetings of standing committees were called as needed, but at least once a week. However, standing committees could not meet when parliament was meeting. Any MP who was not a member of a committee could attend meetings.

If an issue fell within the jurisdiction of more than one committee, the committees held a joint meeting. The meetings were chaired in rotation by the chairmen of the participating committees. A quorum consisted of two-thirds of the "full-time" members or one-half of all the committee members. A simple majority was needed to pass or defeat a motion. A minority of at least three committee members could state a separate opinion, which had to be appended to the majority decision (Article 120 of the Regulations).

Standing Committees in the Legislative Process in AT-AS

It is difficult to give a definitive answer to the question of how much influence standing committees had in the AT-AS in 1990–92. First, empirical evidence on committee activities should be treated with caution because not all activities were properly documented (see Table 7.2). Still worse, some committee minutes and records of proceedings are missing from the Seimas archives.[12] Second, we noticed an imbalance between the formal powers and the de facto products. For example, the low number of laws amended suggests that committees did not use or were unable to use their formal powers fully.

Draft bills could make their way to the standing committees through two channels. First, upon receipt of a draft bill from the government, the secretary of AT-AS could forward it, along with an accompanying circular from the Legal Department of AT-AS, to a committee for a preliminary review.[13] Second, drafts of bills could be forwarded to the committees by the plenary session.

When the parliament was in session, the committees, by law, had to present their opinions within ten days of receipt of a bill. After a committee or committees voted the bill out, and the Presidium of AT-AS made the decision to put it before the House, the draft bill would be added to the parliament's agenda (Articles 184, 187–88 of the Regulations) for a preliminary reading.

During the preliminary reading in the plenary session, representatives from a) standing committees, b) the Legal Department of AT-AS, c) the Presidium of AT-AS, and d) the government delivered brief presentations on the bill. This procedure would take up to ten minutes per speaker. Then the parliament voted on whether the bill should be added to the parliament's docket for the session. If the vote was positive, the date for the first reading was fixed and a principal standing committee as well as other committees appointed to handle the bill. Committees became engaged in the legislative process only after the first verdict on the bill by the house during the preliminary reading.

However, there were two distinctive features. First, the plenary meeting could schedule additional readings without further deliberations in committees. In other words, it could choose to bypass the committee stage. It was not mandatory to utilize committees. Only in 1994, when a new Regulations Statute of Seimas was adopted, was the committee stage firmly entrenched as a part of the overall deliberative procedure.

Second, preliminary reading in AT-AS was not a mere formality. If the opinions of the principal standing committee, the government, the Presidium of AT-AS, and the Legal Department of AT-AS significantly differed, the plenary session immediately initiated debate. The sponsors of the bill, representatives of the four institutions as well as parliamentary parties (*frakcijos*) and individual MPs had a chance to speak on the bill (Articles 188–189 of the Regulations). Only then was the bill placed, or not placed, on the docket. It is important to stress that at this stage no binding guidelines or any principles for three further readings were established. The standing committees had a free hand on how to proceed with the bill once it was referred to them.

After the initial approval by the plenary session, the principal standing committee had to examine the bill for its impact on the budget and on the Program of the Government. Suggestions to reject the bill must be accompanied by an explanation while committee consent could be expressed in three ways: unqualified, qualified, and conditional pending certain amendments.

First reading in the plenary session could begin only after committee stage was completed. It was only then that the main principles and rationale of a bill were debated. The first reading usually began with the principal standing committee presenting its conclusions followed by presentations from supplementary committees. The bill could be rejected in first reading, or the principal standing committee could be asked to prepare amendments and changes as agreed in the debate.

During second reading, the parliament considered proposed amendments to the bill and held a general discussion on the final version of the bill. A special discussion on the final structure of the bill and for a procedure for submission of last-minute changes and amendments, or debate of the separate sections of the bill was held, too. After second reading, a principal standing committee could be asked to summarize the debate and amendment proposals as well as draft the final edition of the text. After the completion of editing, the third and last reading on the floor would take place in four days.

Committees would seem to have formalized opportunities and powers to influence the legislative process from the beginning of the debate to the last stages. However, our data do not support this assumption. The number of amendments introduced in relation to the total number of bills handled suggests that the committees were not very influential. The data (only 32 percent amendment rate from the total of 871 bills handled; see Table 7.2) suggests that this low level of influence comes from the MPs' inexperience in parliamentary procedures rather than from than a weak position vis-à-vis the Presidium or the House. Opinions delivered by standing committees were by no means decisive in the plenary session.

The number of draft bills differed among committees. For example, during the term the Committee of Science, Education, and Culture processed a total of 149 draft bills, the Committee of Budget 140, and the Committee of Municipalities 92. The activity of other committees, measured this way, is significantly lower. The differences can be seen also in the count of amended bills, a measure of committee intervention. The Committee of Budget amended fifty-six bills, Committees of Economy and Municipalities amended thirty-three each, while the rest did not intervene as frequently.

For comparison of the working load of the plenary session and standing committees, we can provide the following data. In 1990–92, AT-AS convened 580 plenary sessions in which 333 laws and 969 resolutions were adopted. Committees, on the other hand, held 1286 meetings in which 871 draft bills (i.e., laws and other legal acts) were considered. Most of the bills were defeated in the plenary sessions. It is our assessment

Table 7.2

Legislative Activities of Standing Committees in Lithuanian Parliament, 1990–1992

Standing committee	1990	1991	1992	Total
Agriculture				
Number of meetings	40	35	43	118
Legal acts handled	22	22	21	65
Legal acts amended	3	11	13	27
Budget				
Number of meetings	61	50	42	153
Legal acts handled	41	64	35	140
Legal acts amended	19	23	14	56
Environmental protection				
Number of meetings	47	57	43	147
Legal acts handled	12	22	24	58
Legal acts amended	2	1	3	6
Economy				
Number of meetings	n/a	11	10	21
Legal acts handled	n/a	26	18	44
Legal acts amended	n/a	22	11	33
Defense and Interior				
Number of meetings	n/a	16	21	37
Legal acts handled	n/a	21	16	37
Legal acts amended	n/a	6	9	15
Mandates and Ethics				
Number of meetings	23	16	24	63
Legal acts handled	4	5	6	15
Legal acts amended	1	2	1	4
Citizens' Rights and Nationalities				
Number of meetings	47	50	37	134
Legal acts handled	29	25	12	66
Legal acts amended	2	4	2	8
Municipal Affairs				
Number of meetings	36	34	24	94
Legal acts handled	31	34	27	92
Legal acts amended	13	13	7	33
Health Care and Social Protection				
Number of meetings	20	13	12	45
Legal acts handled	11	11	11	33
Legal acts amended	0	0	2	2

(Continued)

Table 7.2 (Continued)

Legislative Activities of Standing Committees in Lithuanian Parliament, 1990–1992

Standing committee	1990	1991	1992	Total
Science, Culture and Education				
Number of meetings	60	47	31	138
Legal acts handled	54	53	42	149
Legal acts amended	19	15	5	39
State and Constitution				
Number of meetings	10	40	32	82
Legal acts handled	17	32	11	60
Legal acts amended	10	11	4	25
Legal System				
Number of meetings	44	22	n/a	66
Legal acts handled	26	27	n/a	53
Legal acts amended	13	3	n/a	16
Foreign Affairs				
Number of meetings	69	67	52	188
Legal acts handled	23	20	16	59
Legal acts amended	2	5	4	11
Total				
Number of meetings	457	458	371	1286
Legal acts handled	270	362	239	871
Legal acts amended	84	116	75	275

Notes:

The record does not indicate the source of draft bills in the committees' archives. However, our assessment is that the Government was far less influential as a source of legislation in AT-AS than in the subsequent parliaments.

The term "legal acts" comprises laws and resolutions;

Archival records missing: a) n/a in the table = missing for the entire year – Committees of Economy (1990), Defense and Interior (1990) and Legal System (1992); b) less than one year—Committees of Budget (October–November 1992), Economy (May, and November 1991; March, July and October 1992), Defense and Interior (March and September 1991; September–November 1992); Mandates and Ethics (June–July 1991); Science, Education and Culture (March–19 April 1991); Municipal Affairs (June 1991); Health Care and Social Protection (25 April–15 October 1991, 15 April–November 1992); State and Constitution (March–August 1990); Legal System (June 1991).

that committee opinions were not significant in shaping the final opinion of the House.

One should not be surprised by the high number of bills passed by the first parliament—in comparison, in 1992–96 the Seimas passed 1,035 laws and 595 resolutions.[14] Of course, the hyperactivism of the parliament naturally begs the question whether the quality of laws had not been compromised.

If we consider the political context of these hectic days, then the explanation of these committee differences is easier. First, the higher output of the Committees of Budget, Economy, Legal System, and Municipalities can be explained by the priorities of the new government. It had to restructure the economy, restore and create private ownership, and lay the foundations for the new state. These committees were certainly at the forefront of the legislative process simply because of the policy priorities of the new government. The influence and importance of these priorities was acknowledged during our interviews with the former chairs of some committees.

Second, the committees could not acquire equal importance because of the precarious international situation of the newly born Lithuanian state. Plenary sessions were exclusive arenas in which to debate and pass bills related to the demand for international recognition, security of the state, and relations with the Soviet Union. This agenda worked to the detriment of committees, which could not contribute to a solution of the political and international problems facing Lithuania. The relevance of these committees was slight during the first months of the parliamentary term and in early 1991, during the open Soviet military crackdown in Lithuania. In the first six months, the committees were bypassed routinely.

It was only in early 1992 that the parliament settled down to a normal, "ordinary" agenda. The committees began to receive more draft bills from the Presidium of AT-AS for consideration and the quality of legislation began to improve. However, early elections had to be called in the autumn after *Sąjūdis* had lost its majority in AT-AS in the spring of 1992. Further routinization of the committee system was postponed to the new parliament.

In sum, at the beginning of the term, committees were neither all-important nor autonomous because of the extraordinary agenda of AT-AS. The committees were simply bypassed in favor of deliberations and adoption of legislation on the floor. The committees' agendas were dependent on instructions from the Presidium of AT-AS and the plenary session. The Lithuanian committees were capable neither of speeding up nor of slowing down the legislative processes that for the most part were external to them.

However, the committees' role and importance gradually rose once the extraordinary agenda had been completed and international recognition of the state achieved. For a brief period of time, at the very end of the term in the summer and autumn of 1992, the committees became the only arenas in the parliament where rational discussions could prevail. In a hung parliament with early elections fast approaching, the plenary meetings became dominated by the fighting among MPs. During that period committees helped to stabilize the functioning of the parliament. The stabilizing factor was so important that shortly before the expiration of the term, a debate was initiated about the possible further increase of their legislative and oversight powers.

Relations between the Committees and the Executive

Interaction between the parliament and the government is especially important in the budgetary process, which we will briefly touch upon in our analysis of the Lithuanian case in 1990–92. The secretary of the parliament received the draft budget from the government. However, the government also delivered a brief report to the plenary session on the draft budget, and copies of it were immediately distributed to standing committees and parliamentary parties (*frakcijos*). During the period when the committees worked on the budget, there were no plenary sessions. All committees worked on budget reports, which were forwarded to the Committee of the Budget. The Committee of the Budget summarized all recommendations and wrote a summary report for the plenary session. After the first budget reading and debate on the floor, the budget was returned to the government for amendments. If serious objections arose during the second reading, the budget could be returned to the government again. Otherwise, it was adopted in the plenary session. During the year after adoption, the committees could intervene and suggest amendments on certain expenditure items (Articles 229–241 of the Regulations). At least procedurally, the committees were empowered to participate in the formation of the budget.

The extraordinary agenda of the first parliament itself ensured very close contacts between the parliament and the government. The parliament had the legal means to ensure oversight. For example, ad hoc investigative commissions could be established, inquiries filed, reports from the governmental officials heard and so on. From existing data and interviews with committee chairmen, we established that most of the time, AT-AS either filed inquiries to the government, established *ad hoc* investigative commissions, or referred problems to a standing committee for clarification.

Still, parliamentary oversight of the executive, despite the legal provisions, was short of an ideal check in the first parliament. Political instability and overlap of the oversight functions among committees were detrimental to the effectiveness of this important task. During the first parliamentary term, Lithuania had four governments.[15] When the government changed the composition and structure of ministries was altered, while the committee system in the parliament remained the same. Thus every time oversight functions had to be readjusted among the committees, and, in some cases, contacts with ministries and agencies reestablished.[16]

The institutional weakness of oversight also was dependent on the fact that formal-legal aspects of interaction between the government and the parliament often gave way to informal deals and personal politics. The chairs we interviewed told us that the relations with the government became more complicated during the prime ministerial term of Gediminas Vagnorius. The government became much more autonomous and unwilling to cooperate. The relations even became tense in early 1992, when the government lost its majority in the parliament.

Conclusion

It is difficult to overestimate the importance of the first Lithuanian parliament during the systemic change in Lithuania. It acted as a catalyst of change during the period of enormous institutional and international upheavals. The challenge was further magnified by the fact that the parliament had to establish itself institutionally, as it only inherited Soviet rules, not a functioning system of committees. As noted in chapter 1, institutionalization is intrinsically linked to stability, continuity, and predictability. Against this definition, the Lithuanian parliament in 1990–92 qualifies as only minimally institutionalized.

On the other hand, institutional stability also means adaptability to external and internal changes. The AT-AS score is much higher on this factor. AT-AS clearly displayed adaptability to rapidly changing political, social, and economic circumstances, and its parliamentary work and procedures were not significantly disrupted even by an open Soviet crackdown on Lithuanian independence in January 1991. The eventual failure of the crackdown consolidated popular support for the parliament. The popularity of the first parliament is missed by today's MPs who see the trust in the legislature scoring significantly less than the approval of the government and the president, partly because of political debates in the parliament.

While parliamentary rules and procedures were highly volatile and inconsistent in the first parliament, it is also true that the main procedural principles and practices of parliamentary debate, legislative process, and organization were laid down then. The degree of structuring of the committee work could not be high in a minimally institutionalized parliament. Throughout the term, the role, functions, size, and membership of parliamentary committees constantly changed. Low institutionalization is perhaps best displayed by the fact that the committees were poorly differentiated both in organizational and functional terms. We have to conclude that the committee work was at best only minimally institutionalized as well.

The weaknesses of the newly born party system, and the lack of political differentiation and articulation had a negative effect on the committees. It was only in the second half of the term in AT-AS that MPs finally became bound by party discipline. On the other hand, it was first and foremost a committee system that helped to buffer high political polarization and ensure the continuous, rational, and stable work of the first Lithuanian parliament in 1992.

Now after its first decade of reborn existence, the Lithuanian parliament has gone a long way in institutionalizing and routinizing its legislative procedure. The new Seimas's rules came into force February 1, 1999. The procedural provisions for the legislative process in the new Statute fundamentally reforms organization of parliamentary work. From now on the Seimas's committees unequivocally become the central bodies managing scrutiny of drafts, debates, and adoption of the legal acts.

Notes

Some of the empirical evidence presented in this essay was drawn from the findings of the research seminar conducted by the authors in the Spring 1998 term at the Institute of International Relations and Political Science, University of Vilnius. We want to thank Viktoras Gasiūnas, Dovilė Jakniūnaitė, Giedre Bacevičiūtė, Giedrė Silickaitė, Erika Mockutė, and Deividas Vijeikis for their research assistance. Regina Škuropad, the head archivist at the Seimas, has also been very helpful in providing advise and access to the archives. Last but not least, the editors of this volume, David Olson and William Crowther, suggested many improvements to the first draft of this paper.

1. *Laikinasis pagrindinis įstatymas* was an amended version of the Constitution of the Lithuanian Soviet Socialist Republic. The Soviet Constitution was minimally adapted to democratic politics and stripped of Soviet references. *Laikinasis pagrindinis istatymas* was passed on March 11, 1990 and functioned until replaced by a referendum by the new constitution on October 25, 1992.

2. Hereafter Regulations and Rules.

3. Committee of Mandates was an in-house version of the High Electoral Commission with powers to verify legality of elections in each and every district.

4. Seimas—historical (1920–40) and the new official name of the Lithuanian parliament from October 1992.

5. Due to the undemocratic nature and a rubber-stamp function of the Soviet style "parliaments," it is highly questionable whether high continuity would have been a good thing anyway.

6. Only twenty to twenty-five MPs of AT-AS had previously been members of the Supreme Soviet of Lithuanian SSR or the Congress of Soviet People's Deputies (1989–90). Some of the *Sąjūdis* MPs already had some parliamentary training in the *Sąjūdis*'s Seimas committees. *Sąjūdis*'s Seimas was the political assembly of *Sąjūdis*. In 1988–90 it was an opposition forum to the communist-dominated legislature and its government. *Sąjūdis*'s Seimas claimed to have a true and real representation of Lithuanian society. During the first congress of *Sąjūdis* (October 22–24, 1988), 220 members of Seimas were elected. Later the size of Seimas was reduced to 141. Some of the chairmen of the *Sąjūdis* committees subsequently assumed chairmanships in the AT-AS.

7. The account of the work of committees relies on interviews conducted with five chairmen of AT-AS standing committees, namely, Committees of Environment Protection; Science, Education and Culture; Citizens' Rights and Minorities; Health Protection and Social Affairs; and Legal System.

8. A representative of a standing group of nonaligned (independent) MPs also participated in the allocation procedure because this group enjoyed all benefits of the parliamentary parties.

9. The Secretary of AT-AS was an elected MP to oversee the chancellery of the parliament.

10. Later in March 1990 the Standing Committee of Mandates was renamed to the Standing Committee of Mandates and Ethics.

11. LKP (*Lietuvos komunistu partija*)—Lithuanian Communist Party. Its reformist (majority) wing had just two months before it split from CPSU, while the orthodox communists established their own party, LKP-TSKP (Lithuanian Communist Party on CPSU platform, pro-Moscow communists). LKP-TSKP was outlawed in the aftermath of the abortive August *coup d'état* in 1991, not least because of their support for the January 1991 Soviet military crackdown in Vilnius.

12. The following analysis relies on the archival research conducted in the Seimas from March to May 1998. Unfortunately, only five committees (Agriculture, Budget, Environment Protection, Municipal Affairs, and Foreign Affairs) had a full set of records for the entire term (1990–92) stored in the Seimas archive. Documents of the remaining committees were missing for various periods from a month to one year. See notes for Table 7.2.

13. Legal Department was (and still is) one of the divisions of the chancellery of the parliament. It is charged with analysis of and advice on draft bills from the standpoint of the legal language.

14. It should be borne in mind that AT-AS had a truncated term of thirty-two months, while the second parliament went through the full cycle of forty-eight months. Still, after adjustment for the difference in the cycle, AT-AS would

have passed approximately five hundred laws if it stayed for the full period. They are less than half of the output of the second parliament.

15. The first government, headed by Kazimiera Prunskienė, governed from March 17, 1990, to January 8, 1991; second (Albertas Šimėnas)—January 10–13, 1991; third (Gediminas Vagnorius)—January 13, 1991–July 14, 1992; fourth (Aleksandras Abišala)—July 26–November 26, 1992.

16. There was a substantial overlap of jurisdiction between the Committees of Legal System and State and Constitution. On the other hand, there were committees (Citizens' Rights and Nationalities, Municipal Affairs as well as State and Constitution) that did not have corresponding ministries to deal with. The Committee on Mandates and Ethics was not involved in legislative process at all; instead it primarily dealt with the problem of parliamentary ethics.

References and Bibliography

Kis, Janos. 1998. "Between Reform and Revolution." *East European Politics and Societies* 12, no. 2: 300–387.

Krupavičius, Algis. 1996. "Pokomunistinė transformacija ir Lietuvos partijos," in *Politinės partijos Lietuvoje: atgimimas ir veikla,* edited by Algis Krupavičius. Vilnius: Litera. 1–93.

Lietuvos Respublikos Aukščiausiosios Tarybos reglamentas [Regulations of the Supreme Council of the Republic of Lithuania]. 1992. Vilnius: LR Aukščiausiosios Tarybos leidykla.

Lietuvos Respublikos Aukščiausiosios Tarybos ir Prezidiumo dokumentų rinkiniai [Collections of Documents of Supreme Council and Presidium of the Republic of Lithuania]. 1991–92. Vilnius: Viltis.

Lietuvos Respublikos Aukščiausiosios Tarybos posėdžių stenogramos. Prezidiumo dokumentų rinkinys [Transcripts of Plenary Sessions of the Supreme Council of the Republic of Lithuania]. 1990–92. Vilnius: Viltis.

Lietuvos Respublikos Konstitucija [Constitution of the Republic of Lithuania]. 1993. Vilnius: LR Seimo leidykla.

Lietuvos Respublikos Laikinasis pagrindinis istatymas [Basic Law of the Republic of Lithuania]. 1991. In *Lietuvos Respublikos Aukščiausiosios Tarybos ir Prezidiumo dokumentų rinkinys*. Vilnius: Viltis, 34–56.

LTSR Aukščiausiosios Tarybos reglamentas [Regulations of the Supreme Soviet of LSSR]. 1985. In *Deputatų veiklos normatyviniai aktai*. Vilnius: Mintis, 109–28.

LTSR Aukščiausiosios Tarybos nuolatinių komisijų nuostatai [Rules of Standing Committees of the Supreme Soviet of LSSR]. 1985. In *Deputatų veiklos normatyviniai aktai*. Vilnius: Mintis, 151–61.

Lukošaitis, Alvidas. 1997. *Parlamentarizmo raidos etapai Lietuvoje. 1990–97 metai* [The Development of Parliamentarism in Lithuania]. 1990–1997. Vilnius: Seimo kanceliarija.

Žeruolis, Darius. 1998. "Lithuania." In *Handbook of Political Change in Eastern Europe,* edited by Sten Berglund, Frank Aarebrot and Thomas Hellen. Aldershot: Edward Elgar.

EIGHT

The Impact of Moldovan Parliamentary Committees on the Process of Institutionalization

Steven D. Roper

U NLIKE THE POLISH OR HUNGARIAN PARLIAMENTS, WHICH ARE very active institutions, the Moldovan parliament has not developed characteristics that provide for political autonomy and consolidation. The weakness of Moldovan parliamentary development is at least in part the consequence of an underdeveloped committee system. Based on the framework developed in chapter 1, this chapter examines the internal and external environment in which Moldovan committees function.

Party and Parliamentary Development in Moldova

Moldova's last census in 1989 reported a population of 4.2 million, with 65 percent ethnic Moldovans, 14 percent ethnic Ukrainians, and 13 percent ethnic Russians. Moldova's last Soviet-era parliament was also the country's first post-independence parliament. There was a direct institutional bridge between Moldova's communist past and democratic future. Moldova's last Soviet parliament was elected in spring 1990 and continued its activity until February 1994. This last Soviet parliament was elected during a period in which government authority was deteriorating while ethnic conflict was increasing. In August 1989, the Moldovan parliament, the Supreme Soviet, proclaimed Romanian, which uses the Latin alphabet, as the state language. This decision was supported by Communist Party reformers and opposed by the Russian-speaking community organized around the Edinstvo Movement.

This decision was particularly opposed by those Moldovans living in the heavily Russified areas of Transnistria (the left bank of the Dniester River) and what is now called Gagauzia (southern Moldova). Parliamentary elections were held in this ethnically polarized environment.

Unlike earlier elections to the Supreme Soviet, the spring 1990 elections were marked by generally fair and open competition. Opposition candidates had access to the media and were allowed to campaign. The 1990 electoral law maintained the Soviet practice of 380 single member districts. In districts in which a candidate did not receive 50 percent of the vote, there was a second-round election.

As evidenced by the 1989 language law, there was a strong pro-Romanian sentiment among many Moldovans. The pro-Romanian and pro-unionist party, the Popular Front, became the leading opposition party. This party also received tacit support from many communists, and several leading Popular Front candidates were actually ranking Communist Party members (Crowther and Roper 1996, 144). Following the election, the Popular Front entered into a coalition with several other parties and held over two-thirds of the parliamentary seats.

The 12th Parliament's first session opened in April 1990. This parliament's structure was based on the Soviet model, with a presidium that carried out legislative duties when the parliament was not in session. The leadership of the parliament and the government reflected the dominance of the Popular Front. During this period, the Popular Front pursued a pro-Romanian and pro-unionist agenda (in essence, Moldova's incorporation into Romania) that alienated the Russian minority. In August 1990, the Gagauzi (a Turkic Christian minority) announced the formation of their own republic followed shortly in September by the same announcement from Transnistrian authorities. This ethnic tension erupted into a civil war by May 1992.

By the end of the summer, a cease-fire was declared, but the Popular Front was perceived as largely responsible for the war. In August 1992, several changes within the Popular Front leadership increased the level of tension within the country and within parliament. Finally, parliament was dissolved and new elections for the 13th Parliament were held in February 1994.

Structural Attributes of the Moldovan Parliamentary Committee System

Several trends are becoming evident through analysis of data from the 13th Parliament (March 1994 through February 1998) and the 14th

Parliament (convened in April 1998). The number of seats in the 13th Parliament was dramatically reduced (from 380 to 101). In addition, the 13th Parliament continued to be unicameral. Each member was assigned to one committee.

In the 13th Parliament, there were ten permanent committees.[1] Eight of these committees had ministerial oversight responsibility. While some of these committees had oversight responsibility for just one ministry (e.g., Committee for State Security and Public Order), many of the committees oversaw several ministries (e.g., Committee on Culture, Science, Education and Mass Media). Overseeing multiple ministries places a massive resource and time burden on committees, and erodes the ability of the committee to oversee the government.

Committee membership ranged from six to thirteen members with an average of 9.2, among the lowest in the region. The Moldovan parliament has no subcommittee system. There are no formal subcommittees, and the standing orders do not provide for the formation of permanent subcommittees. Parliamentary parties often carry out work that might otherwise be done through subcommittees.

In the 14th Parliament, several changes were made in the committee system. While previously, members of the Permanent Bureau (the institution responsible for organizing parliamentary activity and committee work) were not allowed to hold committee assignments, Permanent Bureau members in the 14th Parliament were allowed to do so. One Permanent Bureau member actually held a leadership position on a legislative committee. Moreover, the Committee for Social Protection, Health Assistance and the Family counted two Permanent Bureau members among its numbers. The number of permanent committees was increased from ten to eleven.[2] This increase in the number of committees, coupled with a reduction of MPs, slightly decreased the average committee size to 8.9 (see Table 8.2). As in the previous parliament, over half of the committees had multiple ministerial oversight responsibilities, thus limiting their specialization. During the 13th Parliament, there were only six temporary special or investigatory committees on issues such as corruption, privatization and the criminal code. These inquiry or special committees were composed of both MPs and external experts.[3]

One of the complaints raised by Moldovan MPs is that there are too few committee staffers. For the 13th Parliament, there was an average of 3.4 staffers per committee. Considering the volume of bills and the relative small size of the committees, MPs do not have the staff necessary to provide expertise on legislation or assist in ministerial oversight.

Membership

Both the American and comparative literatures on legislatures recognize the central importance of committees. Much of the committee research examines the relationship between committees and the parent chamber in order to understand the distribution of power (Shepsle and Weingast 1987; Hall and Grofman 1990; Krehbiel 1991). Proponents of distributive theories of institutional power (Shepsle 1978; Weingast and Marshall 1988) maintain that committees are composed of preference outliers and that a committee system creates a system of binding jurisdictional agreements for purposes of reelection. Others such as Krehbiel (1991) argue that committees are developed to provide information to the parent chamber. Like Polsby (1968), Krehbiel argues that member specialization yields rewards for the entire organization. While these two perspectives differ, both attempt to understand how committees influence the institutionalization of organizations.

There are some obvious difficulties in applying a distributive model to committee assignments in the Moldova parliament. First, Moldova has been constructed as a single national district since the 1994 parliamentary elections (in 1990 the country did use single member districts). Because MPs are no longer elected from individual districts, the basis of representation has little to do with constituency service. Results of a June 1997 survey of Moldovan MPs in the 13th Parliament conducted by William Crowther and myself highlight the difficulties that result from this electoral system. While 41 percent responded that they represent their party's constituency, 11 percent stated that they represented their party, and almost 39 percent responded they represent the entire electorate.[4] In the 14th Parliament, almost 75 percent of MPs came from the capital, Chisinau. Because MPs are elected from a national single district with closed party lists, it is doubtful that committee preferences are motivated by reelection.

In many ways, parliamentary parties have supplanted committees as the locus of power within the parliament. Parliamentary parties not only exert considerable influence on the composition of committees, but they exert influence on voting in plenary sessions. A committee staff member noted that it was not uncommon for members of the committee to change their vote in plenary session because of the demands of the parliamentary party. The "gatekeeper" function so often attributed to committees in the U.S. congressional literature, resides with parliamentary parties in Moldova.

Because of this situation, it is not surprising that MPs have a negative view of committee power. Our survey of MPs found that over 45 percent regarded their committee's influence as either poor or very poor. In my interviews with Moldovan MPs, policy specialization and expertise were often given as a basis for committee assignments. One indicator of policy specialization is the background of committee members. If members are assigned to committees in which they already have prior expertise, then the committee assignments allow them to further specialize, providing support for the informational model of committee memberships (Krehbiel 1991). In the 14th Parliament, on the Committee for Economy, Industry and Privatization, for example, 60 percent of members were economists and 40 percent are industrial engineers. The Committee for Culture, Science, Education and Mass Media contained 71 percent academicians and 29 percent journalists or other writers. The process of policy specialization was further increased because Moldovan MPs were assigned to only one committee.

The development of policy expertise takes time, and unfortunately in Moldova there is a high rate of committee turnover. During the 13th Parliament, the committee membership turnover rate was 40 percent.[5] This high turnover rate affected all committees. Such a high turnover rate has a negative impact on the ability of MPs to further develop policy specialization, and as a result members also develop a negative attitude towards the committee system itself. In our survey of MPs, over 30 percent believed that the activity of committees was inefficient or very inefficient.

The overall turnover rate for the 13th Parliament was 70 percent, and the rate for the 14th Parliament was 75 percent. As a consequence, in the 14th Parliament there was not an incumbent in two of the eleven committees, including the important Committee for Budget and Finance. Based on our survey responses, the three committees considered most important only averaged 20 percent membership incumbency. In the three most important committees, 80 percent were new members with no parliamentary experience.

Party Composition

Party representation on Moldovan committees deviates from proportionality. For example, in the 14th Parliament there were four parliamentary groups: The Bloc of the Democratic Convention of Moldova (BCDM), the Bloc for a Democratic and Prosperous Moldova (BMDP), and the Party of Democratic Forces (PFD) formed a parliamentary coalition called the Alliance for Democratic Reform with just over 60 percent of parliamentary seats. The Party of Communists of the Republic of Moldova (PCRM) was the fourth party.

As previously noted, the organization responsible for committee assignments is the Permanent Bureau. The Permanent Bureau has historically been composed of nine members (three members of the parliament's presidency and six members from the parliamentary parties chosen by proportional representation). The Permanent Bureau is responsible for directing parliamentary activity and works in consultation with the parliament's presidency, parliamentary parties, and committees. The Permanent Bureau oversees the administration of the parliament, including committee and general staff.

Committee assignments and committee leadership positions are determined by parliamentary party negotiation. The Permanent Bureau sometimes has to modify the parliamentary party choices because of a disagreement between parties.[6] There was substantial deviation from party proportionality in the committees of the 14th Parliament. For example, while the PFD should have 10 percent of the committee assignments, there were two committees in which the PFD had no representation. Even more surprising, the BMDP, which had 25 percent of the parliamentary seats, had no representation on the Committee for Control and Petitions. In fact, the composition of almost every committee deviated from party proportionality, partly due to the small number of members on each committee. These committee assignments reflected party preferences. For example, the BMDP was most overrepresented on the powerful Committee for Budget and Finance.

In the 13th Parliament, defections from parliamentary parties had a significant impact on committee representation. By the end of the last session of the 13th Parliament, approximately 25 percent of MPs had left their parliamentary party, including several committee presidents and vice presidents.[7] The numerous parliamentary party defections are not surprising, given the general attitude towards parliamentary parties among many MPs. In our survey of the 13th Parliament, over 35 percent indicated that the activity of their parliamentary party was poor or very poor. Because the Moldovan parliament, like many parliaments in this region, does not allow for the creation of new parliamentary parties after the first sitting, independent members had no party affiliation in committee (as in Romania).

Committee leadership positions are also supposed to be assigned based on party proportional representation. Each committee has a president (chairperson), vice president (several committees have more than one), and a secretary, proposed by parliamentary parties. However in the 13th Parliament, there was substantial deviation from proportionality in

Table 8.1

Party Share of Committee Officer Positions with Changes in the 13th Moldovan Parliament, 1994–1998

	Officer Positions		
Party	February 1994	January 1998	Change ±
Democratic Agrarian Party of Moldova (PADM)	26	13	–13
Socialist Party and Movement Unity Edinstvo (PSMUE)	5	9	+4
Bloc of Peasants and Intellectuals (BTI)	0	0	0
Christian Democrat Popular Front Alliance (AFPCD)	0	0	0
Independents	0	13	+13
Total	31	35	+4

Table 8.2

Comparison of the 13th and 14th Moldovan Parliaments

Factors	13th Parliament	14th Parliament
Number of Seats	104	101
Number of Committees	10	11
Average Number of Committee Members	9.2	8.9
Turnover Rate (%)	70.0	75.0
Deviation from Proportionality for Committee Presidencies (%)	26.5	5.0

the assignment of committee presidencies (see Table 8.1). Approximately 26.5 percent of committee presidencies were shifted from some parliamentary parties to other parties, particularly to the ruling Democratic Agrarian Party of Moldova (PDAM).[8] In the 14th Parliament, by contrast, the committee presidencies were generally assigned based on parliamentary party proportionality. There was only a 5 percent shift in committee presidencies (see Table 8.2). While the principle of proportionality in the 14th Parliament was violated in the membership of committees, the Permanent Bureau ensured parliamentary party proportional representation in committee leadership positions.

While committee leadership positions in the 14th Parliament were based on proportionality, the importance of committees to which MPs were assigned varied by party. In our survey of the 13th Parliament, the Committee for Legal Affairs, Appointments and Immunities, the Committee for Economy, Industry and Privatization, the Committee for Budget and Finance, the Committee for Human Rights and National Minorities, and the Committee for Agriculture and Industry Processing were considered the most important. In the 14th Parliament, the PCRM had the most committee presidencies (four), but it did not hold the presidency on any of these important committees. The ruling coalition excluded the PCRM from these key committee leadership positions. Instead, the PCRM was given the presidency of committees such as the Committee for Youth, Sports and Tourism and the Committee for Control and Petitions.

Power from Procedures and Rules

All Moldovan MPs have the right to initiate legislation. All draft legislation must be submitted to the Permanent Bureau, which is responsible for creating the legislative agenda. Draft legislation is then distributed immediately to all MPs; however, it is not assigned to a committee until fifteen days later. Unlike most other parliaments, the Moldovan parliament requires every committee to examine draft legislation. While each committee has a primary jurisdiction, each draft goes to every permanent committee for review before the first reading. The Permanent Bureau determines which committee will be designated as the "primary committee," and which committees are advisory. Every "advisory committee" must issue a report.[9]

Committee meetings occur on Tuesday, Wednesday, and Thursday afternoons for three hours. The standing orders provide for closed meetings; although committees can allow the media to attend. Government officials may as a rule attend committee meetings. MPs with amendments to draft legislation have the right to attend meetings, but they do not have the right to vote in committee.

The Permanent Bureau decides the amount of time a committee has to review a draft. While primary committees have up to fifteen days to review drafts, it is normal for a committee to take no more than five days.[10] Moreover, all drafts must be reported out of committee to the Permanent Bureau. No committee can refuse to report a draft to the plenum. While many drafts are unanimously approved, the standing orders allow for minority reports. Because of the large number of drafts, there is no time to carefully consider legislation. One staff member labeled committees and the parliament a "law machine."[11]

The committee report must contain four sections: First, the committee must address the urgency of the legislative issue. Second, the committee must comment on the integrity of the draft's solution in respect to the "sphere of social relations" (*Parlamentul Republicii Moldova* 1996, 55).

Third, the committee must examine the economic and political impact of the draft. The committee can only make modifications to the draft with the author's consent. While the primary committee has much more influence in the legislative process, advisory committees issue reports that can serve as the basis for subsequent amendments.

Another example of the erosion of committee jurisdiction involves committee participation. The standing orders provide the president of a committee the opportunity to participate in the proceedings of another committee. While a primary committee report may request two or three readings of a draft, ultimately it is the Permanent Bureau, not the primary committee, that establishes the number of readings.

Committee Activity

Measuring post-communist committee activity can be very difficult because of poor record keeping. In countries such as Moldova, with limited parliamentary experience, maintaining a legislative history has not been a priority. Especially for early sessions (1992 and 1993), there is a lack of data on committee activity. Most of the data available provide only an imprecise measure of committee activity. However, the data allow us to compare the activity between committees.

The data for the first four sessions (March 29, 1994–December 26, 1995) of the 13th Parliament indicate that certain committees were more active than others in reviewing laws and decrees (referred to as parliamentary documents). The three most active committees included the Committee for Legal Affairs, Appointments and Immunities (156 documents), the Committee for Budget and Finance (141 documents), and the Committee for Economy, Industry and Privatization (107 documents).[12] While all committees must review legislation, these committees were most often designated as the primary committee. As previously noted, these three committees were considered by Moldovan MPs to be the most important. The least active committees included the Committee for Control and Petitions (thirteen documents), the Committee for Human Rights and National Minorities (fifteen documents) and the Committee for Agriculture and Industry processing (thirty-one documents). In the fifth session of the 13th Parliament, 98.5 percent of reported committee documents (either drafts or decrees) were adopted by the parliament (some with and without amendments).[13] Because of the influence of party factions at the committee level, agreement between committees and the chamber indicates the supremacy of the chamber (i.e., party faction leaders) over committees in the legislative process.

Government Relations

One of the complaints raised by many MPs is that the government and president have too much influence in the legislative process.[14] For example during the first four sessions of the 13th Parliament, 592 legislative drafts and decisions were considered. Out of this total, the government initiated 78 percent. Not only is the government the most active branch, government initiatives were adopted by the parliament at a higher rate than initiatives proposed by members (79 percent compared to 68 percent). The influence of the Moldovan government in the legislative process follows a general Western European pattern, in which the legislative process in Europe is often dominated by the cabinet (Olson 1994).

Members do not have the right to compel government officials to provide information during committee meetings. As a consequence, most information gathering occurs at plenary sessions devoted to questions and interpellations. Several MPs have argued that these sessions do not provide effective control of government officials. The written responses of government officials to questions submitted by the plenary were considered insufficient.[15]

A Case Study of the Committee System: Public Administration Reform

One of the most important issues facing the parliament over the last few years has been reform of local government. During the 13th Parliament, the International Monetary Fund (IMF) placed great importance on the reorganization of Moldovan local government. The IMF urged the adoption of a draft law that would significantly reduce the number of territorial units and thus provide a cost savings to the central government. During the 13th Parliament, MPs refused to pass the legislation. Some MPs feared that a consolidation of local administrative units would result in a loss of political power at the local level.

Territorial reform was one of the significant issues during the 1998 elections, and several parties favored the proposed reform. The Permanent Bureau of the 14th Parliament placed this issue high on the legislative agenda; however, rather than reexamining the drafts that had already gone through committee during the 13th Parliament, the drafts that were ultimately submitted to the 14th Parliament were initiated by the government. Once again the government, rather than committee members, originated important legislation.

The Legal Affairs, Appointments and Immunities Committee was delegated primary authority over the public administration drafts. The committee considered a draft on local public administration and administrative-territorial reform. Eugen Rusu, president of the committee, was responsible for gathering the proposals from the advisory committees and issuing the committee's report. This report was presented in a plenary session and approved by the parliament in December 1998.

Immediately after the bill was approved, President Lucinschi voiced concerns over the new administrative structure and vetoed the bill. He argued that the bill failed to create a separate administrative unit for the country's ethnic Bulgarians. He proposed the creation of an administrative county in the Taraclia area (where most of the country's ethnic Bulgarians reside). However, the parliament reconfirmed its prior vote and the law on administrative reorganization was promulgated in December 1998.

During 1999, there was a great deal of discussion concerning the creation of a separate Taraclia county. The government established a commission to examine the status of ethnic Bulgarians in this area, and the Council of Europe also sent representatives to investigate the issue. Lucinschi and members of the BMDP and the PCDM supported amending the administrative reorganization law, and in October 1999 the government submitted to parliament an amendment to the law. Committee President Rusu, a member of the BCDM, argued that the government's position was politically motivated. Moreover, he stated that those MPs who supported the amendment risked destroying the parliamentary coalition. The amendment was passed by the parliament in October. However, because of Rusu's objections, the issue was placed on the plenary agenda by the Permanent Bureau without full examination by his committee. Party power rather than committee power was fundamental to the passage of the law and the amendment. This provides a further example of how the plenary and the parliamentary leadership control committee power.

Conclusion

Several features of the Moldovan committee system hinder the development of parliamentary institutionalization. First, the turnover rate of the parliament and committees limits the ability of members to develop policy expertise. As a consequence, policy formation becomes concentrated in the government. While this is a general feature of parliamentary (and even semi-presidential) systems, the lack of policy specialization undermines the authority of members, committees, and ultimately the parliament.

Second, the small size of Moldovan committees and lack of staff support limit the ability of committees to oversee the government and to perform effectively. Committees are inundated with drafts that they must report out. The lack of personnel and resources constrains MPs and provides a motivation for expediting legislation without extensive discussion. As previously noted, drafts are often reported out of committee in five days. The deliberative function which parliaments serve is thwarted in Moldova because of a lack of resources and small committees. As a consequence, Moldova does not fit either a distributive or informational model of parliamentary committee organization.

Third, much of the legislative process occurs in parliamentary party meetings and plenary sessions, and therefore committee power is supplanted by these other organizations. Moldovan MPs consider committees ineffective in the legislative process because of the power of parliamentary parties. Committees could provide members autonomy from parliamentary parties and the chamber. Parliamentary parties are often accountable to institutions outside of the parliament (e.g., party leadership, government or presidency). Because of the need for a vote of confidence, party discipline supplants member or institutional autonomy.

Without a developed committee system, the Moldovan parliament loses its autonomy to the government and even to the president. Most drafts come from the government, and the government is able to pass its legislative agenda. Until the parliament concentrates on developing the committee system and consequentially becomes more institutionalized, other political institutions will continue to exert primary influence on the creation of policy.

Notes

This research was made possible by the financial support of a Fulbright Fellowship to Moldova. I want to thank Andrei Onea and Ion Umaniuk of the Foreign Relations Division of the Moldovan parliament for all their assistance. I also want to thank Dr. Yuri Josanu for his support.

1. The ten permanent committees during the 13th Parliament included the Committee for Legal Affairs, Appointments and Immunities; the Committee for Economy, Industry and Privatization; the Committee for Budget and Finance; the Committee for State Security and Public Order; the Committee for Foreign Policy; the Committee for Human Rights and National Minorities; the Committee for Agriculture and Industry Processing; the Committee for Culture, Science, Education and Mass Media; the Committee for Social Protection, Health Assistance and Ecology; and the Committee for Control and Petitions.

2. The Committee for Youth, Sports and Tourism was added during the 14th Parliament.
3. Interview with Tudor Olaru, Permanent Bureau Secretary for the 13th Parliament, Chisinau, November 1997.
4. This data set will be deposited at the Parliamentary Documents Center at the University of North Carolina–Greensboro.
5. Some of this turnover was due to members becoming part of the government or assuming a leadership position in the parliament. The Moldovan constitution does not allow an MP to simultaneously hold a government office, and by January 1, 1996, fifteen members had resigned their position. In addition, the 13th Parliament standing orders did not allow members to hold parliamentary leadership positions.
6. Interview with Tudor Olaru, Permanent Bureau Secretary for the 13th Parliament, Chisinau, November 1997.
7. By the end of the last session of the 13th Parliament, four committee presidents and one acting president had either resigned or were expelled from their parliamentary party.
8. I calculated the deviation from proportionality for committee presidencies based on the general formula for deviation from proportionality: $D = (1/2) \sum |s_i - cp_i|$ where D stands for total deviation, $\sum$ stands for the summation across all parliamentary parties, s_i stands for the percentage of parliamentary seats for the i-th parliamentary party, and cp_i stands for the percentage of committee presidencies for the i-th parliamentary party.
9. Most advisory committees will issue a statement saying: "We have no recommendation for this draft." Sometimes they might issue a substantive statement.
10. The standing orders provide advisory committees ten days in which to issue their report.
11. Interview with staffers from the Committee for Budget and Finance and the Committee for Foreign Policy, May 1997.
12. The Committee for Foreign Policy also had proposed 107 legislative documents.
13. I want to thank Ion Umaniuk for providing me these data.
14. This complaint was voiced by many MPs at a workshop entitled "On the Aspects of Parliamentary Practice: The Organization and Activities of Parliament and the Relations Between Parliament and Government," Chisinau, Moldova. February 27–March 1, 1997.
15. The number of government ministries was reduced in May 1998 from twenty to thirteen. This change should assist the parliament in performing its oversight duty.

References

Crowther, William, and Steven D. Roper. 1996. "A Comparative Analysis of Institutional Development in the Romanian and Moldovan Legislatures." *Journal of Legislative Studies* 2:133–60.
Hall, Richard L., and Bernard Grofman. 1990. "The Committee Assignment

Process and the Conditional Nature of Committee Bias." *American Political Science Review* 84:1149–66.

Krehbiel, Keith. 1991. *Information and Legislative Organization.* Ann Arbor: University of Michigan Press.

Olson, David M. 1994. *Democratic Legislative Institutions.* Armonk, N.Y.: M. E. Sharpe.

Parlamentul Republicii Moldova. 1996. Chisinau: Fotojurnalist.

Polsby, Nelson W. 1968. "The Institutionalization of the U.S. House of Representatives." *American Political Science Review* 62:144–68.

Shepsle, Kenneth A. 1978. *The Giant Jigsaw Puzzle.* Chicago: University of Chicago Press.

Shepsle, Kenneth A., and Barry R. Weingast. 1987. "The Institutional Foundations of Committee Power." *American Political Science Review* 81:85–104.

Weingast, Barry R., and William J. Marshall. 1988. "The Industrial Organization of Congress." *Journal of Political Economy* 96:132–63.

PART **5**

Varieties of
Parliamentary Committees

NINE

Committee Systems in New Democratic Parliaments: Comparative Institutionalization

William E. Crowther and David M. Olson

T HE PREVIOUS CHAPTERS COMPARE AND CONTRAST THE COM-
mittee systems among newly democratized parliaments in seven
post-communist parliaments. Our theoretical base, the concept of institutionalization, provides an analytic framework to comprehend the development of new legislative structures and functions. We emphasize the
opportunities to understand the early stages of legislative institutionalization with data across several newly activated parliaments in new democracies that are in their own beginning stages.

As agents of parliaments, committees have the twin objectives of first,
sharing power, and second, performing work tasks. The more important
and efficient the committees as work organizations, the more important
they become for political parties and executives to control. Committees, as
work structures, raise all of the questions of representation and power internal to parliaments, which parliaments themselves attempt to answer in
their wider societies.

This chapter develops three broad categories of degrees of legislative
institutionalization and examines the causal factors in differential institutional development. In the concluding sections, we develop a sequential
analysis of committee institutionalization, and relate that analysis to the
major strands of current committee research.

Patterns of Institutionalization

To understand the processes of institutional formation and adaptation in new democratic post-communist parliaments, we employ seven sets of indicators of committee system institutionalization. We then suggest several hypotheses to account for emerging differences among post-communist legislatures.

In keeping with the comparative empirical basis of the first chapter (chapter 1, Appendix 1.1), we locate our analysis in the research on Western European parliaments. Our indicators of committee system institutionalization drawing from the work of Döring (1995) and Lees and Shaw (1979) include:

1. Committee Structural Attributes
2. Membership Characteristics
3. Party System
4. Committee Relationships with Parliamentary Parties
5. Committee Autonomy
6. Floor Control
7. Government Relations

The new parliaments differ on the seven institutionalization indicators, summarized in Appendix 9.1 of this chapter, as described in our accounts of each of the Central European parliaments.

1. Structure

The committee systems of the new democracies of Central Europe tend to resemble those of the established parliaments of Western Europe in structure. The committees are permanent, tend to parallel the structure of ministries, and tend to number ten to twenty committees per chamber.

Principles of Organization. Central European parliamentary committees do vary in the degree to which they are parallel to the ministries, and also in the extent to which they use both special committees and subcommittees.

The agency-parallel principle is not strictly followed in the Central European parliaments. Contemporary policy topics cross-cut the usual distinctions among the governmental ministries, and further, it is possible for committees and any one ministry to become too closely related for the committee to exercise independent judgment.

One practical reason for the lack of complete parallelism is that the ministries themselves are in flux, which is yet another example of constant change in new democracies. The committees of the Czech Chamber of Deputies, for example, are much more stable than are the ministries. Committees can develop an experience and expertise with policy and process independently, and in spite, of flux within the government.

Instability of governmental structure also plagued the work of the committees in Lithuania's post-communist legislature. Not only were changes in government persons and parties frequent, but they were also accompanied by changes in ministerial structure. Relationships between ministries and corresponding committees were broken, and oversight responsibilities frequently shifted from one committee to another. Yet, in general, policy committees do concentrate on a limited range of ministries, so that each can review budget requests for "its" ministries.

Instability of ministerial structure is a constant problem in the formation of committees in all democratic legislative bodies. The Norwegian parliament's committee system, for example, was restructured in 1993, in part because of variations in the number and jurisdiction of ministries (Rommedtvedt 1998a, 69).

Furthermore, all parliaments examined here have at least some permanent committees that are explicitly transagency in jurisdiction. The preeminent example is the Budget Committee, illustrated by both Hungary and the Czech Republic. For detailed review of segments of the budget, relevant portions are delegated to the other committees with a policy sector and ministry jurisdiction, but they, in turn, report to the integrative Budget Committee, which has lead responsibility to report to the plenum. This type of committee is likewise found in many established democratic parliaments.

The committee concerned with justice and law is another example of a transministry committee. While that committee does have a corresponding ministry (as does the Budget Committee), its jurisdiction is far broader than the single ministry. This committee in several of the post-communist parliaments is an inheritor of communist system practice, in which a single committee, often called the Legislative Committee, held joint jurisdiction with all other committees for technical review of the legal text (Olson and Simon 1982).

In practice, its wide policy scope permitted that committee to become the main source of policy coordination among several committees as the newly democratized parliaments coped with system transformation policy far broader than any one ministry and any one committee. As a direct consequence, however, that same committee was criticized as either a center of power or an obstacle to progress, as in both Hungary and Bulgaria. The Czech Chamber of Deputies has transformed the jurisdiction of that committee, making it more similar to the other committees in its scope of policy and thus position of power within the parliament.

In addition to the permanent policy committees, there are several organizational innovations in the post-communist parliaments, including special committees and subcommittees.

Numerous special committees have been created to cope with immediate problems. While some have been concerned with policy problems and legislation, most have been investigatory. They are sometimes, as in Bulgaria, more often suggested by the minority than approved by the majority. As a result, however, the total number of groupings of members with official status and responsibilities is far larger than our initial number of "committees."

Subcommittees are much more variable in structure, composition, and function among the new parliaments than are standing committees. Just as committees are thought to be more flexible and innovative than the whole chamber, so subcommittees are in some cases becoming locations of innovation and improvisation in the committee systems of newly democratized parliaments. Most subcommittees are temporary; they are expedients to meet immediate needs, and thus are flexible and variable within a single legislature, and much more so among them all.

In the early Czech Chamber of Deputies, subcommittees had external members, in addition to deputies. Dissatisfaction with the influence of external members lead to a restructuring of the committee system as part of broader rules changes. Several of our reports indicate that subcommittees are an opportunity for external participants, whether as "experts" or lobbyists, to work closely with legislators.

The Polish Sejm makes a distinctive use of ad hoc subcommittees: they are a means of multicommittee coordination. When two or more committees share jurisdiction over a bill, they create a special subcommittee of members from each of the parent committees to recommend a common version (Olson et al. 1998), as is also the case with the "desiderata" oversight procedure. Czech permanent subcommittees are also used to coordinate among several main committees on selected topics.

In contrast to these more clearly institutionalized committee systems, subcommittees have had extremely limited use in some of our cases. In Bulgaria, for example, subcommittees have not been established. While early rules provided for this contingency, the rules were altered in the 38th Parliament to eliminate even the possibility of subcommittees.

Number of Committees and of Committee Positions. The number of committees per parliament (or chamber in bicameral systems) ranges from

Table 9.1

Number, Seats, and Size Range of Committees: Selected Central European Parliaments

Parliament and Chamber			Committees		
Name	Size	Number	Net Change in Number	Total Number of Seats	Size Range
Bulgaria	240	20	-4	312	17 to 34
Czech Republic					
Deputies	200	12	1	222	11 to 26
Senate	81	8	0	98	9 to 11
Estonia	101	10	0	97	7 to 12
Hungary	386	19	9	375	8 to 27
Lithuania	141	13	0	158	8 to 13
Moldova	101	11	1	92	6 to 13
Poland					
Sejm	460	27	3	770	4 to 41
Senate	100	15	6	190	8 to 20

Notes:

1. Time period is middle of 1990s, usually in the third democratic term of office of Central European parliaments.
2. Number is at beginning of term.

Sources: Membership Directories for each parliament and data supplied by authors in this volume.

eight to twenty-seven. The Czech Senate has the fewest; the Polish Sejm the most (see Table 9.1).

The number of committees has not increased markedly in the initial post-communist decade, though their jurisdiction, scope of activity, and composition are completely altered from those of the communist inheritance. The greatest changes in number of committees has occurred in Bulgaria, in consequence of changes in governments and their supporting majority coalitions in parliament. Considerable change has also occurred in Hungary and the Czech Republic as a result of restructuring of the committee system. Change through deliberate restructuring, rather than from government majority preference, is an important indicator of differential degrees of institutionalization in the committee system.

The total number of committee positions approximates the size of the parliament. Only in the Polish Sejm are committee seats almost double the chamber size. In most parliaments, the change in total number of committee positions has been modest over the decade. Large changes have occurred in Bulgaria (decrease) and Hungary (increase) resulting from committee restructuring.

Not all parliament members are eligible for committee memberships, however. Chamber officers (Speaker, Vice Speakers) are usually precluded from committee membership, as are government ministers even if they remain MPs, as in both Poland and the Czech Republic. On the other hand, the frequent changes in Estonian governments were responsible for a considerable share of changes in the working membership of the entire parliament. When serving as ministers, elected MPs were replaced in parliament by substitute members. Either way, the practice that ministers come from parliament, especially in small parliaments with rapid changes in governments and in ministerial structure, create extreme conditions of personnel instability. In keeping with Western European practices, the Central European parliaments are attempting to define distance between themselves and the governments they create.

Size Range of Committees. Both within and across parliaments, committees vary in size. The largest committees are in Bulgaria and the Polish Sejm, while the smallest are in Lithuania and Estonia. There is a considerable size range within each parliament, however, by at least a factor of two. Though the number of committees has changed in several parliaments, the size range has been fairly constant within any one parliament. The largest change in size range occurred in Hungary with restructuring of the committee system. The small size of some parliaments (e.g., Czech Senat, Estonian Riigikogu, and Moldovan Parliament) sharply limits both the number of committees and their size.

Both number and size of committees are relevant to the prior consideration of ministry parallelism. In the Czech Republic, for example, there are more ministries than committees. To increase the number of committees would require either a reduction of their size or an increase in the number of committee memberships for individual members.

Numbers of committees, and size of committees relative to the size of the parliamentary chamber, suggest limitations on the capacity of a committee system to accomplish the twin objective of sharing power and performing work tasks. If small committee size might increase efficiency, small size limits the ability of the committee to handle a large number of tasks simultaneously. Small size also limits the capacity of individual members to develop specializations. Small size could also limit diversity, partisan or otherwise, among the members. That is, committees themselves, as discussed in the Polish chapter, have a representative function in the sharing and allocation of power within parliament.

Summary. Though parliaments vary in the extent to which their committees exactly parallel the ministry structure, this consideration does not correspond to differential degrees of institutionalization. With the exception of a very large (or very small) number of committees, the number of committees likewise does not differentiate among categories of parliaments. If small size of committees militates against the achievement of either distributional or informational objectives, the experience of new parliaments suggests that large size, by itself, is not a guarantee of either.

The variety of committees, and changes in the sheer number of committees, however, are indicators of institutionalization. Both diversity and changing number (usually growing) of committees create problems of co-ordination and time management among parliamentary deputies. The response to confusion has been rules changes.

The attempt to clarify the types of committees by both structure and function, to systematize their relationship to the full chamber, and to reduce their numbers is a response by some parliaments which, in itself, is evidence of growing institutionalization. Hungary and the Czech Republic parliaments are prime examples. Poland also has a relatively stable set of committees, not through post-communist rules changes, but through pre-democratic system evolution. Western European parliaments, too, systematically restructure their committee systems, though within a much longer period of time of thought and experimentation, as illustrated by Britain, Norway, and Sweden (Jogerst 1993; Rommedvedt 1998a; Hagevi 1998).

2. Committee Membership

Continuity of committee membership, joined with permanence of committees, provide more powerful indicators of differential degrees of institutionalization.

Number of Committee Assignments. The sheer number of committee positions relative to the size of parliament affects the use of member time. The large number of committee positions in Slovenia, as an example beyond our set of parliaments, coupled with the parliament's small size, means that each member serves on four committees (Zajc 1997). Time is a scarce resource both for individual Members and for parliamentary work groups. The difficulty in meeting quorum requirements, a constant problem for committees in most of the new parliaments, is exacerbated when members belong to two or more committees. In practice, legislators seldom belong to more than two specialized policy committees in Western Europe, though in few are there formal restrictions (Mattson and Stroem 1995, 271; Damgaard 1995, 311).

Not all members are eligible to be considered for multiple committee assignments. Committee chairpersons are frequently precluded from membership on a second committee. They are also sometimes limited in the number of subcommittees they join. On the other hand, the members of small parties carry a special burden; they are needed to cover several committees.

The tendency in the new parliaments is toward single committee assignments. But in Hungary, those deputies who do belong to two committees are a special subset of members. They are distinctively incumbents and are leading persons in their parties and in the chamber. They are, however, concentrated in the nongovernment parties, for the leaders of government parties often have become ministers.

Incumbency. Stability of committee membership may be expected to be the norm, at least within a single electoral term, for the permanent committees of Western Europe. Continued reelection also produces incumbency in established parliaments, leading to a selection criterion for committee chairs. In Sweden, for example, the average tenure of committee chairs in 1980, and also of vice chairs, was almost twenty years (Olson et. al. 1983, 364). Incumbency in the stable parliament of Norway, however, has been declining over the past two decades, while increasing in Germany (Rommedvedt 1998b; Saalfeld 1997, 41).

In Central Europe, members of parliament are continuously new. There has been a high turnover of membership in their two to four democratic elections. How is a parliament affected when typically half of the membership is perpetually new, particularly when the parliament itself is very new? Committees can develop a stable core of experienced members, but only within the limits imposed by the reservoir of experience in the whole chamber (Ágh 1998, 93).

In the new parliaments, there are two types of incumbencies for committees and their members, which greatly complicate our understanding and measurement of that term. One is chamber incumbency, our usual macro-level measure, while the other is committee incumbency, a micro-level trait. In stable parliaments, these two incumbency measures have tended to be identical, while in the new post-communist parliaments, they differ from one another. In the new parliaments, committees vary greatly in their incumbency rates on both measures, and the two measures do not coincide on any one committee.

Table 9.2 shows the committees with the highest proportion of chamber-incumbent members in several parliaments. For all of our newly democratized parliaments, the incumbency rate on the committee—the members of a committee in one term who had served on the same committee in the previous term—is lower than is the chamber incumbency proportion for the members of the same committees.

Table 9.2

Chamber and Committee Incumbency by Committee, by Selected Central European Parliaments and Committees by Terms

Parliament	Term	Chamber Incumbency %	Committees	Committee Size	Incumbency % Chamber	Incumbency % Committee
Bulgaria	37th		Human Rights	17	59	41
			Foreign Policy and European Integration	31	55	32
	38th	30.3	National Security	31	52	16
			Foreign Policy	25	44	20
			Culture and Media	17	29	6
			Agriculture	25	20	16
Czech Chamber Of Deputies	1996–98	51.0	Foreign Affairs	20	65.0	15.0
			Budget	20	60.0	40.0
			Mandate/Immunity	12	58.3	33.3
Estonia	1995	49.0	National Defense	7	71.0	43.0
			Environment	7	71.0	43.0
			Legal Affairs	10	70.0	30.0
Hungary	1995–97	36	Social Organization	16	56	6
			Culture	19	53	32
			Immunity	10	50	10
Moldova	1998–01	25	Legal Affairs, Appointments and Immunities	10	33	33
			Economy, Industry	10	33	33
Poland	1997	48.6	Education, Science, and Youth	35		38.4
			Health	29		28.5
			Social Policy	36		27.5

Notes:

Three highest committees in chamber incumbency of members are listed.

Committee size for Estonia includes all persons who served on committee in a single term.

Sources: Membership Directories and data supplied by authors in this volume.

The difference in the two incumbency rates suggests several questions about committees. In the Czech Chamber of Deputies, for example, the high chamber experience of the Foreign Affairs Committee, coupled with the low rate of continuous committee service, suggests that experienced members, rather than newcomers, are placed on that committee (or actively seek membership on that committee). Either way, the result is to lower the committee-experience rate on their previous committees. The obverse question is: what happens to former members of the Foreign Affairs Committee? In the same parliament, the Budget Committee has the highest rate of continuous service on the committee. It may be that parties place on the Budget Committee some of their important members who then are reelected.

While there is a consistency across terms within each parliament for the high incumbency committees, there is no apparent policy or jurisdictional pattern across parliaments, with the exception of international affairs (e.g., Defense) and internal power (e.g., Immunity).

The percentage rates for small committees in small chambers are greatly affected by idiosyncratic events and decisions, as in Estonia. But small committees within larger chambers can be powerful committees, illustrated by the Mandate and Immunity Committee in many parliaments. Its high chamber experienced membership in the Czech Chamber of Deputies, coupled with low committee experience, may reflect attributes of party leadership—high electoral security, but frequent changes of persons in those positions.

Of particular significance is the incumbency of committee leadership, which tends to outrank that of ordinary members, as in Bulgaria. Ilonzski's examination of Hungary highlights this pattern. Committee membership has become increasingly meaningful to members of the Hungarian legislature. Incumbency rates, for example, are greater for some committees than for the legislature as a whole. Chamber incumbency is higher yet for MPs with multiple committee memberships, and for those with leadership positions on the committees.

Incumbency rates both for small committees and for small parties are greatly affected by the swings in election returns. Within the initial democratic decade in Central Europe, governments are typically defeated in the next election. The previously large and thus government parties are greatly reduced in size, while the previously small and thus opposition parties balloon in size with newcomers. The paradoxical result is that the new government parties have the largest share of inexperienced members, while the new opposition parties have a larger proportion of incumbents as both members and former ministers.

Mid-Session Stability. In some parliaments, the membership of committees changes within a single term; there is stability of membership neither across terms nor within any one term. Estonia, Moldova, and Lithuania, parliaments of low institutionalization, all especially have a high turnover in committee membership within a single term. In these parliaments, the persistence of committee names across terms is illusory. Committee membership within a single term is markedly more stable in the more institutionalized committees of Central Europe.

Attendance and Skills. Many of the new parliaments complain of committee attendance. This behavior is linked both to the number of committees each member belongs to, and to individual member aptitudes and skills. In all post-communist parliaments, the frequent lack of member interest in a committee's jurisdiction contributes to member lassitude and indifference. Some of our accounts stress that members with relevant past education and current occupation concentrate in certain committees. It is precisely their education and occupation which give them a self-interest to participate in their committees. Their skills motivate them to high attendance and equip them to make sound decisions. These positive considerations are stressed in our accounts of low institutionalization parliaments.

In the Polish Sejm and Czech Chamber of Deputies, however, comparatively institutionalized parliaments, the same traits are associated with insider lobbying. The personal affiliations of deputies may constitute a form of "unlicensed" lobby presence and action, as noted in Hungary (Ágh 1998, 90). In a more positive interpretation, it was precisely the energy and initiative of members that stimulated the Sejm committees to be active in administrative review through the unique device of "desiderata."

Some committees have had outside members; non-deputies have become participating and voting members of committees or subcommittees. In Moldova, external persons can be members of special purpose committees. This practice was curtailed in Hungary, for example, through rules changes, and also in the Czech Chamber of Deputies. Limitation of the use of external members was one way to reduce the overt opportunity for insider influence through the committee system. Definition and limitation of this type of committee member is another indicator of increasing institutionalization of the committee system.

Constituency. The degree of constituency relevance to committees, rather than only personal member involvement in committee work, is noted in Western European parliaments (Rommedvedt 1998b; Patzelt 1997, 60–61; Damgaard 1997, 82). The constituency connection, however, was almost completely missing in the post-communist parliaments.

Though both Western and Central European parliaments are elected through proportional representation in large districts, the members of

Western parliaments are attentive to district concerns, while the members of post-communist parliaments are characterized as responsive much more to party leaders than to district voters. Even in the Polish Sejm, with its attention to administrative review, with many of the problems specific to single locales, the district connection was a missing factor in committee activity and member involvement. The distributional perspective on committees is apparently not characteristic of the new parliaments.

Summary. Both chamber and committee member incumbency has been low in the early transition period across Central Europe. This characteristic in itself is hardly surprising, given the high degree of party and electoral instability. Incumbency appears to be be increasing over time, suggesting both the increasing importance vested in committees and increasing stability in the political environment. It may be that incumbency in both chamber and committee across terms will vary more among post-communist parliaments in the second decade than in the first, and would thus become a more useable indicator of institutionalization. Member stability within a single term, and the use of external members, are more apparent indicators of differential institutionalization in committees in the initial decade of post-communist democratic parliaments.

3. Political Parties and the Committee System: Composition

The importance of committees to parliamentary parties is clearly indicated by party composition of both members and officers in the committees. The committee system itself is a negotiated result of interparty deliberations, expressed as decisions of the whole chamber in the adoption of Rules (Soltesz 1995, 65).

The new democratic parliaments usually allocate committee memberships to parliamentary parties on the basis of proportionality. Application of the same distributional principle to committee officers, however, is much more variable.

Members. Committee memberships in Western Europe are usually proportional to party size in the parent chamber, reflecting a consensual rather than majoritarian approach to this potentially contentious issue (Mattson and Stroem 1995, 276). Since most democracies in both Western and Central Europe are multiparty, and governments are usually coalitions, power sharing among the parties may become the typical practice in the new parliaments as it has in the established ones.

Lithuania's experience illustrates a "maturing" process and the pressures that lead to the proportionality principle. As Lukošaitis and Žeruolis point out, the Seimas did not initially employ proportional representation to assign committee membership. Given the domination of the legislature by a single party, and the lack of experience of the first generation of post-communist legislators, committee assignments were not critical, and members were largely able to select their own committees. Only after parliamentary parties began to be formed, and proportional representation of the party groups introduced, did the membership of committees stabilize and begin to function more effectively.

Most of the new parliaments also have independent members, whose number has increased through a parliamentary term in the initial decade. As initial party formations disintegrate, at least some deputies leave their party without entering another; instead, they become independents. Their placement on committees is more problematic than for party-affiliated members. They essentially select their own committee assignments, which can have the effect of altering party ratios on committees. Their importance in these respects increases doubly both as chamber size decreases and as party volatility increases, as in Estonia.

An important consideration is the parliament's definition of the minimum size for a set of members to be recognized as a parliamentary party. Party status entitles the group to committee representation, and often also to membership on chamber steering bodies. The smaller the party, however, the less able it is to provide members for all committees. There can be more committees than party members. Continual controversy over party allocations of committee seats has been noted in Estonia, for example.

But everywhere, small parties want to have at least one seat on every committee, even though that principle produces more committee seats for them than they would obtain under the chamber-wide proportionality principle. Small parties have raised exactly the same demands in Sweden (Mattson and Stroem 1995, 269). In Norway, every party, including the one-seat parties, holds membership on the critical Finance Committee (Rommedvedt 1998b).

But not all committees are equal. Some are clearly more important for the entire parliament (e.g., budget), while others vary in importance to specific parties. That criterion, however, can modify the proportionality distribution principle, especially of committee officers if not also memberships, as illustrated by Moldova.

Committee Officers. The Czech Chamber of Deputies illustrates variation in the interparty distribution of committee officer positions. Following the formation of a majority coalition in the 1992 election, the coalition parties chaired all committees. With the formation of a minority coalition following the 1996 election, by contrast, committee posts were shared among

Table 9.3

Party Distribution of Committee Chair Positions by Government Status of Party in Selected Central European Parliaments, by Parliament and Time Period

Parliament and Chamber	Time Period	Government Status of Party			
		Government	Opposition	Independent	Total
Bulgaria	37th	18	2	0	20
	38th	13	1	0	14
Czech Republic Chamber of Deputies	1992	11	0	0	11
	1996	7	6	0	13
	1997a	4	7	1	12
Estonia	1992	8	0	2	10
	1992a	6	2	2	10
	1995	8	2	0	10
	1995a	9	0	1	10
Hungary	1990	6	4	0	10
	1994	15	5	0	17
Poland	1996	18	7	0	25

Note:

Time period is whole electoral term, except for government or party changes midterm, without election, shown as a, b.

Sources: Membership Directories for each parliament and data supplied by authors in this volume.

most parties (excluding only two non-democratic parties), and, as part of the same set of negotiated power-sharing arrangements, the leader of the largest opposition party became Speaker.

Distributional principles follow the election returns. They are the product of interparty negotiations following each election, which establishes shares of power among the parties. Table 9.3 shows the usual practice of the new parliaments that the government coalition holds all, if not most, committee chair positions.

Party sharing of vice chair positions, however, is more variable. The majority often wishes to induce the minority to share at least some formal responsibility, while the latter are more ready to accept lesser than more visible positions, as illustrated in Bulgaria.

Party vs. Member Stability. While these allocation principles are similar to those of established democratic parliaments, practice is more variable in

Central Europe because of different circumstances of their parliamentary parties. Compared to Western Europe, the parliamentary parties of Central Europe are more numerous, smaller in size, and much less stable (Rose 1996, 151–55; Mair 1997, 182; Olson 1998). As parliamentary parties come and go, the deputies holding committee member and officer positions may not change correspondingly. Thus the proportional distribution principle among parties, though used in the beginning of a parliamentary term, may become irrelevant by the end, as in Lithuania.

Parliaments vary in their response to members of committees who change political parties. In some, members leave their committees, to be replaced by other party members. That is, the committee seat belongs to the party, as in Bulgaria and Moldova. In those parliaments, party stability on committees is high, while personal stability is low. In other parliaments, members retain their committee seats during the entire parliamentary term, even though they individually may change parties. In those parliaments, illustrated by the Czech Chamber of Deputies in the 1996–98 term, personnel stability is high, while party ratios are variable.

Summary. The institutionalized set of Central European parliaments distribute committee memberships proportionally among the parties, like Western European parliaments, but also prefer to keep committee officer positions in the government parties if they have the majority to practice that principle of power monopoly. In the least institutionalized parliaments, the shifting parties undermine the relevance of either party control or representation in the committee system.

The partisan perspective on parliamentary committees presupposes the prior existence of stable parties with a clear pattern of internal decision making. That condition cannot be assumed in the new post-communist parliaments. Parties, like committees, develop from nebulous beginnings in new democratic parliaments.

4. Committee-Party Relationships

As we initially projected, the relationship between committees and parties appears to play a key role in the development of functional legislative committees. Committees and parties are "parallel and interlocking" interactive substructures of parliaments (Longley and Davidson 1998, 6). The relationship between committee members and parliamentary parties is clearer and more predictable in more established parliaments than in less established ones.

In the weakly institutionalized Estonian parliament, for example, party factionalization hindered the development of a stable relationship between committees and parties. It was difficult for committee members in the first two terms to have an accurate view of their parties' policies because of the frequent splits inside the party groups. Under such conditions, when the government through its parliamentary parties failed to dominate the legislative process, there was ample opportunity for the deputies to promote their individual preferences and specialties both within and outside of committees. In Moldova, by contrast, party dominance rather than factionalization has emerged as a key problem. As Roper points out, parliamentary parties have supplanted committees as the locus of power within the parliament, playing the "gatekeeper" function often attributed to committees. But in both the Estonian and Moldavian parliaments, parliamentary parties were the groups through which decisions were made about legislation in committees.

The small size of most of the parties in all three of the least institutionalized parliaments, which themselves are small, prevents them from taking seats on all the committees. In Estonia, only three parties were larger in size than the committees. The parties could not, as a consequence, utilize the committee system for interparty bargaining.

The contrast between these cases and the more effectual committee-party relationships in the more consolidated legislatures is striking. In both Hungary and Poland, committees have played a strong role in facilitating legislative activity through their relationship with the party groups. The committee model permitted and sustained interparty and intergroup negotiation, rather than having been undermined and superseded by party instability.

It is also evident in our case studies, that as particular legislatures become more established over time, the party-committee relationship tends to stabilize. This dynamic is evident in Ilonzski's examination of Hungary. During the initial term, she suggests, party groups served as the workhorses of legislative activity and the role of committees was relatively weak. Over the course of the transition, however, the mediating role of committees has increased, and they have emerged as a significant arena in which interparty coordination can be achieved. The members come to fulfill a dual role as connectors between party and committee. This pattern resembles the party-committee relationship in Austria, Sweden, and Germany (Mattson and Stroem 1995, 302; Johnson 1979).

5. Committee Autonomy

Committees in established legislatures should have greater autonomy than those in less institutionalized ones. They should have more control over their own schedules, have greater latitude in the initiation and amendment of legislation, and make more use of minority reports.

Committee autonomy varies dramatically across the newly democratic legislatures. In Moldova, as Roper points out, committee control of the legislative process is weak, and jurisdiction over legislation is not exclusive. In Bulgaria, as well, committee autonomy is limited. Committees may not initiate bills, and must report government initiated bills that are assigned to them within one month.

In comparison to this limited role, committees in more highly institutionalized parliaments, like those of Poland and Hungary, have been able to develop an independent function within the broader institution. Rather than reduced to a passive role, committees in these legislatures are characterized by Wesolowski and Karpowicz, and Ilonzski, respectively, as crucial actors that permitted and sustained interparty and intergroup negotiation. Perhaps the strongest statement regarding committee autonomy derives from the Czech Republic, where committees are found to be "very strong on procedural issues." Strikingly, as the Czech investigators find that the government has no possibility to interfere in the legislative program of the committee and does not try to do so. "On the contrary, the committees usually force the ministers to change their plans and to come to defend a bill before the committee."

In most of the Central European parliaments, committee consideration of legislation is subject to time controls. In practice, however, the committees of Poland, Hungary, and the Czech Republic have more elasticity of time than in the other post-communist parliaments. At the other extreme, the Moldovan committees in practice report bills within five days, though fifteen days is their limit. In some parliaments, time for reporting government bills is shorter than for private member bills, as in Bulgaria.

Time, however, is relative to workload. The high volume of proposed legislation (quite in addition to everything else) may compel committees to act precipitously, as a consequence of major decisions taken elsewhere, as in either governments or parliamentary presidia, or even parliamentary party meetings. Under the pressures of time and policy, those bodies consider matters that, in less pressured but more stable systems, could be handled through committees.

6. Floor Control

The same general pattern that is evident in committee autonomy extends also to floor control. Committees in more highly institutionalized parliaments have more control over floor proceedings on legislation within their jurisdiction than do their counterparts in less institutionalized parliaments. In Lithuania during the highly unstable early transition period, "committees were simply by-passed in favor of deliberations and adoption of legislation on the floor." Moldova presents a similar case, in which much of the legislative activity takes place in plenary session, and committee members reverse their committee votes during floor debates.

Hungarian committees, by contrast, take an active part in shaping floor debate. After both the first and second readings in the plenary, the committee discusses amendments and takes an active part in legislation. The committee is also entitled to propose amendments and argue for them on the floor.

The new parliaments have developed extensive innovations in the sequence and timing of floor and committee stages. In several, bills are referred to committees prior to first reading. Committee review has, in some, resulted in rejection of bills at first reading stage, and in others, bills never even get to that initial plenary step. Further, committees continue to review bills and consider amendments after both first and second readings. Thus there is, illustrated by the Czech Chamber of Deputies, a decline in the number of bills at each successive stage. Even in the less well-institutionalized Estonian parliament, not all bills reached first reading from the committees; and bills, including government bills, were defeated on the floor, largely in accordance with committee recommendations. Procedural innovations have permitted the exercise of committee autonomy.

7. Government Relations

Governmental relations emerge as a crucial issue across the range of post-communist legislatures. The diversity of practice across the region is striking in the initial post-communist decade.

Clearly, instability of government stands out as a complicating factor in the development of parliaments and their committees. Instability of governmental structure plagued the work of the committees in Lithuania's post-communist legislature. Not only were changes in government frequent, they were also accompanied by changes in ministerial structure. Relationships between ministries and corresponding committees were severed; oversight responsibilities frequently shifted from one committee to another and became purely theoretical.

A second Baltic case, Estonia, presents an example of strong government presence in the legislative committees. Ministers have the right to participate in the committee during the consideration of bills. Committee oversight is limited. Committees do not have the right to compel government officials to provide information during meetings, but can send written questions to the minister. Most governmental information gathering by parliament, according to Ruus, occurs at plenary sessions.

Similarly, in Bulgaria, the oversight and investigative function of committees has been limited. While formal rules permit standing committees to call members of government for questioning, and also permits the formation of ad hoc investigatory committees, the reality thus far in the transition has been that little actual legislative oversight has occurred. Party dominance appears to play a crucial role in committee-government relations. As Karasimeonov points out, oversight activity has been weakest during periods of a stable parliamentary majority.

Even in more established legislative institutions, government-committee relations are far from uniform. In Poland, the government and ministers have an uneasy relationship with the committees. Though ministers can remain as members of parliament, they are precluded from committee membership. Yet they must attend when requested by the committees, to either present their own legislation or to answer desiderata inquiries. The latter are not always welcomed by ministers, who sometimes would prefer to send subordinates.

Hungarian committee members also face substantial limitations when dealing with government. Investigations of government or ministry, while the right of the whole body, are often transferred to both the standing committees and to special investigatory committees. Government agencies, however, regularly fail to provide theoretically compulsory reports to the committees. Furthermore, the working relationship between committees and ministries does not appear uniform. Ilonzski notes that cooperation with the ministries on committee work largely depends on personal and party sympathies and the professional connections between the ministerial staff and committee members. In the established parliaments, relationships with government and ministries are likewise varied (Mattson and Stroem 1995, 286–95). While most legislation comes from the government, all Western European parliamentary committees frequently amend government bills. In addition western MPs find that the government submits legislation late and seeks hasty action (Hansard Society 1992, 10; Hagevi 1998).

Institutionalization Categories in Summary

Based on our indicators, clear differences in institutionalization among our seven examples of Central European parliaments have emerged in their initial post-communist decade. Committees in Poland, the Czech Republic, and Hungary stand out as relatively institutionalized. In each case, parliamentary committees show increased structural stability. Membership appears to be increasingly specialized, and with increasing incumbency rates. Significantly, in each case, committees have not been overwhelmed by party groups. Rather, party and committee function in an "interdependent" manner, as in Western European parliaments. Committees have served as fora within which interparty communication can occur and party positions can be formulated. In each of these cases committees play an active role in the legislative process, and exercise a meaningful degree of control over their own activities.

The contrast between these cases and the less developed legislatures in Estonia, Lithuania, and Moldova, and to a lesser extent Bulgaria, is striking. Committees with less autonomy, less control over the legislative process, and only limited impact on the government, are the norm in these legislatures. In general, they suffer from instability of structure. The number and function of committees have been volatile. Even in those cases, such as Moldova, where committee structure has been stable, differentiation is limited, hampering committee effectiveness. Parliamentary parties are often able to supersede committees. Committee membership is neither stable nor specialized. Finally, and unsurprisingly, committees find it difficult even to influence government ministries.

Explaining Patterns of Committee Institutionalization

The six explanatory factors that we examined as potentially significant factors in the introduction of the volume include (chapter 1, Appendix 1.2):

1. Institutional Legacy
2. Policy Environment of the Transition
3. Party System
4. Institutional Environment
5. The Legislature as Committee Environment
6. Resources Available to Committees

The explanatory value of the variables is summarized in Appendix 9.2 of this chapter. Among the causal or explanatory factors, conditions of the party system exert the most immediate formative influence upon parliamentary committee systems. All the other factors are also present and interact to shape the varied degrees of institutionalization defined by our initial set of indicators.

1. Institutional Legacy

Distinct patterns of legislative development distinguish the former Soviet and Central European cases from one another.

The Moldovan case confirms many of our initial hypotheses about communist and pre-communist legacies. Moldova has no national-level legislative history as a model of democratic institutional experience. The impact of communist-era legislative practice is pronounced. Like the two other former Soviet Republics, but unlike any of the other post-communist legislatures we examine in this volume, Moldova's last Soviet-era parliament was also the country's first post-independence parliament. It was a direct link between Moldova's communist and democratic regimes. Moldova's last Soviet parliament was elected in spring 1990 and continued its activity until February 1994. This parliament's initial structure was based on the Soviet model. Many of the initial MPs (in both the successor Communist Party and the opposition parties) had experience in the Communist Party of the Soviet Union which, we suggest, shaped attitudes about both the role of institutional leadership and the role of party groups.

As in Moldova (and Estonia), Lithuania's inclusion in the former USSR exercised a powerful influence on its transitional legislature. Lithuanian decision-makers, Lukošaitis and Žeruolis point out, were forced to consider "the Moscow factor" in virtually every decision and strategy. They were severely constrained in making initial decisions regarding the pace and direction of change. Institutionally, the Soviet legacy also played a significant role. The Supreme Soviet of the Lithuanian Soviet Socialist Republic (suitably amended) provided the first organizational framework for the independent Seimas until new organizational statutes could be written.

While the "Soviet/satellite" divide is critical, considerable disparities separate the Central European regimes from one another. Bulgaria's historical legacy was clearly not conducive to an easy course to democratization. Little existed in democratic development in the interwar period. A strongly authoritarian Communist Party retained an all but unchallenged position in Bulgarian society until the dissolution of the Soviet Union forced its demise. Both of these factors were conducive to non-democratic patterns of behavior by the transitional political elites (including legislators).

In comparison with these cases, Poland, Hungary, and the Czech Republic all benefited from historical legacies that were relatively benign, at least in this comparative context. Poland and Hungary both have histories as sovereign states with significant democratic traditions. Hungary was well on the way to reform before the collapse of communism. Its communist regime, while authoritarian, was far from the extreme example of coercion seen elsewhere in the region. Poland was the site of a vibrant civil society and high levels of counter-regime political organization for at least a decade before communist collapse. Conditions during late communism in the Czech Republic were clearly less favorable, yet its pre-communist legacy provided a strong basis for the democratic transition. The Czech Republic itself, while not independent within the federation, played a dominant role in Czechoslovakia, probably the region's most successful democratic effort between the wars.

2. Policy Environment of the Transition

Multiple and often extremely difficult policy tasks complicate efforts to consolidate post-communist societies and institutions. The sudden transitions of economy, ethnic relations, and political system, and in some cases state definition, impose extra-institutional agendas upon the parliaments of post-communist democracies, and may shift the focus of political activities to actors outside the legislature all together. Policy conflict may make cooperation among parliamentary party groups impossible, shifting the locus of discourse from the committee to the party group and the plenary.

The negative impact of policy complexity is evident in Lithuania, which, more than any other country examined here, was threatened by direct military attack during its early transition. Soviet intervention was by no means excluded, and serious provocations plagued the newly independent state. Soviet troops surrounded the parliament building (the barricades are now part of an historic exhibit). Not only did these military dangers confront the new legislature with extremely difficult policy decisions; they also shifted the locus of legislative activity to the plenary sessions where issues of fundamental import were debated. A similar outcome is evident in Moldova, where the policy environment was complicated by the necessity of negotiating economic and political reforms, while at the same time addressing critical ethnic issues (Crowther 1997). Ethnic tension ultimately erupted into a civil war and rupture of the state in May 1992. As in Lithuania, the consequence of this intense conflict was the concentration of policy making in the government.

While not threatened by territorial dissolution, Bulgaria also faced fundamental challenges as its leaders struggled to negotiate the post-communist transition. Ethnic conflict, fundamental discord regarding the character of the regime, and division concerning economic strategy all played a role. Karasimeonov's analysis indicates that upheaval during the early transition and the frequent elections that resulted from severe political divisions hindered the development of effective parliamentary committees.

Legislative ineffectiveness allowed the government increased if temporary power.

While all of the post-communist transitions are by their nature turbulent periods in the political histories of their countries, those of the more successfully institutionalized cases are markedly less chaotic than others examined in this volume. Hungary's path to post-communism is characteristic of "moderate" transitions. Ethnic conflict has not produced sharp political divisions that we see in countries such as Moldova. The division between former communists and their opponents, while evident, has remained within relatively moderate confines. The economic transition from communism to capitalism, already well underway before the first democratic elections occurred, did not produce the levels of dislocation seen in the post-Soviet context. Generally speaking the same can be said of the Polish and Czech cases. The break-up of the Czecho-Slovak federation, however, suggests a heavy policy load upon the Federal Assembly, which disappeared as the state was dissolving (Olson 1994).

This "relative tranquillity," we contend, was highly beneficial to the emergence of functional committee systems. "Normal," rather than extraordinary, legislative agendas favored committee rather than plenary deliberation. The lower levels of party conflict seen in these three countries allowed committees to emerge in the role that Ilonzski highlights, as agents for interparty discourse. Increased governmental stability created an environment in which committees were better able to develop relationships with ministries, develop regular procedures, and begin to develop expert and experienced memberships. Nowhere among our examples is the capacity of the committee format to express and resolve policy conflict more dramatically expressed than in the Polish National Assembly, a unique legal form of a bicameral parliament, in which the Constitution Committee worked through two terms in the preparation of Poland's post-communist constitution.

3. Party System

Both single party dominant and highly fragmented party systems were associated with lower levels of legislative committee institutionalization than is evident in conditions of both stable and moderate party competition, consistent with findings from parliaments around the world (Shaw 1979; Mezey 1979).

Unstable party systems are characteristic of the post-communist transitions (Olson 1998; Kitschelt 1992; Mair 1997, 98). Establishing new parties, accommodating newly introduced electoral rules, and

simultaneously addressing the policy demands of mobilized and often polarized constituents produces highly volatile party competition, particularly during the initial phase of the post-communist transition.
Nonetheless, quite distinct patterns of party interaction are evident among
our post-communist cases.

Three of these, Hungary, Poland, and the Czech Republic, stand out as
examples of the early emergence of multiparty competitive systems. In the
Hungarian case, Ilonzski considers a party system characterized by both
the lack of single party dominance, and the lack of extreme fragmentation
and party instability, as essential to the ability of committees to consolidate and to develop an independent function within parliament.

Party fragmentation, on the other hand, greatly inhibits the work of
committees. As is evident in the Estonian Riigikogu, party fragmentation
makes it impossible for members of committees to have an accurate view
of their parties' policies because of frequent splits inside the party groups.
Additionally, party splits lead to both high levels of committee member
turnover, and non-proportional representation of members and committee
leaders.

Bulgaria, Moldova, and Lithuania, at various points in their respective
transitions, all reflect the problems related to single-party dominance. The
general problem is well depicted by Lithuania's early transition. During the
initial session, Saudis controlled the parliament. It was thus not necessary
to develop committees as special vehicles for mediating interparty conflict.
Rather, decisions were made by the legislature's leadership (controlled by
Saudis) or in plenary proceedings (likewise controlled by Saudis). During
Moldova's early transition, parliament was dominated by two powerful
political parties in turn. The Popular Front and the Agrarians both used
the legislature as a vehicle through which to assert their influence. Each
controlled both the general body's leadership, and that of the committees.
With critical decisions taken internal to the party, committees languished.

Conditions in Bulgaria appear much the same. After an initial period
of instability, the BSP and UDF each in turn played an increasingly dominant role in legislative politics. As in Moldova and Lithuania, critical decisionmaking authority consequently passed to party groups, limiting the
consolidation of legislative committees' role in the work of the parliament.

The threshold requirement is one electoral system feature with an immediate, and often disruptive, consequence for party structure within parliaments. The minimum vote requirement (usually at 5 percent) has the
effect of removing whole party groups from parliament. Given the frequency of government defeats in elections in the initial post-communist
decade, another disruptive electoral effect is the large increase in the size of
the new government parties through the entry of entirely new members.

Parliamentary parties are not stable in either size or composition across electoral-parliamentary terms, with disruptive consequences for the party-committee relationship.

4. Institutional Environment

The structure of ministries and the constitutional relationship among president, prime minister, and parliament define the immediate decisionmaking environment within which parliaments function.

A separately elected president, while justified on grounds of stability in the governmental system, has often proved a source of instability in relationship to parliament. In our set of countries, only the Czech Republic and Hungary lack a separately elected president (McGregor 1996; Taras 1998).

In the others, the presidents' interactions with parliament have varied both by party system and by personality. The interactive combination of a powerful president with either a single dominant party or a highly fragmented and unstable party system, has made parliament subordinate to government leadership in each of our countries except Poland. The Polish Sejm, with one of the region's more volatile and early presidents, survived as one of our more institutionalized parliaments (Jasiewicz 1998). In the other countries, however, parliaments have had a less firm internal structure, and thus have been less well equipped to act independently of the president.

As a more immediate consideration, the structure of ministries impacts the committee structure. To provide stability in the committee system, the Czech and Hungarian parliaments have decoupled the committee system from the vagaries of changing ministerial definition, as has Norway in Western Europe. In the latter case, committees were restructured to better serve parliament's own internal purposes and to also break the close relationship between committee and ministry (Rommedvedt 1998a).

5. The Legislature as Committee Environment

Committees and parliaments exist in a symbiotic relationship; though committees are, at least potentially, a source of strength to the wider parliament, it is the latter body that defines the conditions within which committees work.

The experience of members, the party system, and the chamber level leadership structure all impact the committees. Once established, committees can act as an anchor for the entire parliament during difficult periods, as did the Polish Sejm committee system during the early post-communist transition years. A similar observation would apply to the Swedish parliament in the early years of its democratization (Rustow 1955).

But new committees in new parliaments partake of the newness of the entire institution. With everything in flux, as in our instances of low institutionalization, so are the committees. They are both a consequence of, and an indicator for, the condition of the larger parliament.

6. Resources Available to Committees

Many of our accounts emphasize the shortage of rooms, personnel, and funds for the entire parliament. Most parliaments are expanding their space, mostly by acquiring and remodeling existing buildings. The Hungarian parliament, for example, has taken over the building of the Communist Party Central Committee, while the Czech Chamber of Deputies has expanded into adjacent buildings and palaces. The Lithuanian parliament has likewise acquired the use of adjacent office buildings of the old regime, while the Estonian parliament will occupy the entire historic but small building that it now shares with the government.

Within the constraints of the entire parliament, however, there is a competition for resources between committees and the parliamentary parties. Several of our chapters note that parties are better supplied with expert and support staff than are the committees. In crowded buildings, party and committee needs for space are directly competitive with each other. Parliament requires many support staff and specialized facilities, including research and information offices, document preparation staff, and libraries. All of these specialized offices can provide direct assistance to members and committees, as well as to presidia and parties. But they are also direct competitors with committees for scarce resources.

Comparisons and Patterns in
Parliamentary Committee Institutionalization

Patterns of Institutionalization

Even within the short span of one decade, considerable differences have emerged among the newly democratized post-communist parliaments in their relative institutionalization. Poland, Hungary, and the Czech Republic have the most stable parliaments, while the former Soviet Republics, the least. Bulgaria represents an intermediate outcome, which, we would suggest, is representative of conditions in other Southeast European transition states.

In principle of committee organization, number, and size, the committee systems of the new democracies closely resemble those of the established democratic parliaments of Western Europe. There is, however, extensive variation in the extent to which they mirror the structure of ministries.

The newer parliaments are experimenting with a wide range of forms and uses of committees and subcommittees, indicating how committee structure is itself a flexible instrument for legislative adaptation to rapidly changing circumstances. There is considerable organizational complexity in number and variety of committees and work groups among the new parliaments, which is sometimes used as an indicator of institutionalization. Their initial profusion and diversity, however, were more the mark of improvisation than institutionalization.

Reorganization of the committee system, through revised Standing Orders, places both the Czech and Hungarian parliaments in the most institutionalized category. The effect of rules changes has been to simplify a diverse set of working bodies into fewer and more comprehensive types of committees. Poland, over a longer period of development beginning in the communist period, has evolved a set of committees with stable operating rules and procedures. The new Polish and Czech Senates have made the pre-existing committee systems of their lower but more active chambers, the model for their own committee systems.

At the other end of the continuum, Estonia, Lithuania, and also Moldova, have been changeable in their committee number and jurisdiction, have had a constant turnover in committee membership, and have had many changes in committee leadership resulting from both party and government instability. This portrait of instability is intensified by the concentration of our chapters on the earliest years of their independence. Their condition at their beginning is perhaps the clearest expression of the unstable extreme of institutional formation. The chaos of their beginning years was also characteristic of the beginning stages of our more institutionalized parliaments.

The constant change among parties in the newly democratic parliaments is the single feature most distinguishing them from those in Western European parliaments. This attribute is one of the factors most immediately affecting the committee system. In the newly democratized parliaments, party groups are only weakly related to the electoral formations through which they were initially elected. Electoral lists are often amalgamations of small groups and prominent personalities, illustrated by Estonia, Lithuania, and the Czech Senate. Party formations in parliament may differ from electoral coalitions, and neither may be closely related to extra-parliamentary parties. Once in parliament, the members leave existing party groups, and form new ones, or become independents. As party groups disintegrate or are newly created, the basis of government formation likewise is threatened, as in the Czech Republic in 1997.

Developmental Sequence

This review of post-communist parliaments in their initial decade suggests that some characteristics evolve earlier in a longer range process of institutional development than do others. Neither the structural variables nor measures of incumbency now differentiate among these parliaments. Stability of committee membership and leadership within single terms, as well as systematic reorganization, however, are the most apparent sources of differentiation among the committee systems of newly democratized parliaments in their early years.

In the newly democratized parliaments, structure and rules stabilization have preceded increased levels of incumbency in the initial decade. New members appear to learn in a relatively short time how to work within received structure. This pattern conforms to the U.S. case, in which committee structures and floor procedures evolved much earlier than did incumbency (Gamm and Shepsle 1989). We might anticipate that incumbency will increase over time in post-communist parliaments, perhaps more quickly in the more institutionalized parliaments than in the less stable parliaments.

Awareness of, and responsiveness to, district and constituency is notably absent in the newly democratized parliaments, but very apparent in Western European parliaments. Neither appreciation of citizens to be represented, nor even of voter segments, is found at significant levels in the new parliaments. We might anticipate the development of the representation function in the new parliaments in the future, and perhaps more quickly in the more institutionalized parliaments than in the others.

We also anticipate the emergence over time of a closer party-committee linkage. While the more institutionalized parliaments are closer in this respect to the Western European parliaments, in all of the post-communist parliaments the party relationship to the committee system remains volatile. The working relationship between the two components of parliamentary organization, however, most immediately depends upon stabilization of the party system.

This developmental sequence has implications for three major perspectives on committees. Committees in the first decade of the new parliaments examined in this study initially develop an informational and expertise competence on topics within their jurisdiction. Their experience is consistent with the observation that the informational function is preeminent among the committees in established Western European parliaments (Mattson and Stroem 1995, 303). But as our chapters also demonstrate, committee formation itself is a contingent process. In the absence of structure and rule stablization, informational competence is slow to emerge.

Once formed with some degree of stability and continuity, the information function becomes the first clear contribution of committees to the legislative process. The role of committees as agents of interparty negotiation is based on the committee informational capacity and also reflects the conditions of party development within each parliament.

Jurisdictional power and autonomy, as anticipated in a distributional theoretical perspective, seems a derivative of the informational function. Our several post-communist parliaments show how committees gain jurisdiction over a set of issues. Even in the Moldovan parliament, in which all bills are sent to all committees, one committee typically assumes a lead role on any one bill. The other committees, usually within five days, quickly decline to act. In this parliament, committee jurisdiction occurs through default.

In many of the beginning parliaments, members were assigned to committees on the basis of their personal preferences, often reflecting their education and occupation. Their personal concerns were the basis for the definition of a committee's jurisdiction and motive to assert jurisdiction against other committees. More established patterns of jurisdiction develop through negotiation over time, within and across terms. This process might occur during a conscious reorganization effort, illustrated by both the Hungarian and Czech parliaments, or through a slow evolution illustrated by the Polish Sejm.

The initial decade of post-communist parliamentary experience suggests that the sense of rightful and regularized jurisdiction, whether defined by policy topic or by administrative structure, is closely related to both their informational competence as well as an interparty coordination function. The development of committees' functional utilities appears incremental, interactive, and contingent.

New Departures

The newly activated legislatures of post-communist democracies display a wide variety of practices which raise questions about our understanding of more established democratic legislatures. For example, the new legislatures have developed a wide variety of working subgroups to pragmatically meet immediate needs as they unpredictably occur.

If all such work groups are generically "committees," they display a much wider range of organizational form and practice than in established legislatures. One of their features is the use of subcommittees, to which no direct comparisons can now be made to established legislatures, for they have not been noted in the research literature (Stroem 1998, 39). For another, some of the new parliaments permit external members of committees, which practice greatly expands our usual notion of "member" of parliament.

The instability of new parliaments in both membership and in party formation (Olson 1998; Norton and Olson 1996), presents a much wider range of incumbency behavior, and thus of measures, than heretofore noted in established parliaments. We have developed incumbency measures at both chamber and committee levels. Within generally low incumbency rates in the new parliaments, both incumbency measures vary widely among committees. The chapters also show that party changes in committee membership do not always mean personnel changes, or vice versa. These variations in the new parliaments require "thick description" for analysis and comparison among parliaments, both new and established.

The new parliaments have also developed innovations in the sequencing of committee and floor consideration of legislation. Committees often receive draft legislation prior to first reading on the floor. They also have jurisdiction over bills between the several readings. These several additional steps give committees the possibility of more independent thought and action than is implied by the more formally restricted pattern of committee action only following the first reading stage.

Dimensions of Institutionalization

This review of committees in post-communist parliaments suggests more broadly defined dimensions of legislative institutionalization, such as autonomy, formality, and organizational complexity (Polsby 1968; Sisson 1973; Patterson and Copeland 1994; Hahn 1996).

Parliaments vary in their autonomy from government, as do their committees. We have found extensive variation on this dimension, with the committees of the least institutionalized parliaments highly dependent upon the government, and largely incapable of either delaying or modifying government legislation. The more institutionalized parliaments, by contrast, have had much more latitude in their decisions concerning government bills, and have had the opportunity to review the conduct of administration.

Formality of internal structure and procedures has become much more apparent in the institutionalized parliaments than in the others. Committee jurisdiction is stable, and committees have a regularized function in acting upon legislation. The allocation of committee seats in accordance with party size has become stable, though the practice of party proportionality in the selection of committee officers has been seen in only one of the Central European parliaments.

Finally, organizational complexity has been displayed in abundance in all of the post-communist parliaments. Their early improvisation quickly led to a proliferation of working groups, with diverse purposes, composition, and procedures. It is the reorganization of committee systems through rules redefinition that organizational complexity has become regularized and consistent in the more institutionalized parliaments of post-communism.

Institutionalization as an attribute of parliaments, with an emphasis upon stability and continuity, provides a regularized pattern through which dissatisfaction and demands for change can be expressed. Institutionalization is not so much the end of a road, but a clearly marked road. It is not a clearly defined goal, but rather a measurement of the extent to which members of parliament, through their parties and committees, discover stable means to express political aspirations and resolve policy disputes. As the experience of the U.S. Congress and Western European parliaments indicates, there is rarely a shortage of either policy disputes or political aspirations. There can be, however, continuing structures and widely practiced procedures through which rival goals can be articulated and achieved.

Committees are a preeminent parliamentary expression of continuity and stability in the midst of policy disagreement in the world's democracies. They are, as noted in examinations of the Western European parliaments, among the most significant organizational features of modern parliaments (Mattson and Stroem 1995, 303). They provide a crucial means through which parliaments both express and resolve public policy disagreements. Our concentration upon newly activated parliaments in the new post-communist democracies provides a unique perspective on how parliaments begin to develop the internal structures and procedures that enable them to accomplish their purposes in the wider society.

Appendix 9.1

Patterns of Committee Institutionalization

	Low Institutionalization			Moderate Institutionalization	High Institutionalization		
	Moldova	Lithuania	Estonia	Bulgaria	Czech Republic	Hungary	Poland
Committee Structure	Stable Undifferentiated	Fluid Differentiated	Stable Undifferentiated	Fluid Undifferentiated	Reorganized Differentiated	Stable Differentiated	Reorganized Differentiated
Committee Membership	Unstable Unspecialized	Unstable Unspecialized	Unstable Unspecialized	Moderate Stability Unspecialized	Moderate Stability Specialized	Stable Specialized	Stable Specialized
Party Composition	Mixed/ Proportional	Mixed/ Proportional	Mixed/ Proportional	Mixed/ Proportional	Proportional	Proportional	Proportional
Relation with Parties	Party Dominant	Party Dominant	Unstable	Party Dominant	Interdependent	Interdependent	Interdependent
Autonomy	Low	Low	Moderate	Moderate	High	High	High
Floor Control	Low	Low	Moderate/low	Low	High	High	Moderate
Governmental Relations	Low Influence	Low Influence	Low Influence	Moderate Influence	High Influence	Substantial Influence	High Influence
Level of Institutionalization	Low	Low	Low	Moderate	High	High	High

Appendix 9.2
Sources of Committee Institutionalization

	Low Institutionalization			Moderate Institutionalization	High Institutionalization		
	Moldova	Lithuania	Estonia	Bulgaria	Czech Republic	Poland	Hungary
Institutional Legacy	Former-Soviet	Former-Soviet	Former-Soviet	Satellite Repressive	Satellite Repressive	Satellite Reformist	Satellite Reformist
Transition Policy Environment	Complex	Complex	Complex	Complex	Moderate	Moderate	Moderate
Nature of the Party System	Single Party/ Fragmented	Single Party/ Fragmented	Fragmented	Single Party/ Discontinuous	Multi-Party Competitive	Fragmented/ Multi-Party Competitive	Multi-Party Competitive
Institutional Environment	Government/ Party Dominant	Government/ Party Influential	Government Dominant	Government/ Party Dominant	Shared Authority	Shared Authority	Shared Authority
The Legislature as a Critical Environment	Unstable	Unstable	Unstable	Unstable	Stable	Stable	Stable
Resources Available to Committees	Low	Low	Low	Low	Moderate	Moderate	Moderate

References and Bibliography

Ágh, Attila. 1998. "Changing Parliamentary Committees in Changing East-Central Europe: Parliamentary Committees as Central Sites of Policy-making." *Journal of Legislative Studies* 4, no. 1 (Spring): 85–100.

Crowther, William. 1997. "The Politics of Democratization in Post-communist Moldova." In *Democratic Changes and Authoritarian Reactions in Russia, Ukraine, Belarus, and Moldova,* edited by Karen Dawisha and Bruce Parrott. London, Cambridge University Press.

Damgaard, Erik. 1995. "How Parties Control Committee Members." In *Parliaments and Majority Rule in Western Europe,* edited by Herbert Döring. New York: St. Martins Press.

———. 1997. "The Political Roles of Danish Mps." *Journal of Legislative Studies* 3, no. 1 (Spring): 79–90.

Döring, Herbert. 1995. "Time as a Scarce Resource: Government Control of the Agenda." In *Parliaments and Majority Rule in Western Europe,* edited by Herbert Döring. New York: St. Martins Press.

Gamm, Gerald, and Kenneth Shepsle. 1989. "Emergence of Legislative Institutions: Standing Committees in the House and Senate." *Legislative Studies Quarterly* 14, no. 1 (February): 39–66.

Hagevi, Magnus. 1998. "Committees in the Swedish Riksdag." Paper prepared for the international conference "Committees in New and Established Parliaments." University of North Carolina, Greensboro, 30 May–2 June 1998.

Hahn, Jeffrey W., ed. 1996. *Democratization in Russia: The Development of Legislative Institutions.* Armonk, N.Y.: M. E. Sharpe.

Hansard Society. 1992. *Making the Law: Report of the Hansard Society Commission on the Legislative Process.* London: Hansard Society for Parliamentary Government.

Jasiewicz, Krzysztof. 1998. "Poland: Walesa's Legacy to the Presidency." In *Postcommunist Presidents,* edited by Ray Taras. Cambridge: Cambridge University Press. 130–67.

Jogerst, Michael. 1993. *Reform in the House of Commons: The Select Committee System.* Lexington: University Press of Kentucky.

Johnson, Nevil. 1979. "Committees in the West German Budestag." In *Committees in Legislatures: A Comparative Analysis,* edited by John D. Lees and Malcolm Shaw. Durham, N.C.: Duke University Press. 102–47.

Kitschelt, Herbert. 1992. "The Formation of Party Systems in East Central Europe." *Politics and Society* 2, no. 1 (March): 7–50.

Lees, John D., and Malcolm Shaw, eds. 1979. *Committees in Legislatures: A Comparative Analysis.* Durham, N.C.: Duke Univesity Press.

Linz, Juan, and Alfred Stepan. 1996. *Problems of Democratic Transition and Consolidation.* Baltimore, Md.: Johns Hopkins University Press.

Longley, Lawrence, and Roger Davidson. 1998. "Changing Roles of Parliamentary Committees." Special issue of *Journal of Legislative Studies* 4, no. 1 (Spring).

Mair, Peter. 1997. *Party System Change: Approaches and Interpretations.* Oxford: Clarenden Press.

Mattson, Ingvar, and Kaare Stroem. 1995. "Parliamentary Committees." In *Parlia-

ments and Majority Rule in Western Europe, edited by Herbert Döring. New York: St. Martins Press. 149–307.

McGregor, James P. 1996. "Constitutional Factors in Politics in Post-Communist Central and Eastern Europe." *Communist and Post-Communist Studies* 29, no. 2: 147–66.

Mezey, Michael L. 1979. *Comparative Legislatures.* Durham, N.C.: Duke University Press.

Norton, Philip, and David M. Olson. 1996. "Parliaments in Adolescence." In *The New Legislatures of Central and East Europe,* edited by David M. Olson and Philip Norton. London: Cass. 231–44.

Olson, David M. 1994. "The Sundered State: Federalism and Parliament in Czechoslovakia." In *Parliaments in Transition,* edited by Thomas F. Remington. Boulder, Colo.: Westview. 97–124.

———. 1998. "Party Formation and Party System Consolidation In the Democracies of Central Europe." In *Parties and Democracy,* edited by Richard Hofferbert. Oxford: Blackwell. 10–42.

Olson, David M., and Philip Norton, eds. 1996. *The New Legislatures of Central and East Europe.* London: Cass.

Olson, David M., Ania van der M. Krok-Paszkowska, Maurice D. Simon, and Irena Jackiewicz. 1998. "Committees in the Post-Communist Polish Sejm: Structure, Activity and Members." *Journal of Legislative Studies* 4, no. 1 (Spring): 101–23.

Olson, David M., Jon Pierre, and Ryszard Piotrowki. 1983. "Documentary Data in the Comparison of Committee Systems in National Parliaments." *Statsvetenskaplig Tidskrift* 86, no. 4: 356–66.

Olson, David M., and Maurice D. Simon. 1982. "The Institutional Development of a Minimal Parliament: The Case of the Polish Sejm." In *Communist Legislatures in Comparative Perspective,* edited by Daniel Nelson and Stephen White. London: Macmillan.

Patterson, Samuel C., and Gary W. Copeland. 1994. "Parliaments in the Twenty-First Century." In *Parliaments in the Modern World,* edited by Gary W. Copeland and Samuel C. Patterson. Ann Arbor: University of Michigan Press.

Patzelt, Werner. 1997. "German MPS and Their Roles." *Journal of Legislative Studies* 3, no. 1 (Spring): 79–90.

Polsby, Nelson W. 1968. "The Institutionalization of the U.S. House of Representatives." *American Political Science Review* 62 (September): 144–68.

Rommetvedt, Hilmar. 1998a. "Norwegian Parliamentary Committees: Performance, Structural Change and External Relations." *Journal of Legislative Studies* 4, no. 1 (Spring): 60–84.

———. 1998b. "Committees in an Established Democratic Parliament—the Case of Norway." Paper prepared for the international conference "Committees in New and Established Parliaments." University of North Carolina, Greensboro, 30 May–2 June 1998.

Rose, Richard. 1996. *What is Europe?* New York: HarperCollins.

Rustow, Dankwart A. 1955. *The Politics of Compromise.* Princeton, N.J.: Princeton University Press.

Saalfeld, Thomas. 1997. "Professionalization of Parliamentary Roles in Germany." *Journal of Legislative Studies* 3, no. 1 (Spring): 32–54.

Shaw, Malcolm. 1979. "Conclusion." In *Committees in Legislatures: A Comparative Analysis,* edited by John D. Lees and Malcolm Shaw. Durham, N.C.: Duke University Press.

Sisson, Richard. 1973. "Comparative Legislative Institutionaliation: A Theoretical Exploration." In *Legislatures in Comparative Perspective,* edited by Allan Kornberg. New York: McKay.

Soltesz, Istvan. 1995. "The Committee System of the First Parliament." In *The First Parliament 1990–94,* edited by Attila Ágh and Sandor Kurtan. Budapest: Budapest: Hungarian Center of Democracy Studies.

Stroem, Kaare. 1997. "Rules, Reasons and Routines: Legislative Roles in Parliamentary Democracies." *Journal of Legislative Studies* 3, no. 1 (Spring): 155–74.

_____. 1998. "Parliamentary Committees in European Democracies." *Journal of Legislative Studies* 4, no. 1 (Spring): 21–59.

Taras, Ray, ed. 1998. *Postcommunist Presidents.* Cambridge: Cambridge University Press.

Zajc, Drago. 1997. "Committee Patterns in Parliaments: A Global Perspective." In *Working Papers on Comparative Legislative Studies II: The Changing Roles of Parliamentary Committees,* edited by Lawrence Longley and Attila Ágh. Appleton, Wisc.: Research Committee of Legislative Specialists, IPSA. 489–503.

LIST OF CONTRIBUTORS

William E. Crowther, Professor of Political Science at University of North Carolina at Greensboro, is Co-Director of the Parliamentary Documents Center for Central Europe.

Gabriella Ilonszki is Associate Professor of Political Science in the Budapest University of Economics, Hungary.

Georgi Karasimeonov is Professor of Political Science at the University of Sophia, Bulgaria.

Ewa Karpowicz is Assistant Professor in the Academy of Entrepreneurship and Management, Warsaw, and a member of the research staff of the Polish Sejm.

Petr Kolář is a researcher in the Parliamentary Institute of the Parliament of the Czech Republic, Prague.

Alvidas Lukošaitis is Assistant Professor in the Department of International Relations and Political Science at Vilnius University and a member of the Information Analysis Department of the Lithuanian Parliament.

Zdenka Mansfeldová is a Senior Research Fellow in the Institute of Sociology of the Czech Academy of Science, Prague.

David M. Olson, Professor Emeritus of Political Science at University of North Carolina at Greensboro is Co-Director of the Parliamentary Documents Center for Central Europe, and Co-Chair of the Research Committee of Legislative Specialists of the International Political Science Association.

Petra Rakušanová is on the research staff of the Institute of Sociology of the Czech Academy of Science, Prague.

Steven D. Roper is Assistant Professor of Political Science at Eastern Illinois University, Charleston, Illinois.

Jüri Ruus is Lecturer in Comparative Politics in the Department of Political Science at Tartu University, Estonia.

Jindřiška Syllová is Director of the Parliamentary Institute of the Parliament of the Czech Republic, Prague.

Wlodzimerz Wesolowski is Professor Emeritus at the Institute of Philosophy and Sociology of the Polish Academy of Science, Warsaw.

Darius Žeruolis is Assistant Professor in the Department of International Relations and Political Science at Vilnius University.

INDEX

www.ingramcontent.com/pod-product-compliance
Lightning Source LLC
Chambersburg PA
CBHW020702270326
41928CB00005B/232